The Spike Lee Brand

SUNY series in African American Studies

John R. Howard and Robert C. Smith, editors

791.43023
Lee
L

The Spike Lee Brand

A Study of Documentary Filmmaking

Delphine Letort

Foreword by

Mark A. Reid

Published by State University of New York Press, Albany

© 2015 State University of New York

All rights reserved

Printed in the United States of America

No part of this book may be used or reproduced in any manner whatsoever without written permission. No part of this book may be stored in a retrieval system or transmitted in any form or by any means including electronic, electrostatic, magnetic tape, mechanical, photocopying, recording, or otherwise without the prior permission in writing of the publisher.

For information, contact State University of New York Press, Albany, NY
www.sunypress.edu

Production, Jenn Bennett
Marketing, Anne M. Valentine

Library of Congress Cataloging-in-Publication Data

Letort, Delphine.
 The Spike Lee brand : a study of documentary filmmaking / Delphine Letort ; foreword by Mark A. Reid.
   pages cm. — (SUNY series in African American studies)
 Includes bibliographical references and index.
 ISBN 978-1-4384-5763-5 (hardcover : alk. paper)
 ISBN 978-1-4384-5764-2 (e-book)
 1. Lee, Spike—Criticism and interpretation. 2. Documentary films. I. Title.

PN1998.3.L44L48 2015
791.4302'33092—dc23   2014038928

10 9 8 7 6 5 4 3 2 1

I wish to dedicate this work to Ludovic and Joséphine and thank them for their patience and everyday support.

Contents

List of Illustrations	ix
Foreword: Agency as Remembering and Retelling Mark A. Reid	xi
Acknowledgments	xiii
List of Abbreviations	xv
Introduction	1
Chapter 1 The Making of Spike Lee's Nonfiction Joints	9
Chapter 2 History and Memory: The African American Experience	37
Chapter 3 Media and Race	63
Chapter 4 The Legacy of Black Nationalism: Culture and Politics	103
Conclusion	149
Notes	155
Bibliography	189
Index	205

List of Illustrations

Figure 1.1   *When the Levees Broke.* Courtesy of Photofest   26
Figure 2.1   *Four Little Girls.* Courtesy of Photofest   41
Figure 3.1   *Jim Brown: All American.* Courtesy of Photofest   83
Figure 3.2   *A Huey P. Newton Story.* Courtesy of Photofest   98
Figure 4.1   *When the Levees Broke.* Courtesy of Photofest   108

FOREWORD

Agency as Remembering and Retelling

Mark A. Reid*

> The potential that concerns me is that of black filmmaking in this country. By raising funds himself, using blacks in most of the creative positions, and—to the shock of the cynical and jaded—making money, Spike has thrown down the gauntlet at those black filmmakers awaiting the blessings of cinema's "great white fathers."
>
> —Nelson George, The Foreword to *He's Gotta Have It*[1]

Most book-length works, book chapters, and academic and film articles that discuss the work of Spike Lee do not cover his documentaries; and when they do, the article narrowly focuses on a single nonfiction film. I admit that I have done this in all my writing on one of America's most important filmmakers. Therefore, when I was given an opportunity to review a manuscript about Lee's documentary work I welcomed the challenge and found that Lee's talent in telling human stories covers many waterfronts of blackness with passionate visually sincere brushstrokes. CNN reporter and talk show host Anderson Cooper considers Spike Lee as a major figure in contemporary black American cultural politics. This is evidenced in *Anderson Cooper's 360°* interviews with Lee on such issues as Donald Sterling's (former owner of the Los Angeles Spurs basketball team) recorded racist diatribe, the gentrification of New York City's historically

---

*Mark A. Reid is Professor of English at the University of Florida. He is the author of *Redefining Black Film* (U. of California Press, 1993), *PostNegritude Visual and Literary Culture* (SUNY Press, 1997), and *Black Lenses, Black Voices: African American Film Now* (Rowman & Littlefield, 2005).

black communities, and the use of the "N" word in Quentin Tarrantino's *Django Unchained*.

Lee is a late-comer to documentary filmmaking and there exist many highly respected African-American documentarians like Madeline Anderson, Carol Parrott Blue, Stanley Nelson, Michelle Parkerson, Marlon Riggs, Jacqueline Shearer, Yvonne Welbon, and others who paved the way for Spike Lee. Unlike these filmmakers, Lee's entry into nonfiction film comes after a long and critically successful career in writing, producing, and making fiction films. For this reason, a volume on his social documentaries merits our attention.

The Spike Lee Brand makes a very important contribution to scholarly studies of the film-work of Spike Lee by looking at his documentaries. The author's coverage intelligently places Lee in the pantheon of important social political documentarians such as Claude Lanzmann and Emile de Antonio. The volume is probably the first single-authored work that I am aware of that covers Spike Lee's documentaries. It is a finely written piece that should have already been published here in the USA.

The volume is well organized in sections that explain Lee's overall film-works before it examines his documentaries. Delphine Letort's coverage of Lee's work is prefaced with comments on his narrative films, which then are distinguished from the style of his documentaries. She analyzes the different distinguishing elements between Lee's fiction and nonfiction films, while she insists on the similar political qualities that prevail regardless of the two different genres.

Letort's balanced appraisal of Lee's nonfiction films is complemented with discussions about how Lee's documentaries address issues that concern racism in urban America. *The Spike Lee Brand* indicates how Lee's documentaries show black agency through the community's collective actions that demand legal and judicial changes. Each chapter indirectly provides reasons why cultural anthropologists, public policymakers, film scholars, and audiences should invest more attention to Spike Lee's social documentaries and the recorded voices of those who bear witness to their predicament.

Acknowledgments

I started researching and writing this book after watching Spike Lee's documentaries about Hurricane Katrina, which provided insight into the images of distress that had flooded the screens of French television. My study gradually expanded into a full-length book after working on *Four Little Girls* and *A Huey P. Newton Story*, which I discovered challenged the historical narrative of the Civil Rights movement as I was teaching it in my civilization courses. Not only do these films investigate the past in an attempt to reveal untold truths, thus placing Spike Lee among such innovative documentary filmmakers as Emile de Antonio and Errol Morris, but they also convey an African-American perspective which I have endeavored to present to my students. Spike Lee's documentaries have provided useful teaching material, allowing students to further their historical understanding of the periods presented in the films. I wish to thank my students for their enthusiastic responses to the images we screened and commented together, which provided the initial incentive to this project.

I am grateful to my dear colleagues and friends Eliane Elmaleh and Brigitte Felix, who have both been a source of inspiration and unflinching support through the years we have been working together at the University of Maine (Le Mans, France). Through discussion and debate they have helped me gain confidence in various research projects—including this book of which they heard the first words. My thanks also go to John Wilde who has been a very careful reader to most of the pages that follow. His comments helped improve the quality of my writing and I truly appreciate his insight and many suggestions.

My home university granted me a six-month sabbatical leave, allowing me to pursue the research necessary for the completion of this book. I wish to express my gratitude to this institution as well as to my research lab (3L.AM—Langues, Littératures, Linguistique de l'Université d'Angers et du Maine) and its directors Nathalie Prince, Franck Laurent, and Benaouda Lebdai. I have collaborated with my colleagues at the Department of English on various projects or courses, which have helped broaden my knowledge in different fields of study. I want to acknowledge their support through this friendly note: Redouane Aboueddahab, Alban Daumas, Laïli Dor, William Gleeson, Laurence Guillois-Becel, Jeffrey Hopes, Xavier Lachazette, Elisabeth Lamothe, Hélène Lecossois, Laurence Mauger, Brigitte Moriceau, Estelle Rivier, Anne-Marie Santin-Guettier, and Richard Tholoniat.

I extend my gratitude to Nicole Vigouroux-Frey who trusted me a few years ago when I timidly started researching films, following an intuition that she helped sharpen by her insightful questions and suggestions. She has offered her continuous support over the years and I thank her for her friendship, her intellectual rigor, and her pragmatic advice. I also had the chance to attend Jean Rasenberger's film lectures when I was a student at Occidental College; she offered the greatest thought-provoking courses I ever had in film studies, challenging the students into watching art films that I would never have discovered without her guidance.

A great deal of gratitude goes to colleagues who have guided my research in the past few years and furthered my understanding of films—including Hélène Charley, Serge Chauvin, Nicole Cloarec, Emmanuelle Delanoë-Brun, Renée Dickason, Georges Fournier, Georges-Claude Guilbert, Janice D. Hamlet, Anthony T. Larson, Isabelle Le Corff, Gilles Menegado, Monica Michlin, Mark A. Reid, David Roche, Dominique Sipière, Penny Starfield, Taïna Tuhkunen, and Shannon Wells-Lassagne.

Last but not least, I'm exceedingly grateful to Professor Michael T. Martin who has provided me with consistent support for the past couple of years—responding enthusiastically to all my questions and emails. His informative criticism has guided my research efforts, bringing this work into sharper focus. He suggested new paths of study which have enriched my approach to black film studies. He invited me to serve on the advisory editorial board of *Black Camera* (Indiana University Press), which has been an exciting adventure that has broadened my perspectives on black filmmaking and stimulated new avenues of research.

I also owe a great debt to the anonymous peer reviewers whose stimulating, insightful remarks helped me reshuffle the text into a publishable piece.

Support for this publication was provided by:

List of Abbreviations

IGIW	If God Is Willing and Da Creek Don't Rise
WTLB	When the Levees Broke: A Requiem in Four Acts
ABC	American Broadcast Company
BBC	British Broadcasting Company
CNN	Cable News Network
ESPN	Entertainment and Sports Programming Network
HBO	Home Box Office
BP	British Petroleum
FEMA	Federal Emergency Management Agency
HANO	Housing Authority of New Orleans
HUD	Department of Housing and Urban Development
MMS	Minerals Management Service
PBS	Public Broadcasting Company

Introduction

Spike Lee's artistic engagement with racial politics can be traced throughout his film career, which is marred by repeated controversies drawing attention to his persona as a public figure whose outspoken views consistently challenge the myth of the United States as a color-blind society. His fiction films earned him recognition as a committed filmmaker, both disrupting and reviving racial stereotypes while challenging dominant modes of representation in popular culture. While this book is primarily concerned with his work as a documentarian, it is useful to note that the "Spike Lee Brand" encapsulates a filmmaking style and a racial perspective that are disseminated in all of his film productions—whether fiction or nonfiction. Spike Lee expresses his political views through recounting fictional situations that are often based on real stories, prompting heated debates on issues of race, class, and gender that are often eschewed by the mainstream media. Be they box-office hits or financial failures, Hollywood big-budget productions or cheap digital films,[1] Lee's feature films and documentary projects further reflection on those racial matters that provide the focus of his narratives, interrogating the legacies of Jim Crow over the present.

She's Gotta Have it (1986) daringly foregrounds the representation of black female sexuality on screen; *School Daze* (1988) tackles intraracial class and color prejudice; *Do the Right Thing* (1989) questions the intertwined notions of race and class in a multicultural ghetto; *Mo' Better Blues* (1990) romanticizes jazz culture; *Jungle Fever* deals with interracial sex (1991); *Malcolm X* (1992) relates the personal and political path of iconic black nationalist Malcolm X; *Clockers* (1995) delves into the drug and crime business that thrives in the urban ghettoes; *He Got Game* (1998) interrogates the relation between basketball and business; *Bamboozled* (2000) explores the construction of racial stereotypes on screen; *She Hate*

Me (2004) represents homoerotic desire; and *Miracle at St. Anna* (2008) pinpoints the active role of black soldiers during the Second World War.

While these feature films established the cinematographic rules that became idiosyncratic style in his fiction and nonfiction endeavors, they also demonstrate Lee's consistent interest in factual history, which may account for the reason why he turned to documentary filmmaking and continues to devote much time and energy to such ventures. The filmmaker's commitment to the documentary is rarely discussed in the abundant critical literature devoted to his filmic output, which prioritizes the study of his fiction drama and his treatment of taboo subjects—including miscegenation, black sexuality, minstrelsy, etc. Each newly released feature unavoidably stirs up controversy, prompting the opinionated filmmaker to take advantage of every public opportunity to vent his views and engage discussions about the issues that confront African Americans in their everyday life. His controversial statements tend to overshadow his documentary production, which however offers a unique perspective on the effects of race and class in American society.

Ranging from history to sports and music, his documentaries tackle a diversity of topics in an attempt to challenge racial stereotypes and prejudices, furthering the "struggles for representation" that characterize the tradition of African-American documentary. Film scholars Phyllis R. Klotman and Janet K. Cutler argue that the documentary genre has provided African-American filmmakers a tool with which "to interrogate and reinvent history" allowing them "to assert their view of reality."[2] Lee follows in the wake of African-American documentarians who responded to a struggle to be seen and used nonfiction as a means of cultural and political expression, retrieving historical episodes and African-American figures from collective oblivion. His concern for the life of African Americans in the face of Jim Crow's enduring legacies makes him a black documentarian broaching themes that would remain repressed if not tackled by black minority directors—including William Miles, St Clair Bourne, Madeline Anderson, and Marlon T. Riggs, among others.[3] His filmed biographies resonate with a tradition dedicated to telling the fights of black leaders, whose historical input would never make it to the mainstream without the commitment of such filmmakers as William Greaves, Stanley Nelson, and others. Based on investigations into the lives of iconic figures like football player Jim Brown, singer Michael Jackson, basketball star Kobe Bryant, his documentaries bring to light personal experiences that serve to illustrate different aspects of the black experience.

From unearthing the history of civil rights to retracing the careers of sports icons, from documenting New Orleans's reconstruction after

Katrina to retelling the story of Michael Jackson's work ethics behind a glowing career, Lee's documentary filmmaking challenges the stereotypical representations of African Americans across the television spectrum while offering didactic tools to better comprehend the concrete impact of the color line in American society. His films beg to question the politics of representation behind highly mediatized topics, which are reductively epitomized by individuals whom the mainstream media spotlight: Michael Jackson embodies the 1980s' music revolution; Michael Jordan symbolizes the black athlete's exceptional performances; O. J. Simpson represents the archetypal black criminal; Martin Luther King stands for the whole Civil Rights movement, etc. The director considers the power of iconic photographs to frame the viewers' perceptions of events by remediating them in a narrative that complexifies the stories behind them. His biographical documentaries thus rely on a polyphony of voices that are edited in counterpoint to each other in a narrative that questions the racial discourse of the media.

The cable station Home Box Office (HBO) co-produced his first foray into the genre (*Four Little Girls*, 1997), his first sport documentary (*Jim Brown: All American*, 2002) and his two-part series about New Orleans after Katrina (*When the Levees Broke: A Requiem in Four*, 2005; *If God Is Willing and Da Creek Don't Rise*, 2010) whereas Lee's second documentary *A Huey P. Newton Story* (2001) was the first original production of BLACK STARZ! cable channel,[4] *Kobe Doin' Work* (2009) was produced by the Entertainment and Sports Programming Network (ESPN) and *Bad 25* was made in collaboration with the estates of Michael Jackson. Lee's documentaries exhibit the technical devices used in his fiction films, thus guaranteeing the filmmaker leaves his easily identifiable imprint on them, which may however undermine the credibility of his stance as a documentarian. "The documentary tradition relies heavily on being able to convey an impression of authenticity" explains film theorist Bill Nichols,[5] observing that documentary films are expected to produce a faithful representation of the world. While this widely shared belief is derived from the mimetic power of the camera, providing raw access to the world it captures on-the-fly, Lee's staunch stance on race-related issues nonetheless appears as a barrier to overcome should the audience believe in the tight correspondence between the images he records and the reality he portrays. Some commercial documentaries further prompt questions as regards his engagement to retrieve an authentic understanding of the situations he investigates. The financial contribution brought in by Sony Music, which produced some of Michael Jackson's musical videos, may have weighed on the narrative choices undergirding the making of the biographical documentary *Bad 25*. Matt Singer reviews *Bad 25* in the light of *Red Hook Summer* (2012), which broaches the secret paedophilic past of a community preacher, suggesting the filmmaker used the feature film to address the controversies which he eschewed in his documentary project about Michaeln Jackson.[6]

Lee's appropriation of the documentary mode is not seen as artistically creative. In the latest scholarly book devoted to *Spike Lee's America*, film critic David Sterritt deems that the documentaries are illustrations of Lee's hectic filmic output and contends that their informative value prevails overs their artistic quality. Summarizing in no more than a few pages the eight-hour documentary series comprising *When the Levees Broke: A Requiem in Four Acts* (2006) and its sequel *If God Is Willing and Da Creek Don't Rise* (2010), Sterritt observes that "neither film is particularly distinctive or distinguished in artistic terms, but together they comprise a work of humanistic cinema that is as laudable as it is monumental."[7] The two four-hour-long films span a five-year period and provide a sociological insight into post-Katrina New Orleans that makes them unique experiments in the contemporary televisual landscape. They also aptly illustrate Lee's creative appropriation of the various documentary techniques, blending the observational and the poetic modes to convey the emotional dimension of filming history in the making. Much attention will be devoted to the challenging viewing experience represented by this pair of films, highlighting their values as sociological documents and filmic endeavors.

This book aims to demonstrate that Lee's documentaries are as thought provoking as his most controversial feature films. Rather than adopt a comparative approach that would measure up the documentaries to their fictional counterparts, I intend to examine and critique the ideological discourse of Lee's documentaries through the narrative and aesthetic strategies they deploy. His nonfiction endeavors explore events that transformed the relationship of African Americans to American society, adopting a reflective stance that contributes to challenging assumptions and altering perception which, according to Bill Nichols, characterizes the Golden Age of documentaries that began in the 1980s and has continued unabated since.[8] Spike Lee's documentaries give voice to African Americans with a view to constructing a frame of understanding that challenges and undermines racial bias, offering critical insight into a series of events that expose the enduring weight of racial prejudice in American society and in the media. In an interview given to *Cineaste*, Lee expands on the political subtext of his intertextual filmmaking:

> I want people to think about the power of images, not just in terms of races, but how imagery is used and what sort of social impact it has—how it influences how we talk, how we think, how we view one another. In particular I want them to see how films and television have historically, from the birth of both mediums, produced and perpetuated images . . . and a lot of that madness that is still with us today.[9]

This approach undergirds his documentary filmmaking, which questions the media's treatment of and interaction with race while pinpointing the continuing effects of discrimination. Lee abundantly exploits the possibilities offered by montage to fragment the past into multiple perspectives, which confers an interesting polyphonic aspect to the films that incorporate a wide array of primary sources. His documentaries are built on a compilation of documents, either archival photographs or personal items, which reveal the existence of competing truths. Different layers of information mingle: the witnesses' personal accounts combine with archival media footage, shifting the narrative from the past to the present, from the personal to the political, from the intimate to the public. Thus the multilevel narratives call attention to the director's investigative research work into the stories of the past. Lee revives the tradition of the griot as he explores a range of storytelling techniques that exploit the African oral tradition, opening up public screen space for African Americans to testify about their lived experience of race.[10] Even though his documentaries are steeped in racial politics, they offer entertaining stories that widen their appeal to a crossover audience, allowing memory to be shared beyond the color line. This book aims to offer an in-depth study of Spike Lee's documentary filmmaking, highlighting their twofold value as documents providing valuable sociological records and as texts illustrating the director's idiosyncratic worldview.

The first chapter discusses Spike Lee's creative appropriation of the documentary, striving to analyze the shift from the participatory to the performative modes, which characterizes his approach to the genre. Lee resorts to fictional techniques including music and editing to convey the atmosphere embedded in archival footage, slowing down the television flow to counter the audience's viewing habits. The filmmaker induces a contemplative gaze when introducing stills that seem to freeze filmic movement and to suspend the time flow. Most talking head interviews are filmed with a static camera, simulating a fixed gaze that enhances the testimonial act. The combination of archival material and interviews with individuals whose confessed memories express alternative viewpoints complexifies the narrative of the past and the viewers' perception of it. Lee relinquishes the observer's position to engage with the events broached, using a conspicuous handheld camera to express corporeal engagement with the characters he accompanies. Rather than gather the materials through observation, Lee interferes with the situations depicted, entering the frame while standing among the filmed crowd or directly addressing his interviewees. However, Lee would rather remain out of shot and avoid representing his interaction with the people he films in the tradition of the participatory documentary mode. His intervention resembles an invitation for his interviewees to speak their minds freely, to revisit old stories, and to share further their views. Looking straight at the camera, the filmed characters self-consciously engage with the facts Spike Lee urges them to address. French film theorist Jean-Louis Comolli dubs documentary participants "characters" to enhance the fact that the camera captures their own *mise en scène* and their relationship to their environment which he compares to a social stage.[11] Lee's camera pays careful attention to details that build characterization, prompting his interviewees to speak out and to take advantage of the opportunity presented by the camera to address a wider audience. The spoken words combine with Lee's elusive authorial presence, emphasizing the creative process of his documentary filmmaking as a reflexive construction of representation. The interviews are staged and the characters pose as themselves, undermining the illusion that the documentary may capture truth without the mediation of the camera. Conversely, the visibility of the recording apparatus promotes the film as a self-reflexive construction and a carefully crafted representation.

The second chapter delves into the interplay between the visual representation of history and the notion of oral memory, which Lee explores when examining the legacy of the Civil Rights movement. Relying on eyewitnesses' testimonials to reconstruct the untold stories of the past, he uses films as a didactic tool to transmit African-American history from the viewpoint of its actors and to redress the distortions and fill in the omissions of the dominant narrative. Lee offers his films as platforms to his interviewees who share their memories of the past (*Four Little Girls*) or voice their critical views of the present (*If God Is Willing and Da Creek Don't Rise*), thus taking part in the construction of collective memory around specific events. Historian Marc Ferro posits that the study of the relation between history and memory on screen cannot be broached without considering the economic and ideological values pervading the business of filmmaking—which he refers to as the "nonvisible" or the "extrafilmic."[12] The historian's critical approach to films includes the economic and intellectual context of production in so far at it affects the construction of images and narrative structures. His methodology argues for an interdisciplinary perspective that focuses on the images as signs of an extradiegetic reality, opening up film studies to various disciplines: "Consider images as such at the risk of using other forms of knowledge to grasp them even better."[13] The interdisciplinary nature of film studies undergirds the framework of this book, which aims to decipher Spike Lee's documentaries as original contributions to the understanding of African-American cultural memories. It therefore foregrounds a multimethodological approach, combining semiology and narratology with history and ideology to better comprehend the films' critical discourse, simultaneously articulating an analytical perspective on Spike Lee's interpretation of the facts mentioned.

The third chapter examines the interwoven issues of media and race, which Lee addresses through portraying historical events or cultural icons, the perception of which has been shaped by the media—both television and films. Communication Professors Mark P. Orbe and A. Elizabeth Lyons emphasize the multidimensional nature of Lee's work,[14] which mixes social and cultural criticism when laying bare the linguistic biases strategically used by the mainstream media. Lee's intertextual work aims to debunk the visual stereotypes of African Americans reinforcing race and class prejudices in the media. The study of his documentaries provides a stimulating insight into the media politics of representation, for Lee is able to pinpoint and counter the biases of television culture as he retraces the story of the "four little girls" or the humanitarian consequences of Hurricane Katrina. He exposes the injustices of the present and the past, opening up television screen space to African Americans who are eager to bear witness to history in front of the camera, fashioning narratives that allow them to make sense of their life. His documentaries self-reflexively question the images they borrow from the television archives, which have preserved the narrative of the past as captured by the media. Through investigating the aural and visual footage of Hurricane Katrina's devastating blow on New Orleans (*When the Levees Broke: A Requiem in Four Acts* and its sequel *If God Is Willing And Da Creek Don't Rise*), the filmmaker examines the dynamics of race and class that underpins the representation of African Americans in the media.

The fourth chapter discusses Spike Lee's commitment to Black Nationalism, which raises issues of ethics considering the controversial positions the director has assumed throughout his film career. Spike Lee's commercial engagements clash with his activist endeavors, undermining the credibility of his commitment to the ethics of documentary filmmaking. The biased views associated with the controversies sparked by the filmmaker undermine the search for truth which the genre signifies in popular imagination. The director's nonfiction endeavors not only encompass documentaries, but they also comprise promotional videos and commercial ads that pinpoint political inconsistencies that arouse doubts as to the ethics of blackness he seems to endorse. Some of his advertising films have even contributed to producing stereotypes—including his promotional campaigns for Nike. The cultural icons Lee celebrates (Jim Brown, Michael Jordan, Kobe Bryant, Michael Jackson) embody successful African Americans, who have managed to overcome the double prejudice of race and class, while simultaneously contributing to the commodification of African-American cultural production.[15] The "Spike Lee" label has become a trademark that not only connotes the director's commitment to relating stories from the perspective of African Americans, but it also signifies the marketing strategies endorsed by the filmmaker to pursue a career in the mainstream.

CHAPTER 1

The Making of Spike Lee's Nonfiction Joints

Drawing on film theorist Bill Nichols's groundbreaking study of the documentary, which he divides into six modes (poetic, expository, observational, participatory, reflexive, performative), this chapter reviews Spike Lee's television nonfiction filmmaking practices. Rather than lay the emphasis on the documentary's claim to authenticity, based on the supposedly mimetic power of the camera to capture truth without interference, Nichols's reflection builds on John Grierson's 1926 definition of the documentary as a genre that puts forward the "creative treatment of actuality,"[1] evoking the seemingly endless creative possibilities incipient in the relationship between the camera and its subject(s). Nichols pinpoints that filmmakers constantly modify the conventions of the documentary by exploring the interstices between creative vision and factual reproduction with a view to expressing their own perspectives and opinions. "Documentary engages with the world by representing it"[2] contends Nichols, questioning the ethical position of the filmmaker who produces a specific discourse on the world represented—oscillating between persuasion ("*I speak about them to you*") and expression ("*I speak about us to you*").[3] This tension between two viewpoints permeates Spike Lee's documentaries, revealing the degree of intimacy he develops with his subjects and his authorial presence behind the camera. Although Lee does not put forward his body on screen, rarely intruding in the frame, the films nonetheless bear the imprint of his authorial signature. His idiosyncratic voice determines the overall message endorsed by the films, whose strong informative value yet resides in the testimonials of individual subjects invited to tell their own stories in front of the camera. Documentary filmmakers are keen to express their unique view of things, spotlighting their own experiences (in the autobiographic mode) or their interlocutors' to confront commonly held assumptions. Nichols explains that their films should be analyzed as discourses: "What makes it a documentary is that this expressiveness remains coupled to representations about the social, historical world, including the world of the filmmaker as a social actor, going about his life or her life among others."[4]

This chapter discusses the director's creative appropriation of the documentary modes, which he explores to interrogate the values and the structures behind the media portrayal of African Americans. Through pulling together fictional and nonfictional devices, Lee prompts the viewer to take a critical stance at the representation of African-Americans' experiences in the media and to recognize positive role models among ordinary characters fighting for their civil rights. Lee calls attention to ordinary citizens' bravery when suggesting that the struggle of the 1960s continues in post-Katrina New Orleans; he strives to overturn the negative stereotypes foisted on nationalist figures like Huey P. Newton, whose political message of rebellion he endeavors to retrieve from the controversies surrounding the Black Panthers' history. Based on the narrative arc fashioned by the stories of individuals whose names have become renowned (or not) in relation to their deeds, Lee's documentaries exploit the biographical focus that personalizes his approach to the social and historical topics he investigates. The emotional dimension of the endeavor challenges the detached and distanced glance which may be expected from a documentary; however, it promotes debate over racial issues and translates the filmmaker's commitment to fighting prejudice through analyzing concrete examples. Delving into the personal experiences of African-American characters, Lee aims to assess the weight of history and politics on their everyday life, thereby producing an inside view of racism which he is able to perceive through their eyes. A political agenda undergirds Lee's nonfiction filmmaking, geared toward rejuvenating the image of African Americans, whose active historical and social role he wishes to underline.

Rather than adopt the expository mode of documentary filmmaking, which puts forth the indexical quality of the recorded footage and the truth value of the verbal commentary helping shape a logical argument, Lee's documentaries are reflexive tools insofar as they question the informative value of the archival records which compose his film materials. Significantly, Lee unveils the filmic apparatus during his interviews, revealing their staged dimension for example, which may be read as a sign of his desire to lay bare the technical aspects of the film's construction in an attempt to convey authenticity. From the credit montage he develops to introduce the viewers into a complex situation, which was simplified into a few iconic shots and catchphrases in the media, to the narrative construction of the documentary as a television series that investigates the long-term consequences of Katrina, Lee leaves his creative imprint on the genre's flexible formula.

Investigating the Facts through the Camera Lens

Spike Lee's fiction and nonfiction filmmaking practices feed off each other: his feature films include multiple references to extradiegetic reality whereas his nonfiction films exhibit fictional devices that dramatize the documentaries' search for truth. Based in the Brooklyn neighborhood of Bedford-Stuyvesant, *Do the Right Thing* dramatizes the daily misdemeanors which press on individual interrelationships in a multicultural environment. Giving rise to an array of stimulating comments, the film influenced and shaped the popular perception of Lee's cultural politics. Political scientist Catherine Pouzoulet evokes the creative tension between fact and fiction that permeates the diegetic space of *Do the Right Thing*. She draws a list of all the news items that transpire into the fictional representation of New York, highlighting plotlines and tropes that resonate with notorious cases of racist violence.[5] The film's narrative builds on explicit references to "incidents of interethnic violence, such as the killing of Michael Griffith, who, as he was leaving a pizzeria in the predominantly white Howard Beach section of Queens, was fatally beaten by Italian-American youths armed with baseball bats."[6] Lee's storylines unfold against a historical-factual background and allude to real-life events, the individual and community impact of which he explores through emplotment. Fact and fiction characteristically interweave in Lee's filmmaking, allowing crossovers that challenge generic conventions and audience expectations. The warm yellowish tones of the image track in *Do the Right Thing* signify the pull of fiction, which undermines a realistic depiction of the ghetto's societal ills.[7]

The credits of *Malcolm X* cut from a burning American flag to video footage showing the police beating of Rodney King, whereas the opening sequence of *Clockers* includes staged autopsy and crime-scene photographs in a drug-plagued city.[8] *School Daze* opens with a montage of photographs portraying African-American athletes Jackie Robinson, Willie Mays, and Muhammad Ali, thus evoking sports as a cultural background shared by the characters and the viewers. These glimpses of an outside reality are presented as the basis for the dramatic situations presented, suggesting that the fictional characters are enmeshed in plots that are drawn from the commonplace world of everyday experience. Factual and fictional elements are tightly intertwined in Spike Lee's filmmaking following an editing technique which is epitomized in the title sequence of the previously mentioned films. Interestingly, he adopts a similar strategy to introduce the thematic concerns that are developed in such documentaries as *Four Little Girls* and *A Huey P. Newton Story*, ambiguously resorting to fictional devices to engage us with the facts mentioned—including music, editing, and characterization, among others. His documentaries make use of musical scores and carefully stylized filmmaking that affect the meaning of the film.

Four Little Girls examines the psychological impact on both individual and community levels of the terrorist murders of fourteen-year-old Carole Robertson, Cynthia Wesley, Addie Mae Collins, and eleven-year-old Denise McNair, killed by a blast while preparing for a special youth service at the Sixteenth Street Baptist Church in Birmingham, Alabama. The title of the film echoes the label coined by the media which dramatized the fate of the victims into a news flash story: the girls' lives were ended by the explosion of the bomb, which had been planted in the basement of the church and went off during Sunday School service on September 15, 1963. The documentary's explanatory approach to segregation provides valuable insight into the power dynamics of the period, whilst its heterogeneous visual style questions the oral and visual discourse commodifying the memory of the victims.

The opening sequence of *Four Little Girls* interestingly presents the film as a fictional biopic as the voice of Joan Baez sings "Birmingham Sunday" while the camera tracks along a cemetery, capturing through a blue filter tear-blurred images of the graves that dot the landscape. The sequence shifts back and forth between the present and the past, stitching together black and white archival footage of the 1960s' police repression and protests for equality with colored shots of the tombstones. Editing dramatizes the introduction of the four teenagers' photographic portraits resting in the cemetery where they were buried. The entwined visual tracks oppose the peace and quiet of the cemetery where the youngsters now lay to the archival photographs of children proudly marching the streets. The camera zooms in on the boys' and girls' determined, smiling faces standing out in the crowd of demonstrators, thus spotlighting the children's political awareness and commitment. The credits capture the imaginary imprint left by the struggle in a few shots that slowly morph into an animated drawing, depicting three figures holding hands in a chain of solidarity, symbolically linking the present and the past. The abstract images foster poetic contemplation as the voice of Joan Baez transcends yesterday's violence to enshroud the deceased girls with motherly tenderness. The singer recounts the events of that fateful day in a lullaby song, numbering the dead as though she was teaching counting rhymes. Her soft soprano voice creates an intimate proximity with the dead, setting the emotional tone that pervades the film.

Four Little Girls sacrifices the expository mode drawn from the indexical quality of the photographs included in the montage for the poetic affect achieved by the haunting, ghostly quality of the blurry blue-tinted cemetery footage. Nichols argues that "this mode stresses mood, tone, and effect much more than displays of factual knowledge or acts of rhetorical persuasion."[9] The film, although undergirded by an expository purpose and dedicated to the memory of the "four little girls," combines informational and entertaining elements without giving in to sensationalism. While the poetic mode indicates the director's authorial presence, it also metaphorically introduces the film as a remembrance tool and a tribute. The tragedy of the "four little girls" is told from a subjective standpoint, marked by an affective relationship to the past which Lee does not try to repress, for he wishes to grasp and convey the emotional impact of the girls' deaths on the African-American community. Lee is obviously not just concerned with recovering the truth through an investigation that drives him to examine archival documents.[10] Even though he resorts to the same narrative strategies of compilation filmmaking as Emile de Antonio and Errol Morris, collecting interviews and archival material to plumb the past, Lee's endeavor does not aim to produce objective truth. His documentaries blur the boundaries between fiction and nonfiction, thereby putting forth the uncertainties raised by the investigative process. The portrayal of the "four little girls" limits the documentary project, for Lee can only give us access to memories of them, prompting the viewer to imagine their characters from the anecdotes related about them. Nichols contends that the documentary and the nondocumentary films overlap as categories, for filmmakers experiment with the medium to interpret the documents and facts exposed.[11]

Spike Lee's second nonfiction film broaches the radicalization of the civil rights struggle through the emergence of the Black Panther Party for Self-Defense. Rather than retrace the life of Huey P. Newton in a biopic that would strive to capture the elusive personality of the Panthers' leader, *A Huey P. Newton Story* is a recording of Roger Guenveur Smith's one-man show first presented in February 1997 at the Joseph Papp Public Theater on Broadway. While the film plays on the fascination elicited by the nationalist rebel, Spike Lee deconstructs the iconic figure of Huey P. Newton by laying stress on the political reasoning behind the party's call for revolutionary social action. The credits of *A Huey P. Newton Story* are conspicuously edited from an array of archival footage used to convey contextual information and to construct the visual discourse of the film, thus adding Lee's personal perspective to Smith's portrayal of Huey P. Newton. The focus on archival footage anchors the documentary in the 1960s, providing a historical background to the performance. The film starts with a sequence that cuts from a prologue to the informative credits: the story of the Black Panther Party for Self-Defense is encapsulated in a few iconic shots taken from television newsreel archives whereas red typed letters appear over a grey wire netting drawn on a dark screen, giving background information on the making of the film. Cross editing disrupts the narrative flow in *A Huey P. Newton Story*, signifying gaps in the history of the Panthers, whereas the motif of the wire netting metaphorically connotes a prison tale. The opening sequence articulates the distance between the media story of the Panthers and the version endorsed by Lee, signified by the slow musical score which downplays the dramatic media spin. The interstices between the two narrative strands, opposing archival footage to the title credits, shed light on the spectacle of the Panthers' political performances, attracting cameras and reporters in search of sensational breaking news. The *mise en scène* organized by the Panthers themselves creates a *mise-en-abyme* in the film, which challenges the documentary form to engage with the notion of representation.

The events that marked the decade are visually summarized through iconic scenes: the Panthers demonstrated along with peace activists against the Vietnam war; Malcolm X called for change; the counterculture of the hippies blossomed; Angela Davis accused the police of discriminating against African Americans; Edgar J. Hoover warned the people against Newton as a violent revolutionary; Orson Welles characterized Hamlet in one of Newton's favorite plays as "a gangster with a conscience"; the Panthers were dubbed a "threat to harmony" by Oakland's mayor; window posters of Newton were targeted with gunshots; Newton was arrested for allegedly killing a policeman; Fred Hampton and Mark Clark were murdered by "99 shots" fired by the police[12]; Hollywood star Marlon Brando took a public stance in support of the Panthers at Bobby Hutton's funeral; Martin Luther King called for a "revolution of values." Every piece of film divulges incomplete information as though the story of the Panther Party for Self-Defense had not yet been written. Archival footage in the credit sequence spans the events from Newton's arrest in 1967 to Fred Hampton's murder in 1969; it is not randomly organized nor chronologically arranged as could be suggested by the compilation of facts it covers. Fast editing adds to the tense and confused atmosphere of the period, envisioning the Black Panther Party as part of the counterculture movement of the 1960s.

The opening sequence depicts the Panthers' activists demonstrating outside the Alameda courthouse in Oakland with a reporter cynically commenting on the load of work awaiting the Panthers' lawyers working for Newton's defense attorney Charles Garry, considering the high rate of arrests that took place among the Panthers. Another reporter then appears on screen, faltering in his speech and calling for a "cut" that points to the media's everyday *mise en scène* of the world in the news programs. The film cuts from the media spectacle of the Panthers to the responses they provoked. It includes an interview of an African-American woman testifying about gunshots she witnessed in front of the camera which lingers on graffiti adorning the outside wall of a tenement house ("off the pigs"), thus dramatizing the risk taken by the television crew in a Panther dominated area and by the policemen venturing in a quarter that has dangerously run out of control. The close-up on the words defiantly sprayed on the wall draws attention to the engagement of the Panthers, who conspicuously claim the territory with "graffiti style [that] disrupts the aesthetic of authority."[13] Through the insertion of a behind-the-scenes glance at media reporting, the documentarian self-reflexively pinpoints that the positioning of the camera constructs the representation of the world and frames its perceptions.

Based on a one-man show whose narrative Lee interweaves with archival images, *A Huey P. Newton Story* interestingly merges fiction and nonfiction which documentary critic Michael Renov considers as two interrelated narrative modes that share key conceptual and discursive characteristics. Facts and fiction merge when the camera starts rolling, transforming an interviewee's words and body language into acting for the camera. Playing the role of Huey P. Newton and assuming his political voice, Roger Guenveur Smith's interpretation enhances the process of filmmaking surrounding him. Renov notes that the creative power embedded in the documentary when stating that "nonfiction contains any number of 'fictive' elements, moments at which a presumably objective representation of the world encounters the necessity of creative intervention."[14] Nonfiction filmmaking relies on the same processes of narrativization and characterization that underpin fiction films, making use of stylistic elements including angle shots and editing to dramatize the nonfiction stories investigated by a conspicuous camera. Lee resorts to recognizable tropes such as low-angle shots reminiscent of *Do the Right Thing* and musical tunes used in other fiction films,[15] which signify his presence behind the camera and contribute to the transformation of his interviewees into characters.

From the Participatory to the Performative Mode

In *Issues in Contemporary Documentary*, Professor of communications Jane Chapman assesses the state of current documentary film practice through a series of case studies that explore the creative tension between two contradictory intents within the genre:[16] she argues that the performative documentary oscillates between "two poles of either letting the event speak for itself (observation) or providing a single authoritative voice (narration)."[17] The consistent appeal of the documentary resides in its conflicting approach to the real world, opposing an unmediated reflection to a subjective perspective. Spike Lee's documentaries draw their fascinating power from this negotiation between two viewing modes: apart from a few questions that can be overheard, Lee remains in the background and offers screen space to his filmed subjects, whose stories he shapes into a narrative. The voices of the characters interviewed come to the fore: witnesses testify to the truth of events they recount, voicing their views and feelings toward the situations they mention.

Characterization is best achieved through performance in Spike Lee's documentaries, empowering the interviewees who directly address the camera, eagerly staging their speech and action to make themselves heard. Following Nichols's documentary classification, Lee's nonfiction films interweave the participatory and performative modes. Although they mainly revolve around a web of interviews, illustrating a pattern of collaboration between filmmaker and subjects, they nonetheless bring the emotional intensities of embodied experience and knowledge to the fore through characterization. Nichols explains that "performative documentaries intensify the rhetorical desire to be compelling and tie it less to a persuasive goal than an affective one."[18] Spike Lee develops characterization to overcome the boundaries of the participatory mode, prompting his interviewees to bring in such props as photographs and objects presented as pieces of evidence that characterize their relationship to the past. The documentary participants therefore seem to pose as themselves, which turns the whole filmmaking process into an empowering experience for them. Lee's camera operates as a go-between between the personal and the public, allowing private comments to become political statements as they are broadcast on television, reaching a wider audience.

The documentary series *When the Levees Broke: A Requiem in Four Acts* and *If God Is Willing and Da Creek Don't Rise* provides an illuminating example of the power which can be drawn from the camera, reversing the dynamics of filmmaking: the camera's investigative function is reduced by each interviewee's *mise en scène*. Rather than being the object of the gaze, the interviewees become the authors of their speech, which they embody and interpret in front of the camera eye. The two films illustrate the journey of Phyllis Montana-Leblanc whose story is disseminated throughout the episodes of the series, making her a familiar figure by the end of the first season of the series. A few minutes before the ending credits of Act 4 in *When the Levees Broke: A Requiem in Four Acts*, she speaks to the camera in a direct address. Sitting inside her Federal Emergency Management Administration (FEMA) trailer, she reads a very intimate statement about her experience of Katrina, which testifies to the relationship of trust and confidence that has developed between herself and the filmmaker:

> Not just the levees broke, the spirit broke, my spirit broke
> The families broke apart
> I want my mama back, I want my sister back, I want my nephew back.
> The auction block broke from so many African American bodies.
> The sense of direction was broken because of all the darkness
> There was light from time to time but they broke away and left us.
> My being together broke when I fell apart.
> The smell broke away from my skin when I came out of the waters
> The waters that came and stood, still, with the bodies of my people.
> The dogs, shit, pigs, rats, snakes and "heard of" alligators.
> The broken smile, the broken minds, the broken lives.
> And you know something? Out of all this brokenness I have begun to mend
> With God and my deep deep commitment to infinite strength, to never give up

> I am mending, God willing, for a long long time.
> So when you see the waters, when you see the levees breaking,
> Know what they really broke along with them. [*WTLB*, End of Act 4]

The commentary soundtrack of the DVD discloses unexpected details as to that scene: Lee explains that the woman proposed to read a poem she had composed the night before and he turned the camera on, sensing that it would provide further insight into post-Katrina New Orleans, where chaos was still visually and psychologically overwhelming. He asked her to re-enact her reading in order to adjust lighting and framing, which provides a highly moving and thought-provoking moment in the film. One stops gazing at the spectacle of destruction to ponder on the words the woman utters, her voice betraying the deep emotions she struggles with. Viewers sense that her statement was indeed no improvisation: she reads out the poem articulating what it means to go on living after Katrina has torn her life apart, giving vent to her frustration and disappointment with the authorities in charge. As an active participant in the film, she self-consciously opened the door of her FEMA trailer to expose what her life had become to outside observers, thus reversing the relationship which the camera establishes with the filmed subject: she would not content herself with being a witness whose testimony was recorded, for she was determined to reach out to the outside world. Her private thoughts become political statements as she sits reading in front of Spike Lee's camera, which represents a window onto the world for the woman who grabs the opportunity to make herself heard. Her comments are not unlike the rap songs of Shelton Shakespeare Alexander with their blend of politics and poetry; the young man sings his own rap at the end of Act 2 to recount his experience of Katrina (*WTLB*). Talking in front of Spike Lee's camera obviously became part of the healing process for Phyllis Montana-Leblanc—and other filmed participants, for she made efforts to jot down the words she wanted to communicate and to have the audience listen to. She even wrote a book after the film, which Spike Lee prefaced, thus pursuing the autobiographical narration she had started in the film.[19]

If God Is Willing and Da Creek Don't Rise begins with a prologue by the same Phyllis Montana-Leblanc who delivers a two-minute soliloquy and stages her performance in stark contrast to her final appearance in *When the Levees Broke: A Requiem in Four Acts*: she was seated in a FEMA trailer then, bending over to read her text in a low voice, whereas she delivers her speech like a rap song with fast rhythm and alliterations that underline her bold defiance in the sequel to the film. One can only be struck by the change of tone that permeates her voice as she endorses the role of a spokesperson for New Orleans African-American community. As a witness and a survivor, she has relinquished the first person narration to enhance the political overtones of her comments, using the plural "we" to convey collective sentiment. She raises her voice and her arms to physically embody the resilience she has developed over the past five years, thus fostering aliveness in her performance of resistance. The background provides a theatrical setting that points to the integration of ruins into local landscape: the woman stands in front of a rundown house whose barred windows suggest the place has been abandoned, maybe even condemned for safety reasons, visually exhibiting the traces of Katrina's devastating impact on building structures. Rather than convey an image of destruction, the façade has been painted over with graffiti depicting New Orleans skyline, thus hinting at the redeeming power of art. Phyllis Montana-Leblanc's introduction to the film discloses the psychological journey she has made since Katrina, transcending her frustration and depression into an activist commitment that pervades every line she speaks out loud.

In *When the Levees Broke*, the woman recounted that she had cried for help on a drowning rooftop, desperately watching helicopters hover about and away. At the time she was concerned with bearing witness about her experience of Katrina whereas she draws a list of political demands in *If God Is Willing*, demonstrating that she has engaged in a healing process by reflecting on the political and collective dimension of Katrina. Calling for change with the past, Phyllis Montana-Leblanc's presentation foreshadows the documentary's thematic concerns: poverty, death statistics, education, levee maintenance, politicians' lies, health care, corporate greed, environmental issues will be broached, widening the scope of the documentary beyond the racial issues Spike Lee brought to the fore when dealing with Katrina in *When the Levees Broke*. Her opening lines point to the prejudices that victimized the low-income residents in New Orleans, suffering from the cold-blooded contempt of those "in tailored suits" whom she accuses of being responsible for the deaths she metaphorically evokes as "hooded white sheets." The recurring line "If God Is Willing and Da Creek Don't Rise" evokes a natural cycle that cannot be broken, suggesting that New Orleans's fate belongs to forces that are beyond man's power to control. The speaker, however, uses the anaphora "no more" to suggest Katrina should prompt a rupture with the racial, segregated past of the city:

No more weeping mothers as their child's body lies in the streets.
No more hate from those whose tailored suits still resemble hooded white sheets.
If God Is Willing and Da Creek Don't Rise
No more closing schools in all-black neighborhood meant to teach.
No more lying about the numbers they said they couldn't reach.
If God Is Willing and Da Creek Don't Rise
No more nightmare of breaching levees, black waters that did come, murder and drown.
No more silence, Tea parties, racial division, poverty, yes, we can.
The pavements we will pound.
If God Is Willing and Da Creek Don't Rise
No more leaving poor folks to die because they cannot afford medical care.
No more singing we shall overcome 'cause we're already there.
No more political pushers who use our time to sell their lies.
No more sacrificing the American people leaving us with nothing but sighs.
No more total audacity, explosive fire is gone. Bodies are nine plus two.
No more corporate oil wanting their lives back. Indictment of criminal charges, the whole damn crew.
No more use of our Gulf Coast waters, wetlands, heritage and soil.
No more "up yours, Louisiana."
But we all know there's blood in the BP oil.
If God Is Willing and Da Creek Don't Rise.

Phyllis Montana-Leblanc's stance of individual fortitude is both appealing and disconcerting, expressing her sense of outrage and frustration in the face of continued perceived injustice.

The last but one line of her soliloquy evokes the 2010 Gulf Coast oil spill, known as the Deepwater Horizon incident, which destroyed a significant amount of fish and wildlife before it was finally contained. The oil slick caused havoc that affected Americans along the Mississippi Gulf Coast beyond class and race. As she channels her rage into powerful lines that connote the unending struggle which underpins individual and collective survival in the "new New Orleans," Phyllis embodies a civic stance that has reverberated throughout the city, giving rise to a network of citizen initiatives led by individual celebrities such as Brad Pitt and by the collective mobilization of civil society. Sociologists J. Steven Picou and Brent K. Marshall note that "countless private citizens from New Orleans and the Gulf Coast have volunteered both time and resources to initiate a grouping of their neighborhoods and communities"[20] and to organize life after Katrina. Lee develops what could be dubbed a "citizens' documentary" through *If God Is Willing and Da Creek Don't Rise*, articulating the concerns of all those who have been affected by the neoliberal choices guiding reconstruction in New Orleans. The film highlights the commitment of a group of citizen activists among the interviewees who, while addressing such issues as education, housing, labor, and crime on a local level, testify to broader national and international dynamics. As he investigates further the conditions of reconstruction in post-Katrina New Orleans, Lee provides an overview of the impact of neoliberal policies, which more often than not are perceived in a negative light by the African-American residents. He adopts a militant tone which is missing from the other films, proposing models of action through the characters he accompanies.

Spike Lee's documentaries are mainly built around a web of interviews, providing a host of individual perspectives on the stories which constitute the narrative backbone of the films. This technique allows the filmmaker to grasp some events such as Katrina from various angles, assessing the multiple consequences of the breach of the levees for a diversity of people. The films achieve an overview by combining an overlay of archival material with the voiceover of witnesses, whose views either converge or diverge, thus constructing a dialectical relationship between the present and the past, the private and the public, articulated to issues of race and class. This type of construction enhances the discourse built around characters or events, the perception of which was reductively framed by the media. Not only are the "four little girls" fleshed out by the memories confessed in front of the camera, but Michael Jackson is also humanized through the voices that recall him in *Bad 25*. The interplay of several documentary modes highlights the prominent role given to interviews in Lee's films; however, they are incorporated in a filmic discourse that first and foremost displays the director's creative input and political views.

Discerning the Authorial Voice

Contrary to Michael Moore who conspicuously stages himself as a filmmaker in search of truth,[21] Spike Lee remains almost invisible in his nonfiction films. The overall narratives nonetheless betray his pervasive authorial presence: his musical scores poeticize the filmed landscapes; editing produces dramatic effect and conveys his reasoning; low-angle shots express his presence behind the camera as he strives to empower his interviewees through framing; he may even orally intrude in some of the filmed testimonies although he is nowhere to be seen on screen. Lee draws attention to racial prejudice by interviewing characters whose speech endorses stereotypical views. The filmmaker's voice can first be heard in Act 2 of *When the Levees Broke: A Requiem in Four Acts*, asking Emil Dumesnil, a white man, whether he was looking for Bin Laden when he returned to the Lower Ninth Ward with a 9mm handgun. Lee's mocking tone exposes the racial bias of his interviewee's fear-induced self-protective violence, whereas the question enhances the shocking irony of the situation he wishes to denounce as fear prevailed over solidarity. His selection of interviews undergirds the dramatic arc of the films, retaining the most outrageous statements among white characters whose racist views he thus spotlights.

Spike Lee's interviewing technique echoes Claude Lanzmann's obsessive search for technical details when investigating the processes of human destruction in *Shoah* (1985). The directors thereby dig up stories that account for the crushing psychological trauma their interviewees have been through. When Will Chittenden explains he has been on medication for months, for sleep would never come after Katrina, Lee asks him to name the type of medication he has been taking. The man gives a long list of brand-name pills, which attests to the trauma he has undergone and to its enduring effect in the present. Paris Ervin restrains his tears when recalling that he discovered his own mother's corpse in a house that had not been searched by FEMA contrary to what the markings on the door indicated, which prompted him to imagine her death more vividly as her body was found crushed under a refrigerator [*WTLB*, Act 4, 14:00]. Editor Sam Pollard explains that he selected from among a hundred and thirty interviews the stories which fit into Lee's narrative of devastation in New Orleans. Gathering together the pieces of a jigsaw puzzle, he helped produce a film which puts forth the witnesses' experiences instead of the filmmaker's authorial voice. His editing work consisted in organizing the film's narrative from the witnesses' accounts, whose emotional authenticity he strove to retain:

> Everybody's got different pieces of the story, and someone who might be good at the beginning is not so good when it comes to talking about the evacuation. Someone who doesn't

say much in the beginning is great when it comes to talking about the flooding. So I'm trying to find the rhythms of these people, to create a journey, an arc. . . . If you find the right characters, the right interviews, they can give you a visceral sense of immediacy, of being there, so you feel emotionally connected to it. When this man tells you about finding his mother's body under the refrigerator, because she hadn't gotten out . . . [. . .] You try to get out of the way, not to condense too much, edit too much.[22]

Emile de Antonio's *In the Year of the Pig* (1969) provided the model that many documentary filmmakers emulated in the 1970s and 1980s, combining a rich variety of archival source material with trenchant interviews to recount the background to the Vietnam War in a way radically at odds with the American government's official version.[23] Drawing from the compilation montage which de Antonio turned into a powerful discursive device, Lee constructs a multiple perspective narrative, which confers an interesting polyphonic aspect to the films. Different layers of information are interwoven as narrative levels mingle, shifting from the past to the present, from the personal to the political, from the intimate to the public. Experimenting with Sergei Eisenstein's concept of intellectual montage, which puts forth the use of colliding shots as a structuring principle, Lee questions the representation of African-American figures on screen. The witnesses' personal stories either combine or collide with archival media footage, challenging the monologic discourse of the media with an array of anecdotes that testify to a diversity of experiences.

Even though the performative documentaries put forth the witnesses' acts of bearing witness, Lee introduces a critical edge into the films' enquiries—either endorsing his subjects' testimonies or interrogating the truth of their comments. While grounded on the collaboration between filmmaker and interviewees, the narrative is fashioned by the filmmaker whose views pervade the film. Dramatic camera angles function as indices of his authorial role, articulating a critical view throughout the narratives and even conveying his own judgment on his interviewees' statements. Lee heightens the urgency of the message his interviewees wish to get across by physically engaging with them. In *If God Is Willing and Da Creek Don't Rise*, he uses a tracking shot to film the housing projects that have been closed since mandatory evacuation suggesting through the camera's movement that the process of demolition cannot be prevented. His camera becomes a powerless witness; the panorama created depicts a landscape of desolation as the red brick buildings have been abandoned, boarded up, and the windows sealed out to prevent anyone from getting in.[24] The filmmaker's physical commitment is made conspicuous as he walks behind M. Juakali with a handheld camera which captures the images of a walled city. The Saint Bernard projects, which M. Juakali explains were built during the Roosevelt era, have disappeared from view behind the panels that hide the demolition site. The activist's commentary provides an explanatory voice-over to the blocks of empty apartments, filmed in a long tracking shot that underscores the absence of residents:

> All of this area here—we had 1500 families, mostly poor, black women with children. And right now, it's empty. These are the kinds of building they had before the storm, solid brick, they were built by the Works Progress Association during the Roosevelt era. During the storm hardly anyone evacuated because we felt we could survive. We had three-story building and we felt it was better than going to a shelter. [*IGIW*, Part 1, 34:49]

Not only does Lee offer his interviewees a platform to address an audience his camera will give them access to, thereby expressing his engagement with the issues mentioned, but he also includes them in a critical discourse through analytical editing. Some interviews are used in counterpoint to each other, blatantly pointing to the distance between the speakers. The director thus reveals institutional forms of white supremacy when filming Mitch Landrieu (lieutenant governor of Louisiana, today's mayor of New Orleans) standing in front of his New Orleans mansion, which rises clean and undamaged in the background, reflecting a different social status to the displaced, ruined houses of the Lower Ninth Ward.[25] The documentary lays bare racist tensions underlying the *façade* of American life,[26] expressing Lee's critical views through angles and jump cuts that are easily identified as recurring features in the director's fiction films—including *Do the Right Thing* (1989). The famous "racial slur montage" through which the characters of the film express their anger at each other, based on their own prejudice in a multicultural community divided by race and class, is transferred to *If God Is Willing and Da Creek Don't Rise*: the camera abruptly cuts from upward medium close shots to frontal close-ups of a man wearing a tee-shirt that features New Orleans black and gold striped flag, standing for the "Who dat nation" in reference to the community of supporters behind the Saints' football team. Quick editing dramatizes the words of the speaker as he bellows a series of variations on the acronyms of British Petroleum, labeled as "billionaire pirates" and "belligerent plunderers," thus leveling mounting criticism at the firm's environmental policies after the 2010 Deepwater Horizon oil spill in an entertaining fashion.

Lee may not conduct ambush interviews; however, he metaphorically comments on the events recounted through the choice of a setting that denotes the witnesses' experience.[27] The images of *When the Levees Broke: A Requiem in Four Acts* consistently point to the relationship between interviewees and place: the storm shattered the witnesses' sense of place and the filmed landscape conveys the extent of destruction on their everyday landmarks. Whether they stand in a derelict landscape or sit still in front of the camera with a colored wall in the background, the witnesses' tales of displacement and memories of terror are reflected by the setting around them as all landmarks have been turned over or shifted away by the flows of the flood. When the camera tracks along a street amidst the rubble with Terence Blanchard playing his trumpet in a deadly silent neighborhood, trying to appropriate the place by filling it with music [*WTLB*, Act 3, 41:00], the film must needs grasp a feeling of estrangement from an environment that seems to resist the people's return.

Wherever they speak from, the interviewees look lost in their immediate surroundings, which display no personal or intimate connection: the pink wall used as a background to the interview with Clovina "Rita" McCoy and Catherine Montana Gordon (Phyllis Montana-Leblanc's sister and mother) shows no personal item as though the two women had been cut off from their past by moving away from their home city to Humble, Texas. Their testimony points to the disruption of the affective relationship between individuals and places: the women stand in front of the house they bought in Humble, which however displays their indifference to the place. There are neither trees nor any flowers adorning the garden around the house, which does not seem to have been invested with affection. Humble is the site of no cultural or family memory for New Orleanians who look back at the Big Easy as their home city. Still, Lee tries to counter this feeling by creating a sense of belonging as he specifies each interviewee's name along with the quarter where they live or lived in the city, thus symbolically trying to restore the broken link with New Orleans. Just before the fourth episode's ending credits, every person interviewed in the series gives their names and address, speaking through painting frames that invite us to see them as characters belonging to the same community. The frame serves as an iconographical reminder of the director's spin on their stories, further underlying the role of portraits in his filmmaking.

26 / The Spike Lee Brand

Figure 1.1. The closing sequence of *When the Levees Broke: a Requiem in Four Acts* shows all the characters interviewed in the film through the frame of a painting, which signifies the ambiguity between fiction and nonfiction that characterizes Lee's documentary portraits. Phyllis Montana-Leblanc stands at Armstrong airport, where she was stranded for hours before boarding a plane. *Courtesy of Photofest*

Jane Chapman observes that contemporary documentaries are grounded in the experiences of the filmed characters who are granted a form of authorial voice through the films that stage their stories: "The participants seem to be generating their own cinematic text, rather than being guided. This gives the impression that they are integral to the text and to the production device, rather than merely being recorded by it."[28] This ambiguity pervades the portrait documentaries dedicated to Jim Brown and Kobe Bryant—two African-American figures whose achievements the filmmaker wishes to underline by giving them a voice. The critical distance that seeps in such historical documentaries as *Four Little Girls* seems to disappear as the two men contribute to drawing their self-portrait. *Jim Brown: All American* (2002) begins as a sports documentary dedicated to the charismatic figure of Jim Brown, whose exceptional career as a football player paved the way for his success in Hollywood as a hyper-masculine hero in the Blaxploitation cycle. While the biographical documentary maps out the structural barriers Jim Brown encountered on his way up and down the social ladder of American society, leading him from the limelight to the tabloids' gossip columns, the first-person narration endows Jim Brown with an authorial voice, which allows him to pose as the hero of his own life story and to refurbish his tarnished public image.

Brown lingers on the practical details of his game and his self-imposed strenuous training when addressing Lee's camera, unlike Kobe Bryant who indirectly speaks to the intrusive cameras when devising team strategies during a game which he retrospectively comments on in voice-over. *Kobe Doin' Work* (2009) does not tell the personal story of Kobe Bryant, giving neither biographical detail nor personal information about the player who skipped college and integrated the National Basketball Association straight after high school. *Kobe Doin' Work* draws attention to Bryant's dynamic role within the Lakers and captures his determination to win, expressing the filmmaker's fascination for the Lakers star player whose glowing career has nurtured many more hoop dreams. Close shots betray the aficionado's passionate gaze at the game, focusing on Bryant's outstanding talent at throwing down dunks and delivering blind passes when his team played San Antonio Spurs at the Staples Center on April 13, 2008. Bryant's voice-over strives to demystify basketball by depicting it as his everyday life, presenting himself as a worker on the court under the guidance of coach Phil Jackson. Spike Lee and Kobe Bryant can be heard discussing the technical details of the game, which may sound quite boring unless the spectator is a keen basketball follower. The interview happens out of shot and the duration of the game generates a sense of frustration, enhancing the split between Bryant's image as a Lakers star player and his view of himself as an ordinary basketball player.

As suggested through the latest example, Lee disrupts the spectacle of his films by resorting to self-reflexive techniques that prompt the viewer to question the very images he is watching. Ellen C. Scott points out the duality which characterizes Spike Lee's films, using "the power of the word to challenge the image track" and exploring "the ability of sound to provide a cultural depth of field—a rich store of information about culture—that challenges the stereotypical, flattening tendencies of the screen image."[29] While the interstices between the visual and oral tracks more often than not convey the author's critical voice, articulating an illuminating perspective on the tackled subjects, they also reveal the ethical underpinnings of his engagement.

The Reflexive Mode of Engagement

Although Bill Nichols approaches documentary filmmaking through a chronological lens, for example underlining the fact that the development of portable synchronous sound recording devices underpinned the growing popularity of the observational and participatory modes, he also emphasizes that the different documentary modes provide but a loose frame of affiliation.[30] Spike Lee's documentaries are best defined as nonfiction films, a term that signifies their ambiguous status considering they exhibit qualities common to all the proposed modes. Nonfiction writer and senior editor at *The Atlantic Monthly* Robert Vare argues that "narrative nonfiction bridges those connections between events that have taken place, and imbues them with meaning and emotion,"[31] merging nonfictional data with such fictional devices as narrative spines, characterization and suspense. Narrative nonfiction therefore draws its entertaining power from the fictional devices it employs to report factual events. Lee's documentary filmmaking practice resonates with this definition, enhancing the power of fictional strategies to capture more than the facts.

Lee's documentaries operate in several modes, shifting from the poetic (e.g., the credit sequence of *Four Little Girls*) to the expository (through a compilation of archival footage), merging the participatory (based on interviews) and the performative (allowing the witnesses to perform their speech at their pace). His films are not only characterized by formal heterogeneity, but they also call attention to the principles that underlie the four modes. The filmmaker's engagement with the issues broached in the documentaries is made visible through visual cues that undermine the illusion of unmediated access to the real. Whether he verbally intrudes in an interview through an ironical remark or a sincere comment or visually expresses his presence through a few skewed angles, Lee points to the film as a construction or a representation. When juggling with archival newsreel footage and personal photographs in a compilation montage, the filmmaker deconstructs the elements of a visual culture that has shaped the viewers' knowledge of the past or their perception of iconic African-American figures. Spike Lee's documentaries are highly self-reflexive works, which prompt us to interrogate the representation at work in his own films.

The title of *A Huey P. Newton Story* epitomizes this practice, hinting at the fluid boundaries between fiction and nonfiction by turning the biographical endeavor into "a" story, which suggests that characterization may only allow a limited aspect of a multifaceted personality to emerge from the documentary film. Actor Roger Guenveur Smith's performance received critical acclaim in the *New York Times* with Peter Marks commenting on his voice as "a soft, pinched whine at times carelessly feminine and always comically out of tune with the intimidating message of the legendary black power grip that Newton founded with Bobby Seale thirty years ago."[32] The remark pinpoints the discrepancy between the Panthers' carefully constructed iconography of strong masculinity and their leader's poor oratory, which the actor explored to portray the contradictory nature of the man. Smith introduces ambiguity and complexity into the characterization of Newton, pointing to paradoxical traits of his personality. The filmmaker exhibits the stage of the performance, maintaining distance between his camera and his subject—Huey P. Newton as impersonated by Smith—by including the standing audience in the frame. Archival footage is projected behind the actor on the background wall, creating a visual context to the play and a cultural frame of reference. Instead of giving in to the fascination Newton could elicit as a self-made icon, Lee endeavors to recover the Panther's political message by subduing the mediated images, which turned the Panthers into a threat that had to be contained according to FBI Director J. Edgar Hoover.

The reflexive dimension of Lee's documentaries promotes political reflexivity and prompts awareness of the ideological underpinning of visual representations. Nichols argues that formal and politically reflexive documentaries open a gap between knowledge and desire, provoking "awareness of the assumptions that support a given social structure."[33] Spike Lee achieves this effect in *A Huey P. Newton Story* by heightening the viewers' awareness of the artificiality of the film they are watching: lighting, microphone, audience, setting are part of the props used to dramatize the one-man show, emphasizing the construction of a political rhetoric that lays stress on representation. The introduction of archival footage in counterpoint to Smith's show prods the viewer to question the image of Huey P. Newton and the politics of representation adopted by the Panthers.[34] The figure of Newton seems to emerge from Smith's body, with the physical resemblance between the two men reinforcing the confusion between fiction and nonfiction. The camera constantly moves around Smith, underscoring tense body language as the actor twitches about in his chair. While Smith portrays a character whose jerky speech and nervous pose convey Newton's embarrassment when taking center stage in front of ogling cameras and curious viewers, Lee highlights the poor stage performance of the iconic figure by visually enclosing him in an intense bright focused beam of light.

Spike Lee develops strong characters in his biographical documentaries; nonetheless, the use of self-reflexive techniques evokes the deception of filmmaking and the limits of such endeavor. The interviews garnered from former friends and collaborators of Michael Jackson reveal but an imperfect portrait of the singer, whose personality remains a mystery by the end of *Bad 25*. The documentary retraces Michael Jackson's musical career since his 1987 blockbuster album entitled *Bad*, conveying Lee's admiration for the singer's artistic talent as the "king of pop" who revolutionized the music industry through original musical compositions, dance performances, and marketing strategies, exploiting the market of musical videos to entice a crossover audience. Lee reconstructs the character of the star whose image was tarnished by later scandals which the filmmaker would rather not mention, for they draw attention away from his achievements as an African-American iconic figure. The film closes with the star interpreting *Man in the Mirror* on a concert stage, capturing the artist as a shadow standing with his arms stretched in a backlit pose of crucifixion, suggesting the film has lifted only part of the mask he was wearing. The narrative construction of *Bad 25* is evocative of a failed biographical attempt that echoes the narrative puzzle of *Citizen Kane*. Each interviewee holds a piece of the puzzle which the filmmaker strives to put together, achieving but a flawed portrait of the man who remains an enigma.

In the prologue (which was added to the DVD version) of *Kobe Doin' Work*, Lee explains that filming the basketball player was an exciting adventure: thirty cameras were set up to follow Bryant during the whole game, either on the court or in the secrecy of the locker room, from a variety of angles. Lee's portrait documentary gives in to the fascination elicited by the star athlete by emphasizing the player's athletic performances through a careful choice of angles that exhibit individual skills. Lee deems basketball is an "art form" in *The Best Seat in the House: A Basketball Memoir*[35] and idealizes the figure of Kobe Bryant as a star athlete. The film's rhythm is hectic, intensifying the velocity of the game by following motion and action through quick cuts, close-ups, and zooms on Kobe Bryant's concentrated and excited face. "Basketball is sexy, showing glistening and well-honed male bodies in a state of semi-undress, clad in skimpy jerseys and shorts" argues media scholar Douglas Kellner, alluding to the homoerotic spectacle of professional basketball.[36] Lee turns the game into such spectacle through aestheticizing the black bodies, indulging in the pleasure of watching the athletes move and pass the ball according to the defensive tactics and offensive strategies they devised.

Much of the game is made of repetitive actions, which also accounts for the impressive number of cameras used: the filmmaker counterbalances the sense of repetition that grows as the film unfolds by changing shot angles. With thirty cameras around the court, Lee is able to magnify the spectacle of television basketball which Douglas Kellner considers as the ideal sport to be viewed on the small screen, because it is "fast-paced, full of action, and resplendent with spectacle. Hard-charging full-court action, balletic shots, and ubiquitous instant replays make basketball the right sport for the era of MTC and ESPN."[37] By slowing down the pace of the game, the documentary adds to its spectacular qualities. The camera is often placed close to the floor, capturing the bodies in action from below and looking up to their flying figures.

Even though the results of the game were well-known when the film was released, Lee reintroduces suspense by filming the bodies at close range. The viewer can spot details and realize how body contact and fouls may affect a player's move on the court. Although dedicated to Kobe Bryant, the film dramatizes Lee's acute perception of the game by focusing on the quick moves that make basketball so lively; the musical score includes jazz themes that combine with the energizing atmosphere produced by the competition, with the voices of supporters singing or blowing the horn in the background. Although no fiction film, *Kobe Doin' Work* depicts basketball as "a site for fantasy play shaped by discourses of imagination, projection, dreaming, desire, yearning and longing. Sport [. . .] has historically provided a fantasy space in which black bodies can be gazed upon."[38] Lee aestheticizes the game when he cuts to black-and-white stills freezing the athlete's movements into photographic poses, allowing the viewer to revel in the pleasure of the gaze which objectifies the black body. The filmmaker drops a light piano melody over the cries and applause of the crowd, creating a distance between the spectacle recorded live and the retrospective glance, which plunges the viewer into a dreamlike atmosphere. These black-and-white stills punctuate the narrative of the game, suspending time and deifying Kobe Bryant's athletic figure. Either suspended in the air or dunking the ball into the hoop, Kobe Bryant embodies grace and virtuosity on the court, inheriting the flying mythology which was born with Michael Jordan—a figure of transcendence according to Cheryl L. Cole.[39] These shots depict the effortless art of dribbling the ball while underlining the beauty of the athletic body. *Kobe Doin' Work* being coproduced by ESPN, Lee was expected to fulfil the expectations of the sports-entertainment network by enhancing the athlete's iconic status. Try as he might to give him a voice by offering him the opportunity to comment on the game, Lee cannot counterbalance the reifying power of the media gaze which has turned Kobe Bryant into a commodity.

The first sequence is filmed outside the Staples Center in Los Angeles and captures the glittering image of the Lakers through a low-angle shot that signifies the distance between the man on the street and the players whose portraits adorn the top of the façade, embodying the myth of success that undergirds their elevation to the status of sport celebrity. Bryant's voice-over may be used as a self-reflexive tool intruding on the pleasure of the gaze, for it is detached from his body and ironically connotes the fact that the film does not relate him to a world beyond basketball; however, it does not allow him to assert himself as a subject. Kobe Bryant's personal characteristics merge with his identity as a player; the film portrays no social commitment beyond the court, nor any political insight. In the closing sequence, he is seen leaving the arena in a glass-tinted car that offers no glimpse of his face, thus marking the barrier between his private and public life. The camera will not penetrate the intimacy of a shielded environment, thus restricting the subject of the film to basketball. The ending sequence of *Kobe Doin' Work* echoes the closing credits of *Bad 25* when backlighting reveals a shadow that may indicate a crack in the constructed image of Michael Jackson. The documentaries do not achieve narrative closure and these characters seem to evade the camera, pointing out the limits of the documentary genre itself as it can only grapple with appearances of truth.

By tackling conspiracy theories as relevant information and through the focus on the testimonies of New Orleanians who debate possible explanations for the government's mishandling of the crisis that developed in the wake of Katrina, *When the Levees Broke: A Requiem in Four Acts* self-reflexively challenges the power of the documentary to uncover truth. Rather than investigate the facts, the film explores the flood of rumors engendered by the rupture of the levees that caused the drowning of the city. The title indicates a focus shift away from the scientific investigation into the Gulf hurricane disaster to the polemics aroused by the levees' breach. Lee treats the rumors of sabotage that fuelled conspiracy theories as serious information by having experts comment on them, thus weakening the documentary's ability to unearth truth, but enhancing the suspicious narratives shaped by survivors. Lee resorts to the techniques of mock-documentary which, for films scholars Jane Roscoe and Craig Hight, seek "to construct a particular relationship with factual discourse which often involves a reflexive stance with regard to the documentary genre."[40] Conspiracy theory is evoked in the first episode of the series, with Act 1 devoting only five minutes to the notion of conspiracy, yet the questions raised cast doubt on the whole series' power to grapple with truth. Were the levees dynamited and the Lower Ninth Ward flooded "in order to save some of the more expensive property in the lakefront area" as suggested by Gina Montana recalling what happened during Hurricane Betsy [*WTLB*, Act 1, 25:00]? The investigation discovers elements that can only be interpreted in light of the theory presented: whether it exposes the corruption of police officers stealing goods in a supermarket like other looters or pinpoints the negative impact of budget cuts on New Orleans' hurricane protection system, the film seems to trace the ramifications of a larger conspiracy targeting the city's African-American poor. Lee exposes the underlying political and economic dynamics of a system that sustains oppression in a documentary that explores the self-reflexive mode to denounce political forgeries relating to Katrina.

The witnesses entertain doubts about the discourse produced by political figures, suspecting the media of participating in a conspiracy of silence: they believe that the levees were blown up and the Lower Ninth Ward was sacrificed to save the touristic French quarter. Their testimonies are crafted into a narrative that theorizes the breach of the levees into a conspiracy, which Lee rationalizes by collecting scientific and historical evidence. The film shifts from hearsay to conspiracy theory as Lee uses editing to create an interpretive frame: witnesses retrospectively tie together the events they remember, fashioning a narrative that aims at revealing a form of order and structure to the failures of the levees and floodwalls in and around New Orleans.[41] The survivors' search for a rational explanation is signified by the words that crop up in their testimonies: Harry "Swamp Thang" Cook first depicts sounds in onomatopoeias ("boom") [*WTLB*, Act 1, 22:00], which Gina Montana then qualifies as an "explosion" possibly due to an "electrical transformer, something popping up in the distance" [*WTLB*, Act 1, 23:00]. The words are repeated in the mouths of witnesses ("boom, boom") who recall they felt the ground shake. Witnesses retrospectively identify the boom as the blast of a bomb—Joycelin Moses heard echoes in the distance and so did Michael Knight. The survivors are confident that they could sense the moment when the levees were blown up—Audrey Mason confidently asserts that she "felt the explosion" [*WTLB*, Act 1, 23:45].

The interviewees explain what they are convinced happened whereas Lee turns the impressions collected into a system of beliefs that paradoxically undermines his attempt at clarifying the enigma. The characters envision different possibilities to account for the explosion heard: either the levees gave and the water gushed through or a barge hit the levees and provoked their collapse. Try as they might to connect events and causes in meaningful order, they only expose the failings of the documentary to approach the truth, blurring facts and fiction by prioritizing subjective views.[42] Truth just seems to vanish as more hypotheses are conjured up: the more possibilities, the more confusion. The film edits different types of footage into a semiotic chain that pinpoints conflicting views of the situation: from the officials' reassuring messages to the media's sensationalized spectacle of disaster to the witnesses' retrospective critical accounts, the polyphonic web of voices compromises the coherence of the whole narrative structure.

Commemorating the five-year anniversary of Katrina through two episodes assessing the progress achieved since Katrina swept through New Orleans and the Gulf Coast, *If God Is Willing and Da Creek Don't Rise* further illustrates the self-reflexive dimension of Lee's documentary filmmaking. Aired on HBO on August 27 and 28, 2010, the two parts of the film examine the policies that were enforced as regards reconstruction programs, schools reopening, health structures, among others. New faces crop up to address issues that have arisen since the immediate aftermath of Katrina, which provided the focus of interest in the first season of what might now be termed a series. Lee revisits the witnesses whose voices he made familiar if not famous in *When the Levees Broke: A Requiem in Four Acts*, using some of the shots that have become iconic images for the failures of the government to cope with the situation. The two films complete each other, articulating the dynamic relationship between the past (2005) and the present (2010) through intertextuality, which demonstrates that the civil rights fight is a continuous struggle that has not yet ended. The themes broached, including access to education, emphasize the parallels between the fights of the present and those of the past.

A compilation montage follows the prologue of *If God Is Willing* [*IGIS*, Part 1, 01:54], creating a parallel with the credits to the third act of *When the Levees Broke* [*WTLB*, Act 3, 00:40]. The same narrative structure is replicated, plying between the same archival footage of New Orleans landscape of rubble and broken houses and close or medium-close shots of the film's new participants, posing in front of backdrops that help characterize their relationship to the city. The footage selected from *When the Levees Broke* [*WTLB*, Act 1, 02:00; Act 3, 00:40] functions as self-referential devices prompting reflection on the highly symbolic images of Katrina. The witnesses may have moved on, but archival footage depicts scenes of chaos that have not been forgotten: a crowd of hungry people waits for help outside the Superdome and the Convention Center; a pile of broken children's bikes denotes the broken lives of as many families; a naked black baby in diapers stands by a soldier's gunpoint; an army helicopter flies low, rescuing people from the flooded city; an empty school bus lies crushed under the barge that notoriously hit the Industrial Canal floodwall; graffiti on the walls say "Bush sucks. Where is FEMA!" and spray-painted crosses indicate which houses have allegedly been searched and how many corpses have been found inside—if any.

Only the characters presented in the credit sequence have changed: new faces appear while others have grown older. The presence of Will Chittenden and Kimberley Polk functions as narrative hooks, arousing curiosity as to what their life has become since Katrina. Contrary to *When the Levees Broke*, which showed many New Orleanians in exilic environments rather than in their homes, *If God Is Willing* portrays most participants in New Orleans. Cecile Tebo, NOPD Crisis Intervention Unit Administrator, is filmed in her white uniform leaning on her service car [*IGIW*, Part 1, 02:14]. Some backdrops do signify idiosyncratic views of the city, displayed as a skyline on the horizon reflecting Dr Calvin Mackie's critical distance from the city [*IGIW*, Part 1, 02:16]. The water has receded leaving but a cement block instead of a house, anticipating the location chosen for Harry "Swamp Thang" Cook's nostalgic interview about the Lower Ninth Ward [*IGIW*, Part 1, 02:33]. The interviewees' characterization contributes to fictionalizing the series, suggesting that the five-year time gap between the two films has a lot to unveil. Public figures appear alongside ordinary citizens: Michael Brown will be given the opportunity to retrospectively comment on his decisions as FEMA director; Brad Pitt has gotten involved in the reconstruction process; Mitch Landrieu has risen to prominence by becoming the mayor of New Orleans. Their faces are icons of the "new New Orleans" that has begun to emerge, signifying a shift in politics since 2005.

Terence Blanchard's score further creates musical continuity between *When the Levees Broke* and *If God Is Willing*; his trumpet recalls the tragedy in a few notes that immediately strike an emotional chord. The musical and visual intertextual references ironically imply that progress is slow to reach all the quarters of the city—even worse, some parts have not been refurbished yet. The repetition of the same images is disturbing, for it metaphorically suggests a state of paralysis that has made progress impossible to achieve. Instead of moving forward as one could expect considering the time lapse between the two documentaries, the impression conveyed by the first images of the film evoke an all-too-present past. These quotations from another film can also be understood as flashbacks, which generate a sense of fatality and entrapment: houses are still crumbling as though the storm happened only a few months ago and people have not yet returned to the ghost city.

The credits to the second part of *If God Is Willing and Da Creek Don't Rise* incorporate very few intertextual elements from *When the Levees Broke: A Requiem in Four Acts* except for its elegiac score by Terence Blanchard and the haunting image of a dead body floating in the "toxic gumbo" as were dubbed the dirty waters drowning the city, carrying all types of toxic waste from the surrounding factories. The British Petroleum oil spill that struck Louisiana in 2010 is evoked through air photographs of the endangered wetlands and a snapshot of cemetery crosses indicating the names of all the endangered species of wildlife in the Gulf Coast area, a still of Barack Obama crouching on the beach and footage of citizens demonstrating their anger. The picture of the oil-soaked birds at the end of the sequence symbolically announces a shift from race and politics to environmental and economic concerns.

According to filmmaker and writer Sheila Curran Bernard, "documentaries should demand their [viewers'] active engagement, challenging them to think about what they know, how they know it, and what more they might want to learn."[43] Lee's nonfiction films achieve this objective through the polyphony of voices that intensifies the narratives' multiple layers of signification, allowing the director to shed light on some aspects while omitting others. The collected testimonies inform the perspective which he favors, conveying an insider's point of view that focalizes on the intimate experience of African Americans. The reflexive dimension of his filmmaking is geared toward debunking stereotypes while promoting a sense of collective identity and memory by retrieving hidden secrets and refurbishing the images of possible role models among African-American iconic figures. The panel of interviewees and the presentation of data collected demonstrate that Spike Lee belongs to this generation of filmmakers who, Bill Nichols contends, are concerned with telling history "from below, history as lived and experienced by ordinary people, rather than history from above, based on the deeds of leaders and the knowledge of experts."[44] The documentaries exploit the emotional appeal of memory by crafting an intimate version of the past from a series of interviews that tend to equal personal memories with historical truth. They depict the racial context that underpinned African-Americans' life experience in the Southern states, including after Katrina's devastating impact on New Orleans, merging memory and history.

CHAPTER 2

History and Memory

The African American Experience

The role of historical films in the construction of collective memory has been widely studied since French historian Marc Ferro posited that the cinema represented a neglected source of knowledge. His seminal *History and Cinema* (1993) relates the cinematographic reading of history with the historical reading of film, laying stress on the ideological and economic constraints of the production context underlying the semiotic construction of film. Marc Ferro contends that films are best approached from a variety of viewpoints which help grasp the visible and the nonvisible that seeps into the film's discourse, conveying either resistance to or complacency with the dominant ideology. The reflexive work of many filmmakers exploring the limits of genres, breaking the conventions that rule representation, expresses a creative awareness that Marc Ferro noted when writing that "thanks to popular memory and oral tradition, the historian-filmmaker can give back to society a history it has been deprived of by the institution of History."[1] The French critic invites us to look beyond the frame of a film to understand how cultural politics shape collective memory through contemporary cinema, constructing its historical discourse through the lens of the present. Not only do films enrich the knowledge of the present by practicing a specific mode of writing about the past, but they also provide a blurred window into the past by preserving memory traces. This theoretical background undergirds my approach to Lee's historical perspective in documentaries that articulate the dialectical relationship between the present and the past through the interplay of archival documents and interviews. While his documentaries delve into the past, using primary sources such as archival photographs to further comprehension of the African-American experience, they are also active agents of memory culture putting forth some events and omitting others.

The struggle for the civil rights is a recurring subject in Spike Lee's documentaries. From *Four Little Girls* to *A Huey P. Newton Story* to *Jim Brown: All American*, the filmmaker understands the relation between history and memory through the prism of race, underlining the role of Black Nationalism in the construction of African-American historical consciousness. Lee, however, has eschewed the brunt of criticism he bore after making *Malcolm X*, whose memory he was accused of commodifying and merchandising,[2] by committing himself to documentaries that address the lived experience of race. Prominent among these are the two television series devoted to the reconstruction of New Orleans after Hurricane Katrina's destructive sweep across the Gulf Coast and the breach of the levees which caused the Big Easy to flood, revealing the historical legacy of race on the disproportionate number of African Americans among the dead and the displaced. Although the documentaries play on the illusion of a faithful rendering of history by incorporating the voices of experts whose informed views reinforce the film's overall demonstration, they actively share in the construction of collective memory, highlighting the sense of resilience among African-American ordinary citizens and the determination of black nationalists.

When broaching historical subjects or reconstructing the narrative of events that are deemed crucial for understanding the present, Spike Lee partakes in the memory work which Pierre Nora defines as an artificial construction and a self-conscious effort, observing that "the less memory is experienced from the inside the more it exists through its exterior scaffolding and outward signs—hence the obsession with the archive that marks our age, attempting at once the complete conservation of the present as well as the total preservation of the past."[3] Based on the testimonies of witnesses whose individual stories illuminate some unknown aspects of history, the director's documentaries participate in the construction of collective memory, helping shape a sense of collective belonging by allowing viewers to share in the past. According to art historian Alison Landsberg, the technologies of mass culture spread memories to crossover audiences—regardless of skin color, ethnic background, or gender.[4] She develops the concept of "prosthetic memory" that "emerges at the interface between a person and a historical narrative about the past, at an experiential site such as a movie theater or museum. [. . .] the person does not simply apprehend a historical narrative but takes on a more personal, deeply felt memory of a past event through which he or she did not live. The resulting prosthetic memory has the ability to shape that person's subjectivity and politics."[5] Not only do films help preserve individual memories, which cement the community around historical landmarks, but they also incite people to appropriate and incorporate them into their own life narrative, thus erasing the historical color line between black and white Americans.

Spike Lee's documentaries contribute to this memory-sharing process by retracing how African Americans went through pivotal historical events like the civil rights fight. By interviewing witnesses who are willing to testify in front of his camera, Lee gives meaning to archival footage and allows untold stories to come forth. *When the Levees Broke: A Requiem in Four Acts* illustrates this point as it foregrounds the specific historical resonance of the moment when Katrina's storm surge broke the levees surrounding New Orleans. While addressing the plight of African Americans trapped in the travails of destruction, Lee pinpoints the parallels between the present and the past to suggest that discriminatory policies have not disappeared and continue to produce feelings of victimization among African Americans. Lee underlines how the combined notions of race and class impact individual experiences of history, thus challenging the addressed audience with alternative historical narratives. Appropriating the documentary form to rewrite the narrative of the past and allowing African Americans to testify about their own experiences of history, Spike Lee broadens the viewers' perspective on the roles of African Americans in American society.

Following his discussion of the central function of narrative in the construction of historical meaning,[6] Paul Ricœur contends that narrative configurations are ideological tools for the manipulation of memory, which implies an arbitrary process of selection between events to be commemorated and others to be forgotten.[7] Although the historian emphasizes the fact that memory can be manipulated through narrative configurations, which may deprive individual actors of their power to recount their actions themselves, he also argues that narrative emplotments can be used as a source of empowerment—which Marc Ferro intimated through a different path of reasoning when evoking oral history as a possible primary source for the historical filmmaker. The lesson provides a methodological frame to the analysis of Spike Lee's historical documentaries: while the past can be a site of contested memory overshadowing the present, the narrativization process can foster alternative forms of historical understanding and help formulate challenging versions of the past. Although Spike Lee's historical nonfiction films further a critical stance as to the perception iconic images breed of specific historical events, they articulate an awareness of films as tools of memory favoring certain narrative configurations, which may generate distortions that need to be interrogated. Historian Paul Ricœur was concerned with "the competition between memory and history, fidelity and truth,"[8] which I argue is of special relevance to Lee's documentary filmmaking.

Family Recollections of Segregation

In his groundbreaking work *On Collective Memory*, Maurice Halbwachs devotes a whole chapter to the notion of "the collective memory of the family," arguing that the remembrance of a single event may actually encapsulate the summation of an entire period. Reading from Chateaubriand's record of family life in *Mémoires d'outre tombe*, in which the narrator depicts the sequestered life of the nobles of the period, Halbwachs is able to expand on the monotony of provincial existence.[9] Although the French philosopher and sociologist argues that family memories offer a window into the collective past, considering that customs and traditions culturally organize family life into rituals and social frameworks, he also draws attention to the fact that "each family member recollects in his own manner the common familial past,"[10] thereby suggesting that memory develops according to individual consciousness. In an attempt to challenge the media discourse of the Civil Rights movement, Lee delves into the past through the prism of individual memory, retrieving different versions of the family stories which compose *Four Little Girls*.

The documentary discusses the history of segregation through the lens of family memories, exploring how an event that became collective memory affected individuals differently. Spike Lee draws an intimate portrayal of 1960s Birmingham through the stories collected from relatives and friends of Carole Robertson, Cynthia Wesley, Addie Mae Collins, and Denise McNair. The tragic deaths of the four teenagers made the headlines as their torn corpses were recovered amid the rubble of the Sixteenth Street Baptist Church in Birmingham, Alabama. The 1963 tragedy is evoked as an event that marked the narrative of the civil rights fight, underlining the director's desire to use film as a tool of memory transmission from one generation to the next. Investigating among the witnesses who open up in front of the camera, Lee's filmmaking work parallels that of a detective who endeavors to gather the missing pieces of a criminal case. Lee's film may have played a pivotal role in bringing about justice considering the "four little girls" case had not yet been closed in 1997 when it was released. Even though Robert Chambliss had been convicted and sentenced to life for the murders in 1977, other suspects were never worried by the prosecutors until Doug Jones was nominated as the United States Attorney of the northern district of Alabama by President Clinton on September 2, 1997. Jones pursued prosecution and secured murder indictments against the two suspects still alive:[11] twenty years after Robert Chambliss was tried and declared guilty, newly discovered evidence led the FBI and the Alabama police to reopen the case, causing Tom Blanton and Bobby Frank Cherry to be indicted and sentenced to life in prison in 2001 and 2002, respectively. While these arrests are no doubt linked to a mentality change, they may also reflect the impact of *Four Little Girls* as the film helped raise awareness on the issue of racial injustice.[12]

Figure 2.1 Mrs Alpha Robertson shows a photo of her deceased daughter, Carol Robertson, in *Four Little Girls*. The snapshot is used as a memory prompt, signifying the mother's nostalgic longing for the past. *Courtesy of Photofest*

Walter Benjamin's study of photographs draws from Halbwachs's sociological perspective when he observes that looking at the world through the camera reveals more than expected: "Evidently a different nature opens itself to the camera than opens to the naked eye—if only because an unconsciously permeated space is substituted for a space consciously explored by man."[13] Photographs capture an unconscious space that preserves more than the moment photographed, revealing its social organization as regards gender and class for example. Not only do candid snapshots mimetically reflect an ideological organization embedded in the image of the past, but they also engrave one's relation to the photographed subject, which accounts for the dual role of images used either as artifacts in photo albums, permitting the construction of family memories, or as icons of a collective past.

It is no surprise, then, that *Four Little Girls* includes a host of family photographs to propel the narrative, illustrating both what is being said by the interviewees and offering their own stories to the eye. Lee pieces together the teenagers' life stories from various archival footage, which symbolically provides the backbone of an investigation that focuses on intimate moments of family life, allowing us to grasp glimpses of the social environment in which they grew up. Based on a series of interviews with the deceased girls' relatives, which complement the visual narrative fashioned by the family album photographs, *Four Little Girls* is undergirded by a twofold approach to the past: not only do the filmed witnesses communicate a subjective recollection of a family story, but their narrated memories also immerse us in the past of a family life that bears the imprint of a segregated society. The witnesses interviewed evoke their family life in Birmingham, giving the viewer a glimpse of the constraints the segregated city imposed on the family's socialization experiences. They recall vivid details that flesh out the characters of the missing girls and help translate the psychological effects of enforced segregation.

Fleeting images of the teenagers' childhood are integrated as a visual backdrop into family members' or friends' testimonies, providing a retrospective overview of family lives, moments of which were captured by candid snapshots. A moving camera instills life in the still portraits of Denise McNair, echoing the words used to characterize her. Her parents, her aunt (Helen Pegues) and her neighbor (Queen Nunn) recollect some of the girl's habits, portraying her character as "aggressive," "inquisitive," "caring," and "friendly." These comments invite us to take a second look at the photographs of Denise McNair, which are stitched into the film's visual narrative as artifacts that need probing below the surface. The camera focalizes on photographic details, blurring the right-hand side of the frame for example, to highlight some idiosyncratic attitudes of the girl—including a smile or a gesture; still, it fails to recreate her body motions, thus making her absence more acutely visible.

Susan Sontag contends that photography is an art that testifies to time passing when she writes about the feelings that photographing a subject may arouse. It is an act that confronts the fragility of life with the immanence of death: "All photographs are *memento mori*. To take a photograph is to participate in another person's (or thing's) mortality, vulnerability, mutability. Precisely by slicing out this moment and freezing it, all photographs testify to time's relentless melt."[14] While the photographs of the deceased youngsters are presented as slices of the past and generate a poetics of absence in *Four Little Girls*, the filmic montage disturbs the "incitement to reverie"[15] triggered by contemplation. The film does not linger on the pathos which enshrouds the photographs of the dead, incorporating them in a chain of images that does not privilege one still over another. Filmic movement transforms the meaning of still photographs and transcends the nostalgic power of the photographic medium by turning it into a dynamics of time. The narrative crafted through the editing of photographs points out the fact that the past encompasses stories that need to be told. The interplay between the archival material and the interviews creates a dialectical relationship between the present and the past, developing two narrative threads that endow the figures of the deceased with mystery. The girls' faces neither speak nor move, which heightens an awareness of the discourse produced on them. The effect produced challenges the viewer's critical sense while disrupting the nostalgic feelings aroused by still photographs that captured the girls' camera poses.

The selected photographs compose a family album, shedding light on family rites—including baby portraits, school photographs, family snapshots, birthday pictures, representing the fragments of lives that did not blossom into adulthood. Siegfried Kracauer comprehends photographs as "traces of the past" that lose their power to be understood once they are disconnected from the moment when they were made; they alienate the beholder because the camera mechanically retains elements that are shorn of their significance in individual memory: "In a photograph, a person's history is buried as if under a layer of snow"[16] he observes. Film counters the reification process Kracauer identified by inserting the photographs in a narrative that endows them with meaning. The act of filming may draw attention to previously unseen details by lingering on a single shot and panning various details in close-ups. The film introduces a duration effect, which vanishes in the frozen movement of the photographed subjects, translating the rupture between the present and the past instead.

Spike Lee makes visible the distance between the present and the past by filming the photographs and inserting them in a temporal sequence, which enhances the chromatic change that has transformed the snapshots and dramatizes the emotional tone that pervades the voices of parents and friends disclosing their memories of the girls. The only photograph that stands out in *Four Little Girls* is an enlarged black-and-white portrait of Denise McNair, which is framed with golden wood and posted on the livingroom wall behind her mother while she is being interviewed. The portrait has a very specific place in the home, illustrating the symbolic value it acquired in relation to the story behind it: the girl's father remembers the moment when he shot that particular photograph, for Denise asked him to use her little Brownie camera. Chris McNair recalls that "she was sitting in the bed playing with her doll and said 'Make a picture of me, Daddy.' " The picture did not come out properly because he stood too close to her and took it on the spur of the moment without bringing the care he usually did to the mechanical process (including light, framing, and composition). He was all the more stricken when he went back to the print after his daughter died and stumbled upon a photograph that conveyed more than the girl's features, for it captured this moment of spontaneous complicity shared with Denise: "When the film was developed I saw that the negative was way over exposed and I never worried about it anymore until after she died. And, I went back to the negative and I reduced it and then made a print of it, and I realized what a jewel I had." Chris McNair had an epiphanic experience when he realized how good the photograph turned out to be, echoing Roland Barthes's intense emotional response to a photograph of his late mother, which he explains provoked "a living resurrection of the beloved face."[17] Barthes recounts that he reveled in the discovery of a snapshot that gave a visual shape to his mental image of his mother, perfectly coinciding with his memory of her:

> Hence I was leafing through the photographs of my mother according to an initiatic path which led me to that cry, the end of all language: "There she is!": first of all a few unworthy pictures which gave me only her crudest identity, her legal status; then certain more numerous photographs in which I could read her "individual expression" (analogous photographs, "likeness"); finally the Winter Garden photograph, in which I do much more than recognize her (clumsy words); in which

I discover her, a sudden awakening, outside of "likeness," a *satory* in which words fail, the rare, perhaps unique evidence of the "So, yes, so much and more."[18]

The print may have faded, but the emotions it arouses have not. As a space-time marker, the photograph represents "an illogical conjunction between the *here-now* and the *there-then*" according to Barthes,[19] reviving the pain of absence associated with the type of consciousness it provokes. The photograph thus turns "the past into an object of tender regard,"[20] which is symbolized by the central place it occupies in the home and the fondness with which the father holds it on his laps when telling the story of his taking it in *Four Little Girls*.

Although the film camera strives to replace the eye sweeping the photograph with a glance, it fails to convey the intensity of the revelation that only a loved one can sense. The filmed photographs may provoke empathy on the part of the viewer; however, they do not awaken the same intimate emotions as a personal snapshot might, capturing the familiar features of a beloved figure. While personal photographs may trigger long repressed feelings about the period they cover, leading to the return of the repressed as illustrated by Barthes's exploration of the photographed past in *Camera Lucida*, the editing of *Four Little Girls* defuses the pathos of the situation by consistently switching from the past to the present, thus refusing to dwell on the nostalgic effect produced by stills that imprison the girls in their youth. As suggested by Valerie Smith, editing draws attention to the time gap between the events referred to in archival footage and the present of the shooting:

> The liberal use of family photographs interspersed with the interview footage emphasizes the impact of time on the bodies and faces of the witnesses. [. . .] Frequent off-center close-ups zoom in on the young girls' now middle-aged friends and siblings. [. . .] The faces and bodies of their friends and relatives thus underscore the fact that time is frozen for Addie Mae, Cynthia, Carole and Denise, forever imprisoned on the image of their childhood and adolescent photos.[21]

The present and the past are connected through cross-editing, highlighting either the dichotomy or the coherence between the two interwoven narrative threads: one is devoted to reconstructing the past with archival material whereas the other conveys the retrospective, subjective perspective of the witnesses. While some of them have come to terms with the pains caused by a history of racial violence, others are still shaken by the traumatic memories epitomized by the iconic photographs of the era. The photographs are not just to be gazed at, for the interviewees speak over them, reconstructing the narrative behind them through stories that help make sense of them. Lee focalizes on photographs as though he was digging up memories from the subconscious of his interviewees, questioning Chris McNair about his feelings as a father whose self-image was tarnished by the impossibility of addressing his daughter's wishes in a segregated society. His testimony illustrates that memories can help fill in the gaps in the visual track, which does not encompass the whole experience of life in the segregated South. The film intersperses personal photographs retracing the girls' individual stories with impersonal snapshots depicting segregated water fountains and signs ("No nigger here") that are nowhere to be seen in the family albums [09:00]. The visual interstices between private and public photographs allude to all the unsaid in the family's history.

The interviewees confide memories which have left no visual records, for segregationist symbols have been omitted from the family portraits, which more often than not depict the characters against a blank background. The girls may pose in disguise, but they are neither seen mixing with white children nor photographed in public spaces—other than in staged school photographs. There is no snapshot of a holiday outside Birmingham, suggesting that the family lived a secluded life in the black quarters of the city. Only the voices evoking the past and the use of newsreel footage allow the viewer to imagine the context of the girls' childhood. The family albums illustrate a careful selection of images fashioning the narrative and the memory of family life by purposely obstructing some events and privileging others. As Susan Sontag puts it: "A way of certifying experience, taking photographs is also a way of refusing it—by limiting experience to a search for the photogenic, by converting experience into an image, a souvenir."[22] All references to segregation are censored in the family albums, which replicate the idealized model of the American family, emphasizing the fact that the girls lived in a protective environment. The photograph of eleven-year-old Denise McNair holding a poster that reads "Register to vote" conveys the stirrings of her political awareness [47:20]; yet it was taken at home and not on the street—suggesting demonstrating may have been an indoors game. Lee's camera zooms in on her blurry face whereas her mother recalls her daughter's accusatory questions on the reasons why she, as an adult, would not march. The visual and oral tracks combine and call attention to all the unsaid in the film. The photographs seem to prompt a host of questions, which pinpoint the limits of the film to address all the issues. American film philosopher Stanley Cavell notes that the "screen works as much by what it excludes as by what it includes, that it functions less to frame than to mask."[23] The film constructs an incomplete narrative by focusing on the family photographs, which illustrate the self-conscious selection process implied in the making of a family album. While the families disclosed part of their intimate life story to the filmmaker's camera, they also carefully arranged the artifacts they put on display, thereby posing as a harmonious family despite the constraints endured under Jim Crow.

Significantly, Spike Lee appropriated the media label of *Four Little Girls* to evoke a family story that provides a counterpoint to the impersonal, sensational media accounts. Through a close examination of press articles and photographs dating back to the 1950s and 60s, art historian Martin A. Berger analyzes the negative framing of the media label, which distorted the public's perception of both the crime and the victims:

> The often-repeated 'four little girl' mantra effectively erased the part of the victims' identity that made them targets in the first place. In 1955, as in 1963, the media coverage of and white reactions to the deaths of blacks strongly suggest that white sympathy for victimized children masked a disinterest in the suffering of blacks.[24]

The focus on the dead girls downplayed the systemic violence that prevailed in Birmingham during the 1960s, triggering an emotional response that drew attention away from the political demands of civil rights fighters and the causes of suffering in the black community. While *Four Little Girls* exploits the emotional appeal of the story by crafting an intimate version of the civil rights fight, it also depicts the racial context that underpinned African-Americans' life experience in the Southern states, accounting for the climactic violence of the Sixteenth Street Baptist Church bombing. The viewer viscerally experiences the feelings of terror inspired by the brutal repression that tore the city apart in the summer of 1963 as the camera zooms in and out of photographs depicting raging dogs barking and biting people lying on the ground, whipped by the water pressure of the hydrants that had been turned on to contain the flood of demonstrators defiantly marching through Kelly Ingram Park on May 3, 1963 [47:00]. The hectic montage of photographs and newsreel footage testifies to the trauma that past violence inflicted and that cannot be forgotten by African Americans who confess the paralyzing fear that confined some of them inside their homes at the time.

The film does not include outside elements about the families interviewed, which film scholar Valerie Smith contends had an impact on the significance of the film at the time of its release. She emphasizes the central role of Chris McNair as "a symbol of the community's ability to heal and flourish even after traumatic loss" because he had achieved political and professional success since his daughter's death.[25] The scholar also refers to Chris McNair's condemnation in a sewer bribery and corruption scandal in 2007, which according to her subsequently weakened the demonstration of the film.[26] Even though the film's role in collective memory may have changed due to the credibility loss of the central character, the individual trajectories of the participants do not affect the historical narrative fashioned by the film, which relies on a challenging combination of oral testimonies and visual archives.

Oral History and Public Memory

Four Little Girls stitches together oral testimonies that offer intimate knowledge and individual insight into the daily experience of segregation. The complex web of interviews collected and selected shapes the film narrative, articulating a subjective perspective on the past or on the characters it portrays. The confessed memories testify to different personal experiences, which highlight various status levels between the people, often linked to race and class issues. The contributors' stories may even complete or contradict each other, thus pointing out the subjects of contested narratives. *Four Little Girls* provides a case in point as the film juxtaposes private memories of segregation in counterpoint to statements of former white officials, thus exploring the racial divide through the narrative of the past. Cross-editing emphasizes the distance between the blacks' and the whites' living conditions in Birmingham, which produce two distinct narrative tracks that join and overlap in the iconic photographs of the Civil Rights movement, testifying to the violent encounters between blacks and whites. While these snapshots provide historical records of the civil rights riots, they also represent the traces of a traumatic past for African Americans who either attended the events or watched them on television and read about in the printed press.

Historian Michael Frisch argues that interviews are primary sources of information and can be used as "a powerful tool for discovering, exploring and evaluating the nature of the process of historical memory—how people make sense of their past, how they connect individual experience and its social context, how the past becomes part of the present, and how people use it to interpret their lives and the world around them."[27] In other words, filmmakers may use interviews to challenge some assumptions about the past, actually shedding light on the subjective dimension of remembering the past: from the defense strategies Southern Christian Leadership Conference (SCLC) activists remember discussing and even arguing about (such as the involvement of children in the marches [44:00]) to memories of African-Americans citizens who testify about how their everyday life was affected by the violence raging through Birmingham in the summer of 1963, *Four Little Girls* unfolds a multiple narrative structure which emphasizes the bearing of one story over the other.

The filmmaker uses parallel editing to confront diverging memories of the South and to underline the stark opposition between two ways of life: Chris McNair expands on his painful experiences in Birmingham, a segregated industrial city where his university degree was of little value, which contrast with the happy memories the city inspires to former southern segregationist Arthur Hanes, Jr., Robert Chambliss's Defense Attorney. The film cuts from one interview to the other in order to point out the social distance between the two men, who did not go through the same life experience although both lived in Birmingham: Arthur Hanes, Jr., proudly recalls that the city provided a golden opportunity for the barons who came from the north in the nineteenth century; yet African Americans like Chris McNair did not enjoy the flamboyant career that even working-class whites expected in the fifties as they flocked into the so-called "magic city" [08:27]. The violent and racist acts originating in the city's labor force and rural background, mentioned by *New York Times* Editor Howell Haines as distinctive features of Birmingham's history, do not mar the idyllic vision projected by Arthur Hanes, Jr. The informal atmosphere generated by the family stage does not alleviate the tension that pervades a dual narrative structure, recreating the oppressive feeling of 1963 Birmingham and pointing out the fact that racist attitudes endure. When Helen Hughes comments on the "ugly," degrading behavior of adults opening up fire hoses on children and Cynthia Wesley's sister remembers the "children being washed down the street," the film cuts to Judge Arthur Hanes who recalls he had to downplay the event in front of New Jersey students and professors who were shocked to read about such riots on the *New York Times*' front page.[28] This editing technique reinforces a Manichean view of southern society, defined by the socioeconomic rift between black and white citizens.

Lee lays stress on the image of Birmingham, portrayed as a dangerous city from the African-American viewpoint: Reverend Wyatt Tee Walker, former executive of the Southern Christian Leadership Conference, refers to one black section of Birmingham as "Dynamite Hill" because of the blast he heard on his first visit, targeting the houses of black families living in a quarter that sparked envy among their white counterparts [15:00]. Reverend Fred Shuttlesworth comments on the Klan-affiliated policeman who advised him to leave after his house was blown up, owning up to the fact that the police would not ensure his safety [15:54]. The commonplace conversations spotlight the devastating impact of segregation on individual lives as the interviewees recall anecdotes that unveil the traumatic experiences of being black in a socially discriminating environment. Maxine McNair picks up the narrative thread to complete the story her husband is telling [10:40], conveying a different snapshot of a situation, which she considers was less humiliating for her than for Denise's father. She casts an analytical glance back to the past, articulating the view that segregation emasculated African-American males. Public places deprived black men of their dignity as explained by Maxine McNair and later confessed by Chris McNair, who remembers being barred from buying a sandwich which his daughter Denise naively asked for in an all-white restaurant, thus alluding to the excruciating humiliation he endured as a man and a father under Jim Crow.[29] The details of the story, which took place at Kress's at Christmas time, give us insight into the significance of segregation from the point of view of an African-American family. Chris McNair cannot hide the pain he felt when explaining to his daughter that "she couldn't have a sandwich because she was black," failing as a father to spoil her. When Lee asks about the girl's reaction, Chris McNair painfully adds that it was as if "a whole world of betrayal had fallen on her." The interviews thus reveal the imprints left by segregation and the wounds it opened, which have neither healed nor been completely overcome.

Marc Bloch posits that "historical facts are, in essence, psychological facts."[30] The film plies between personal memories of victimization and footage of police repression to spotlight the violence of segregation and its devastating impact on an individual, psychological level. Chris McNair expresses contempt at the white community, whose members quietly endorsed Eugene Bull Connor's patrolling the streets on board his threatening white tank, which he could not have done "without the nods from the status quo people." His remark is laden with irony, suggesting that neither the Civil Rights Act of 1964 nor the efforts made to commemorate the civil rights struggle have quelled his resentment [33:00].[31] Segregation was legitimized by institutional figures such as Governor George Wallace, who publicly argued for "segregation now, segregation tomorrow, segregation forever" in his inaugural address on January 14, 1963. Even when he is interviewed thirty odd years later, seeking for "redemption" as Maxine McNair puts it, he still embodies the old South, using his African-American servant Ed as a ploy to make amends.

Testifying in front of the camera brings up memories which move the interviewees, shattered by an overflow of emotion ranging from anger, rage and rancor to pain and tears. Not only does the camera capture these excessive responses in close-ups, but it also highlights the weight of the past over the present, exposing the enduring effect of coercive practices developed during segregation. The interviewees' silence emphasizes the grasp of painful memories, symbolizing the point at which "memory will not enter speech."[32] Media and cultural studies Susannah Radstone connects the notion of memory with images, which may crop up in the present and bring back repressed memories of trauma:

> Memory, a way of thinking as figurative as it is literal, fuses the imaginative world with everyday life, dramatizes and recreates the past as it is retrieved. Most of what happens is forgotten, yet nothing of past life perishes, Freud believes. Image, scene, or other person is cannibalized, infused with primitive (infantile, visceral) feeling, combined, condensed, and transposed and might erupt in bodily feeling, dream or nightmare; meanings transmute with ever retelling.[33]

Lee conveys the atmosphere of the civil rights struggle by filming moving moments, when his interviewees are overwhelmed with feelings they obviously cannot repress, testifying to the memories of traumatic encounters with segregationist violence. The involvement of the younger generation in the Civil Rights movement did have an impact on family life, nurturing the fear that caused Barbara Nunn's mother to dream about "blood pouring out of that church." A friend of Cynthia's (Dr Freeman Hrabowki) remembers being jailed along with hardened criminals for taking part in the children's marches [46:00] whereas Maxine McNair had to hide her shame when Denise asked her why she would not join the marches [48:00]. Even if she did support the cause, she was too afraid to risk being jailed, as was Gwendolyn White [49:49]. Speaking about the past arouses feelings and creates stories, which the camera records as oral history.

The process of remembrance emphasizes the film's reflexivity, turning the words into a narrative that makes private memories public history. Yet it also points to the limits of the film project, which endorses a subjective view of the past, encompassed by the objects presented as "souvenirs" of the girls—such as Carole Robertson's sash and Bible, which her mother kept as an affective symbol of the past, signifying the memory of her daughter and her absence in *Four Little Girls*. While the trials may have brought narrative closure to the tragic story of the "four little girls," the film may also have contributed to the healing process by allowing private memories to become available to a wide audience, introducing new perspectives on the larger historical framework. George Lipsitz defines countermemory as "a way of remembering and forgetting that starts with the local, the immediate, the personal."[34] Lee focuses on a microscopic approach to history, delving into family memories to grasp the zeitgeist of the civil rights fight. Such endeavor undergirds his documentary series on post-Katrina New Orleans, thereby bringing to light some unknown details about the events that unfolded in front of the cameras.

The Unofficial History of New Orleans

When the Levees Broke: A Requiem in Four Acts was first broadcast in New Orleans on August 16, 2006, as a tribute to the victims of the floods that followed Katrina's destructive landfall on Louisiana and the breach of the ill-maintained levees. The film was to be watched as a funeral requiem, a musical offering dedicated to the dead who never received proper burials, paving the way for the reconstruction of a community shaken to its core. The series is composed of four one-hour episodes that are dialectically constructed to posit a study of New Orleans social fabric and racial inequalities as they are blatantly exposed by the accounts of witnesses and experts. *When the Levees Broke: A Requiem in Four Acts* investigates New Orleanians' experience of Hurricane Katrina and the ensuing human catastrophe, as the authorities were slow to respond to the needs of those left behind. Testimonies give us an inside view of the events, which witnesses recall from their individual perspectives. Depending on where they lived and how much money they could garner at the time of Katrina, the inhabitants did not go through the same ordeal. Of special interest to Spike Lee is the social and racial background of the city, which he metaphorically depicts by filming from above and from street level, capturing a dual landscape: the dry areas around the Superdome and the Convention Center are in stark contrast to the drowned streets of the Lower Ninth Ward, where all geographical and national landmarks vanished. The traces left by Katrina on the landscape testify to the disparities between New Orleanians whose experience of Katrina was shaped by two entwined factors: their social status and their home location. In a sense, the social level of Lee's interviewees can be assessed through the landscape around them, displaying either the physical traces of devastation or the sense of exilic displacement. Film and media scholar Janet Walker points out that the testimonies metaphorically construct a racial geography of a city which is "noticeably segregated by race and income where middle and upper-middle class white residents [. . .] are [. . .] nowhere to be seen."[35] While some residents had returned home only a few weeks after the storm, others were still stuck in their FEMA trailers or forced to remain in exile after six months. Lee underscores that reconstruction was slow to reach all the quarters of the city by lingering on the sights of debris-filled streets. Even though the Lower Ninth Ward and the Lakefront area suffered equally severe damage, the progress achieved in the two quarters was not identical over the same time period. Reconstruction policies were guided by geographical priorities—that, however, intertwine with race and class illustrating the legacy of the segregationist past of the city.[36] The value of property differs widely from one neighborhood to the other, which had a direct impact on the priorities defined by reconstruction policies.

Lee turns to historian John M. Barry, author of *Rising Tide, The Great Mississippi Flood of 1927 and How it Changed America*, to decipher black-and-white archival footage depicting flood victims, thus demonstrating that the same events have just reiterated. New Orleans flood and hurricane history unveils a pattern of discrimination against the poor, which the following study pinpoints through a chronological approach:

> In its 288-year history, New Orleans has had 27 major river or hurricane-induced disasters at a rate of one about every 11 years. A pattern of three responses runs through that history. After each event, the city rebuilt and often expanded, small differences in elevation determined the location of the well-to-do and the poor, and levees were rebuilt and often raised. [. . .] Inequity in the location of neighborhoods and the distribution of flooding burdens appears early. When levees failed in 1816 and again in 1849, high water drove many of the city's poor, found in the lowest location, from their homes

> for up to a month. [. . .] In general, the poor remained in the city and often occupied low areas vacated by those leaving for the new suburbs.[37]

Quite surprisingly, natural disasters have recurrently hit the city and prompted the same inefficient policies. Even though the authors of the above-mentioned paper note that the poor have again and again been victimized by the strategies developed on a local level, they fail to discuss the relationship between race and poverty, which is endemic to the city of New Orleans. John M. Barry is repeatedly interviewed in the film and argues that the "similarities" between the 1927 flood and Katrina are disturbing [*WTLB*, Act 1, 28:00].[38] The levees were dynamited south of New Orleans on April 29, 1927, to protect the economic assets of the city, yet sacrificing the parishes of St. Bernard and Plaquemines.[39] By having the scholar speak about the 1927 flood in voice-over while the image track cuts to some archival footage, thus adopting the argumentative techniques of the expository mode,[40] Lee lends credibility to the rumor that the poor quarters of New Orleans were voluntarily flooded to protect the city's most attractive features (such as the French quarter) from being ruined. Not only do the scientific grounds presented by the academic legitimize the conspiracy theories argued for by eye-witnesses, but they further help Lee articulate their worldview.[41] When the decision to blow up the levees was made in 1927, the governor of Louisiana responded to the pressure of New Orleans's powerful businessmen, creating a threat that still hangs over the present.[42] Legal scholar Mark Fenster contends that conspiracy theory creates a dialectical relationship between power and the course of history: [43]

> In this sense, the conspiracy narrative is a melding of fact and fiction, and attempts to tell a particular kind of story about the injustice of present conditions through reference to an historical wrong turn initiated by a grand, conspiratorial crime that is ongoing. Thus, most conspiracy narratives by definition oppose, or at least question, the current distribution of power.[44]

The witnesses obviously express private anxieties through the narrative they give shape to, dreading hidden dangers that are reminiscent of the Jim Crow era with its stories of conspiratorial acts implying both "overt and secret state-sponsored racial subordination."[45] The paranoia that pervades the speculative narrative of conspiracy theory is given social and historical underpinning by Marc Morial, the former mayor of New Orleans, who still wonders why no investigation was conducted to clear up the rumors dating back to Hurricane Betsy in 1965: "It became almost an article of faith with people in the community, that the 9th Ward flooded because there was an intentional breach of the levee. It was never investigated. It was neither proven nor disproven" [*WTLB*, Act 1, 26:00]. These comments suggest that the lack of official recognition merely heightened public anxiety, nurturing conspiracy theories that encompass an underground plot or secret scheme according to Mark Fenster, who does treat the subject as a serious issue, associating the notion of conspiracy with the fear for "some kind of agency which is preventing us from discovering the truth, from connecting events and causes in a correct manner."[46] Douglas Brinkley, author of *The Great Deluge*,[47] completes the historical portrait of New Orleans drawn by the film with sociological remarks spotlighting the racial dimension of the city's geographic structure. He points out that conspiracy theorizing is a mode of cognition, arguing that the past victimizations of the black community have nurtured a feeling of insecurity that may explain why "the urban myth that it [the levee] got dynamited" prevails [*WTLB*, Act 1, 27:00].[48]

When the Levees Broke: A Requiem in Four Acts foregrounds the echoes between the failures of the government to cope with the crisis that unfolded in the days following the rupture of the levees and the segregationist and discriminatory practices of the past: Lee consistently highlights the parallels between the African-American diasporic experience and the treatment of African Americans in the wake of Katrina. Some of his interviewees become his mouthpiece as they give vent to their criticism: cultural studies scholar Michael Eric Dyson grants the evacuation process a symbolical value as it re-enacted the traumatic dispersal of the slaves. He observes the fact that "they [the authorities] were treating them like slaves in the ship. Families were being separated. Children were being taken from their mothers and fathers. Those more weary and those who were more likely to be vulnerable were separated from those who were stronger . . . The separation of the evacuation where people lost sight and lost sound and lost sense of their loved ones" [*WTLB*, Act 2, 53:00]. There was a police roadblock on the Gretna Bridge to Jefferson Parish that was reminiscent of the confrontation between segregationists and civil rights activists on Pettus Bridge in Selma in 1963 [*WTLB*, Act 2, 03:00]. The degrading comments made by President George W. Bush's mother who expressed her opinion that "so many of the people in the arena here, you know, were underprivileged anyway, so this, this is working very well for them" [*WTLB*, Act 3, 20:00] as she visited the makeshift camp in Reliant Park in Houston, Texas, resonated with racist views that recalled the humiliations endured by the homeless blacks gathered in the "concentration camps" set up after the 1927 flood to shelter "refugees."[49] *If God Is Willing and Da Creek Don't Rise* further explores the issue of police corruption as seven policemen were indicted for misconduct in the days that followed Katrina. Henry Glover was shot when attempting to cross the Danziger Bridge; the police officers involved in the case let him bleed to death before they burnt his body in his car [*IGIW*, Part 2, 33:00]. Such examples of overt racism mar the New Orleans Police Department's reputation, fuelling distrust among African-American citizens, paving the way for more theory conspiracies.

Lee dramatizes the documentary through editing snippets of the witnesses' statements together, thereby enhancing the emotion that pervades their testimonies and the shocking power of the scenes they recall attending. Their voices convey the feeling of pain that does not seem to have dwindled with the passing of time; medium shots preserve the intimacy of the speakers who do not appear in close-ups while capturing their dismay through body language. The recorded testimonies highlight the "belated impact" of the events that continue to haunt them, which trauma theorist Cathy Caruth links to the definition of post-traumatic stress disorder:

> The experience of trauma, the fact of latency, would thus seem to consist, not in the forgetting of a reality that can hence be fully known, but in an inherent latency within the experience itself. The historical power of the trauma is not just that the experience is repeated after its forgetting, but that it is only in and through its inherent forgetting that it is first experienced at all.[50]

The documentary underlines the trauma of Katrina by linking media images to archival footage, thereby suggesting that the visuals showing the long wait of the people left behind revived previous wounds that did not heal.

Oral history does not provide a relevant approach to the past for historian Thomas Doherty who reproaches Lee with encouraging "the babble, blathering, ranting, and raving" through the interviews he conducted among New Orleanian residents in *The Journal of American History*.[51] Lee may be accused of highlighting controversial statements when broaching conspiracy theories and giving voice to Katrina's survivors who vent their resentment against the authorities; their disparaging comments are based on their intimate beliefs that the government's failures laid bare the extent of racial prejudice. Lee nonetheless exploits these statements to indict official figures (Mayor Ray Nagin, Governor Kathleen Blanco, President Georges W. Bush, FEMA director Michael Brown) for replicating the discriminatory practices of the past.

The wide array of testimonies collected for the documentary series provides valuable sociological information as to how New Orleanians have been going through Katrina's devastation and the city's reconstruction. The collected interviews allow the director to fashion an informing historical narrative that counters the media short-term and flagging interest in the drama of Katrina. By interweaving history and memory through the combination of archival footage and oral testimonies, *When the Levees Broke: A Requiem in Four Acts* prompts the viewers to empathize with the filmed subjects, who confide deeply felt anxieties in the face of life-threatening events. They convey a subjective perspective on historical events, which the film exploits to foster critiques of the political system, whose perceived failures are interpreted in the light of past discriminatory practices.

"Living History": Private Photographs vs Iconic Images

Modeled on the compilation documentary, Spike Lee's nonfiction films shed new light on historical moments, which he investigates by searching among scraps of both private and public life. The filmmaker strives to recover a lost narrative about the African American experience, working like a historian who looks for historical truth by digging through primary documents.[52] While the historian scholar plumbs the past though written records and first-hand accounts (such as journals and official reports), the historian filmmaker resorts to visual and oral sources without taking into account the difference between private and public archival material: newsreel footage is challenged by eyewitnesses' testimonies whereas family photographs compete with iconic images. The historical value of Lee's documentaries is however limited by his desire to focus on African Americans, which implies a selection among the documents he retains. No objective rendering of the past should be expected from watching a "Spike Lee Joint," for the director is keen to highlight the practical impact of race on everyday life. His nonfiction film projects are based on the concept of "living history," which Manning Marable defines as follows:

58 / The Spike Lee Brand

> Reconstructing the hidden, fragmented past of African Americans can be accomplished with a multidisciplinary methodology employing the tools of oral history, photography, film, ethnography, and multimedia digital technology, an approach I call "living history."[53]

In his methodological conceptualization of "living history," Marable posits that history may be best mapped out through a diversity of approaches that favor "interpreting its totality."[54] Marable advocates the integration of material traditionally considered unreliable by historians—including oral history and photography. However, recovering the silenced stories of African Americans implies a different type of research.

Significantly, Lee's documentaries engage with the concept of "living history" by exploring the interstices between private photographs and iconic images, interweaving interviews conducted among ordinary citizen and political officials, whose views allow for a cross-examination of the events depicted. Private memories complexify the narrative of the past or the portrayal of public characters, enriching and challenging the notion of public memory. Lee uses editing to pinpoint the semiotic gaps between private photographs that convey ordinary moments in everyday family life and iconic photographs that contribute to shaping the public perception of headline events. The film enhances the distance between the visual documents, crafting a double narrative of the stories they cover.

Interestingly, *Four Little Girls* cuts twice to the same lynching photograph depicting the corpse of a black man, his limbs hanging loose from the rope tied around his neck amid a crowd of white men, dressed in elegant suits as they pose proudly in front of the photographer, displaying the dead man's body as a hunting trophy [08:00]. The camera zooms in and out whereas the musical score uses drumbeats to dramatize the horror of the scene. The shredded corpse stands for the cruelty of a coercive system, which perpetuated white domination in the South into the twentieth century. The snapshots are presented as visual evidence of the racist ideology and brutality that underpinned segregationist Birmingham: quick close-ups indict the complacent and complicit faces of the white characters in the crowd, including a child who innocently gazes at the camera, attending the hanging as a spectacle. In *Regarding the Pain of Others*, Susan Sontag underlines that lynching photographs were staged to implicate the viewers into the act of watching, which is disturbingly replicated in the film. She explains: "The lynching pictures tell us about human wickedness. About inhumanity. They force us to think about the extent of the evil unleashed specifically by racism. Intrinsic in the perpetration of this evil is the shamelessness of photographing it . . . the display of these pictures makes us spectators, too."[55] The still photographs inserted in *Four Little Girls* produce a visual shock pointing out the denial in the voice of Arthur Hanes Jr., whose comments are introduced in counterpoint to the archival footage, epitomizing a state of "knowing-but-not-knowing" in Freud's words. Arthur Hanes, Jr., recalls the city as "a wonderful place to live and raise a family" in the 1960s [08:33] whereas archival photographs display the vicious spectacle of lynching which most people prefer not to remember—including Arthur Hanes, Jr., who portrays a colorblind city. The film heightens the opposition between the archival photographs and Hanes's testimony, suggesting the man has not yet acknowledged the African-American experience of lynching and continues to believe in the superiority of the whites over the blacks. The mismatch between the visual and oral tracks serves to reveal and to denounce the enduring threats of racism. Film critic Christine Acham comments on the irony of the dual construction, which both "questions the validity of Hanes's comments" and reminds viewers that "historical memory is not only subjective but subject to revisions over time."[56]

In her stimulating book dedicated to *Imagery of Lynching: Black Men, White Women, and the Mob*, Dora Apel discusses the embarrassment which viewing lynching photographs may cause, for they point to the acts of torture behind the victimization and the objectification of the black body:

> When we look at lynching photographs today, we try not to see them. Looking and seeing seem to implicate the viewer, however distanced and sympathetic, in the acts that turned human beings into horribly shamed objects, as if viewing itself were a form of aggression. Most of us would prefer not to look.[57]

These photographs build a narrative that explicitly indicts the agency of white men, who staged their power through vicious and cruel *mise en scènes* for their friends to revel in, simultaneously looking to intimidate African Americans into subjecting themselves to coercion. As editor and political activist, W. E. B. Du Bois repeatedly used the lynching photographs as evidence of danger and unremitting threat. He had some of them published in the NAACP's monthly magazine, *The Crisis*, in an attempt to promote anti-lynching campaigns.[58] By exhibiting lynching imagery as visual reminders of racism, Lee posits that the prejudices of the past have neither disappeared nor lost influence over the present. He remediates the lynching photographs to underline the threat of racial violence posed by the Ku Klux Klan's parades on the streets of 1960s Birmingham—the archival pictures appear in counterpoint to each other, pointing to the coercive power of the visuals used to enforce segregation [08:00]. The sense of menace was still bearing on the minds of the African Americans who gathered around the families during the funeral of the "four little girls" after the Sixteenth Street Baptist Church bombing.

When the television broadcast the images of many unidentified black bodies lying dead on the streets of New Orleans after Katrina, it reactivated the same visual regime of racism and provoked strong reactions of rage and anger among African Americans. Illustrative of an enduring racist legacy are the photographs of New Orleanian African-American victims, which Lee includes in a musical sequence at the end of Act 2 in *When the Levees Broke: A Requiem in Four Acts*. Lee edits together still photographs and film footage depicting straying bloated dead bodies, scattered on the streets like house debris. Most of them are lying face down on the ground or floating in the dirty water, which is evocative of the ordeal individuals went through during the storm. Literary critic Evie Shockley compares the situation in New Orleans with the crisis in Iraq to underscore the hypervisibility of Katrina's black corpses in opposition to "the contrasting prohibition on media images of the remains of military personnel killed in Iraq,"[59] suggesting that the families of fallen soldiers were demonstrated more respect than those of the drowned in New Orleans. The film's tempo slows down to allow the viewers to gaze at the still photographs of the dead, thus breaking with the pace of television and opening up the wounds of memory. Lee accompanies the images with a jazz requiem on the soundtrack, offering a symbolic funeral to the corpses of men and women who died alone in the wake of Katrina. The musical score transcends the spectacle of horror into a requiem, thus reappropriating and remediating the images of the dead, which were perceived as icons of racism by African-American viewers when they were broadcast on television or published in the press. The visual treatment of the black dead bodies resonated with the coercive use of images of lynching, for the figures photographed were turned into objects to be displaced. Visual culture scholar Nicole R. Fleetwood's ironic statement conveys the emotional shock produced by "visual media [which] exposed bodies emoting, bodies suffering, bodies bloated and decaying, bodies— live and dead—as obstacles to be removed so that 'disaster capitalism' could begin its work of rebuilding what has been described as a dead city."[60] The film actually offers the dead the funeral rites they were not given, inviting the viewers to share in the film procession. Wynton Marsalis, jazz musician who sings a capella the lyrics of "St. James Infirmary" during a sequence exclusively composed of still photographs, expresses both the pain and the resilience of the characters trapped in the shots [*WTLB*, Act 1, 39:00]. The photographs show single human figures wading in the flooded streets whereas the voice-over dramatizes their plight and isolation, singing a blues song whose lyrics tell the story of a dead one: "I went down to St. James Infirmary. Saw my baby there. Stretched out on a long white table. So cold, so sweet, so fair. Let her go, let her go. God bless her. Wherever she may be. She can look this wide world over. But she'll never find a sweet man like me." The words confer a tragic dignity on the figures made prisoners of the water in the photographs. One of them describes an African-American woman dressed in patterned African garb in a flooded street, which connotes the conditions of so-called third world cities—thus questioning the Americanness of New Orleans.

Through remediation and narrativization, Lee is able to counter the reification process associated with the act of photographic mechanical reproduction. Walter Benjamin interestingly argues that films challenge the viewers' perceptions, revealing new structures to the eye, endowing the cinema with a revealing power that does not extend to photography. Film cameras record movement, which makes viewers see what is otherwise invisible to the eye:

> By close-ups of the things around us, by focusing on hidden details of familiar objects, by exploring commonplace milieus under the ingenious guidance of the camera, the film, on the one hand, extends our comprehension of the necessities which rule our lives; on the other hand, it manages to assure us of an immense and unexpected field of action. [. . .] With the close-up, space expands; with slow motion, movement is extended. The enlargement of a snapshot does not simply render more precise what in any case was visible, though unclear: it reveals entirely new structural formations of the subject.[61]

Such is the effect Lee obtains when panning over a photograph, which he prompts the viewer to see from different angles. The credit sequence of *If God Is Willing and Da Creek Don't Rise* [*IGIW*, Part 1, 04:52] ends with two snapshots that appeared in *When the Levees Broke: A Requiem in Four Acts* and have become iconic images since: one of them features a family of four pushing their way through the dark water, carrying backpacks loaded with a few possessions saved from their drowned home. Lee creates movement into the stills by digitally tampering with them: the human figures seem to stand out from the frame, turning into three-dimensional shapes that, however, cannot escape their bleak environment. This photograph and another one depicting an old black woman sitting amid a crowd of tired faces, waiting for help outside the Convention Center, symbolize the African Americans' resentful experience of Katrina and its aftermath. Literature and film scholar Anna Hartnell's gaze was drawn by the singular figure of this older woman wrapping herself in the American flag:

> It is hard not to read this image in the context of the wider African American experience on US soil; the face that the flag encircles captures a sense of misery that transcends its immediate temporal and spatial location. [. . .] While the flag apparently acts as a source of comfort for this woman sitting outside New Orleans' Convention Center, there is a deeper sense that it also represents her source of pain. Perhaps even more than the opening scene of *Malcolm X*, this photograph strains, questions, and possibly severs the relationship between blackness and the national cloth.[62]

Hartnell lays stress on the use of iconic photographs in the construction of an ideological discourse that permeates Lee's every camera movement. Rather than foreground the historical discourse encapsulated in the archival documents, Lee uses such cinematic techniques as editing and close-ups to appropriate them in his own reasoning. They are incorporated as arguments shaping the racial underpinning of his interpretational grid.

While discussing the indexical relationship of the documentary to the real, Bill Nichols states that "the film as a whole will stand back from being a pure document or transcription of these events to make a comment on them, or to offer a perspective on them."[63] The iconic photographs selected by Spike Lee represent the moment when the images of the past collide with the filmmaker's perspective. His films produce a critical discourse through the juxtaposition of various archival materials, which question the ethics of media culture as well as his own.

CHAPTER 3

Media and Race

The memory of the twentieth century was fashioned by the media, which recorded most watershed events that occurred in the world and can provide archival footage to craft an illustrated, informative, historical narrative of the past. Lee's nonfiction films interrogate the ideological framework that underpins this narrative, offering stimulating insight into the media politics of representation. The filmmaker displays an acute awareness to his cultural environment and endorses the role of social and cultural critic[1] when broaching the notion of stereotypes. The remediation of television footage allows him to debunk the construction and the representation of the racial subject in popular media while articulating a critique of the political intent and content encapsulated by stereotypes. Lee's films ironically incorporate archival footage to question media biases, using intertextuality to deconstruct and undermine the ideological construct of African-American archetypes.

Underlining this strategy is the crucial role given to iconic photographs, which the media reproduce to convey the zeitgeist of a period. In *No Caption Needed*, Robert Hariman and John Louis Lucaites argue that the rhetorical appeal of iconic images gives meaning to the concept of American democracy. From Dorothy Lange's portrait of *Migrant Mother* (1936), signifying the pressing need for social reforms which the Roosevelt Administration strove to enforce, to Nick Ut's photograph of *Accidental Napalm* (1972), which visually shocked many Americans into supporting the growing anti-war movement,[2] the authors contend that iconic photographs "activate emotional responses such as civic pride or outrage that are overtly political, while others communicate feelings of pleasure or pain that become complexly political as they are folded into historical tableaus."[3] In other words, they analyze iconic photographs as emotional constructs that equal spectatorship with citizenship. Their work provides a methodological framework for the analysis of iconic images, which are remediated in Spike Lee's documentaries. Interestingly, the filmmaker inserts many images to which the American viewers were repeatedly exposed, in order to spotlight the failings of visual democracy. Using iconic photographs that were not included in the corpus of images selected by Hariman and Lucaites, Lee sheds light on pictures that will not be used to further the democratic debate beyond the color line, signifying instead the limits of integration and assimilation. The photographs he puts forth center on the black body, which will not be incorporated in a colorblind reading of topical events. In an attempt to resist the commodification of the black body, Lee prompts his interviewees to publicly recount their own stories, thereby turning his documentaries into tools of empowerment for the African-American community.

They are participatory documentaries which, Bill Nicholls demonstrates, intertwine the personal and the political to "yield representations of the historical world from specific perspectives that are both contingent and committed."[4] Taking advantage of this particular documentary mode, Lee explores the dialectical relationship between the media representations of the past and the verbal accounts of witnesses recalling the same events, fashioning a dual narrative that pinpoints media biases regarding the portrayal of African Americans. Editing allows him to expose the racist ideological spin that undermines the authenticity of news reports: drawing attention to words and images that express a skewed perspective, his films reveal the biases encompassed in the cultural construction of blackness. Through the compilation montage, which juggles with a diversity of oral and visual footage, Lee endeavors to make visible and reveal the prejudices that most viewers may be unaware of. Film critic Richard Dyer notes that "the multi-colouredness of whiteness secures white power by making it hard, especially for white people and their media, to 'see' whiteness."[5] Dyer argues that whiteness is conceived as norms through which to view the world, making viewers blind to their own prejudiced approach. A close examination of the narrative crafted by the media around such figures as Jim Brown and Huey P. Newton enables Lee to identify the tropes of such discursive practices in the mainstream media. Both the athlete and the Black Panthers' leader embodied a threatening hypersexual black masculinity which, according to African-American studies scholar Cornel West, expresses the "white fear of black sexuality."[6] While *Jim Brown: All American* tackles the black athlete's tales of success as a deceiving myth, celebrating the alleged "natural" superior athletic capabilities of the black body instead of an individual achievement permitted by practice and discipline, *A Huey P. Newton Story* calls attention to the distance between the Panthers' community programs and their image in television archives, pointing out the enduring power of racist stereotypes over the characterization of the black male body.

Media scholar Brian A. Monahan argues that the role of the media has been transformed over the past thirty years by the development of 24-hour television news networks such as MSNBC and the Internet. News workers have been driven away from long-standing values that used to define the core of their profession, including "objectivity, public interest, the pursuit of truth,"[7] and encouraged to shape compelling stories into "newsworthy" information that "make it sell." The infotainment trend leads them to prioritize highly dramatic and emotional news items that include "stirring accounts, heartfelt moments, captivating images, harrowing encounters, and compelling characters."[8] News workers play up the dramatic stories of news items through words, statistics and images that sensationalize the events; they create plots and shape characters to dramatize storylines. *When the Levees Broke: A Requiem in Four Acts* unveils the media's slant on the crisis that developed after Katrina as reporters and news presenters downplayed the humanity crisis unfolding in the flooded city, focusing on the high rates of crime that signified a shocking state of chaos instead.

Spike Lee's documentaries build a critical discourse on the media, embedding sequences which he strives to reveal as artificial constructions producing what Jean Baudrillard defines as a "hyperreality," the nature of which is determined by large-scale corporations and their allied government. *Simulacra and Simulation* argues that there is no objective reality anymore, for it is a concept that has been fundamentally altered by the emergence of a highly mediatized environment, marked by the development of news cycles which include an endless list of updates and events to be commented on. Baudrillard refers to various headline cases to demonstrate that the media erase the distinction between a "real" event and its mediated representations,[9] which Spike Lee illustrates by confronting media archival footage to witnesses' testimonies, sometimes completing the stories that were turned into "public drama" with a more intimate version. Compared to the media footage he introduces, Lee slows down the viewing experience by focalizing on his interviewees' faces and inserting still photographs that prompt a contemplative gaze—instead of a voyeuristic impulse.

Deconstructing the Media Spectacle of Hurricane Katrina

Spike Lee examines the media representations of Hurricane Katrina in a compilation film that questions the ideological frame of television reporters and presenters by producing a dialogical narrative around a selection of archival footage, which he prompts the audience to review from a retrospective, informed standpoint. *When the Levees Broke: A Requiem in Four Acts* is thematically constructed, thus grasping the numerous connotations which the reference to Katrina carries with it. The authors of *Katrina's Imprint: Race and Vulnerability in New Orleans* explain that the phrase "Hurricane Katrina" has become synonymous with an array of issues that stretch beyond the natural catastrophe to include its political and socioeconomic consequences:

> The mention of Hurricane Katrina conjures up more than just a violent storm that unleashed nature's destructive force on an American city. Hurricane Katrina is now also recalled as a political event that issued a black mark on a presidency, an epic media story that produced collective trauma far beyond those physically affected, a breakdown of order that shredded the American social fabric (as demonstrated by the divergent reactions of black and white Americans) and an economic calamity that has produced one of the most dramatic urban transformations in modern times.[10]

When the Levees Broke: A Requiem in Four Acts points to Katrina as the signifier of economic developments that disregarded local geography and the necessary preservation of the wetlands around New Orleans; it reveals the wave of gang violence that followed the hurricane as a sign of extreme poverty, resulting from the relationship between poor education and crime; it demonstrates that the slow reconstruction of New Orleans was first due to land-hungry promoters and corrupt insurance companies. Lee highlights images that never reached the news media, aiming to expose media collusion with power. By examining the media footage of Katrina that he remediates in his narrative, he sheds light on the confusion that permeated all media and political accounts as the hurricane was approaching the Gulf coast, sending contradictory messages to a population that was left to cope on its own.

Lee selected television news extracts that illustrate how the media exploited the crisis that unfolded in New Orleans to produce dramatic narratives. When looking back at the unfolding events on screen, Lee is able to identify the elements of an unstable discourse: rather than put across a warning message, the media and the political officials bred confusion by divulging inconsistent information. The opening sequence cuts from Mayor Nagin's address to a Congress Hearing (December 2005), during which he emphatically claimed to speak on behalf of all Hurricane Katrina's survivors, to Michael Brown's promises made during an interview with Betty Nguyen on CNN, dating back to August 28, 2005, the day before Katrina hit: "We're ready, we're going to respond [. . .] We're going to do whatever it takes to help the victims" [05:00]. Both versions of the events contrast with the eyewitnesses' narratives, conveying the distance of these official figures from street level people. These public statements suggest that the story of Katrina was a disputed subject before the storm hit and has remained a bone of contention since. Instead of moving forward, the narrative goes backward with Brendan Loy reading out loud from his blog entry on August 26, 2006: "At the risk of being alarmist, we could be 3 or 4 days away from an unprecedented cataclysm that could kill as many as 100,000 people in New Orleans. Such a scenario is unlikely. The conditions would have to be just right . . . or rather just wrong" [05:22]. Young Brendan Loy appears on screen, a second-year law student recalling the warnings issued by meteorologists:

> There were forecasters out there, there were legitimate meteorologists who were saying "This is a threat." And the National Hurricane Center was saying there's a wide range of area that could be hit by this hurricane, ranging from the Florida panhandle all the way over to Louisiana. So New Orleans was within their strike target.

Editing emphasizes the contrast between Brendan Loy and Mayor Ray Nagin, opposing the young man's rational statements to the public authorities' lack of preparation.

The film then cuts to Phyllis Montana-Leblanc as she recalls that she first heard that Katrina had been designated as a threat on August 26. Her interview is part of a re-enactment since she speaks from Armstrong airport, where she found herself stranded like many other New Orleanians after the city flooded. A few close-ups on newspapers' headlines are interspersed with more interviews: Dr. Calvin Mackee remembers that he urged his family to leave when Katrina was classified into a Category Five hurricane; New Orleans former mayor Marc Morial explains that he was attending a funeral when the news was issued; Will Chittenden recalls he had his family evacuate their Metairie home on the morning of August 28; actor Wendell Pierce was visiting his parents when the exodus started and decided to stay; Michael Seeling preferred not to leave his uptown house which he had not boarded up in time; musician Donald Harrison did not evacuate because his mother-in-law believed Katrina could not be worse than Hurricane Betsy which she weathered in 1955; Herbert Freeman, Jr., stayed with his mother in Central City as the two were not afraid of another storm. Both Mayor Ray Nagin and Governor Kathleen Babineaux Blanco are interviewed on the same studio stage as the previously mentioned ordinary citizens, recalling they took the first steps in planning evacuation on August 26. However, no official announcement had been made at the time nor a state of emergency officially declared.

This web of interviews is opposed to newsreel footage retracing the growth of Katrina into an increasingly threatening menace. The archival shots point to the spectacle provided by evacuation scenes with cars queuing on the flooded streets of Florida. Although the news depicted trees bending in the wind and the voice-over announced Katrina had already caused six deaths on her path, television presenters downplayed the danger for New Orleans considering there was but a "possibility of this storm shifting further west" [*WTLB*, Act 1, 09:08]. As the narrative unfolds and Mayor Ray Nagin was once more interviewed about mandatory evacuation, the viewer can only be struck by the gap between his retrospective statement and his speaking live on television on August 27, when he declared that "we should take heed to it." Never did he mention mandatory evacuation in public before August 28 when it was already too late for many to leave. Nor did he organize evacuation for the carless in New Orleans, which could have been done in the "eight-hour window" between Saturday 28 and Sunday 29—according to another interview he gives in *If God Is Willing and Da Creek Don't Rise*. The archival footage is used in counterpoint to the mayor's retrospective narrative, highlighting the inconsistency of his position. The film thus proffers an accusation against his lack of leadership, using a diversity of newsreel footage as proof of his weak and ineffective planning.

Lee points to contradictory statements that generated a sense of confusion as to the right path of action: the threat posed by Hurricane Katrina was minimized until it was all of a sudden dubbed a "monster of a storm" and became breaking news on CNN on August 28 [*WTLB*, Act 1, 13:02]. Brendan Loy's Internet blog record entries mentioned above testify to an awareness of danger forewarnings that strangely contrasts with the euphemisms in public discourse; the lack of visible public action may have deterred many from leaving. The documentary questions the responsibilities of both the media and the city representatives through a dialectical construction that opposes personal memories to public statements in a narrative that pits the isolated individuals against the political body. This dichotomy underpins the film's progress as the news extracts are interwoven with eyewitnesses' pictorial and oral accounts, thus exploring contrasting tones and voices that dramatize this nonfiction film. Editing further highlights the gap between the testimonies collected, which expose the socioeconomic rift between New Orleanians: some explain they couldn't afford to leave, whereas others decided they could not withstand the storm because they had not stored enough groceries for the days to come. Some sheltered in the hotels located on higher ground in the city center, whereas others started to queue to enter the Superdome. The storm triggered various responses which demonstrate a lack of coordination that resulted in the chaotic situation that followed.

Lee focuses on themes that allow him to depict situations which reveal "the color line"—defined by W. E. B. Du Bois as the problem of the twentieth century at the outset of *The Souls of Black Folk*.[11] He uses editing to demonstrate that much of the media coverage after Hurricane Katrina adopted a "blame the victim" posture and passed negative judgment on these families that did not evacuate before the storm. Psychologist Nancy Boyd-Franklin also underscores the negative framing that pervaded press and television reports; those who remained behind were accused of irresponsibility in failing to take mandatory evacuation as a serious warning. The facts that most of them were trapped because they were unable to stretch over their monthly budget as the end of the month approached and that no transportation had been made available to facilitate their evacuation was never disputed on screen. Lost in the media coverage was the determination and resilience of the survivors, particularly those who stayed behind to defend their homes or to care for elderly relatives who were unable to leave.[12] Television revealed an extreme state of destitution among poor African Americans who were abandoned without food or water on the interstate highways, outside the Convention Center, and in the Superdome, shocking viewers who vicariously experienced the situation as an example of blatant racism. Although Lee does not put forward the survivors' social background as their main motive for staying in New Orleans, much archival footage testifies to the level of poverty in New Orleans. Sociological studies highlighted the social and racial dimension of the humanitarian crisis:

> Of the 270,000 Katrina survivors stuck in New Orleans, 93 percent were black. And those left behind shared characteristics that are often unevenly distributed by race. They were predominantly poor and unskilled: 77 percent had a high school education or less, 68 percent had neither money in the bank nor a useable credit card, and 57 percent had total household incomes of less than $20,000 per year. Poverty is one of the major reasons why many of the evacuees did not manage to leave before the storm [. . .]. 55 percent had no car or other way to evacuate.[13]

The black underclass became visible through the gaze of the media, which recorded the unending wait for relief around the Superdome and the Convention Center. Although *When the Levees Broke: A Requiem in Four Acts* includes media footage of the Superdome, the voices of the black underclass seem to be missing from Lee's narrative. In an attempt to debunk the myth of the underclass, Lee interviews survivors whose social profile does not fit the stereotype and underscores the status of homeowners among the black residents in the Lower Ninth Ward. The interviews conducted with African American New Orleans residents, many of them located in the middle-class quarter of Gentilly, portray individuals who do not correspond to the image of the "underclass" popularized by the media. Sociologists James Jennings and Louis Jushnick note that the word stigmatizes the poor, detracting attention from wealth inequality to focus instead on personal failure—including a lack of work ethic and a sense of personal responsibility:

> The portrait of the *underclass*, a pejorative term used by conservatives and liberals alike, has been created as another myth to prove the deleterious consequences of programs that benefit the poor, thereby justifying policies of policing and containment and reminding good, normal, hard-working middle-class citizens that they have nothing in common with "them."[14]

While much of media attention on African Americans was on the black poor,[15] reinforcing entrenched views about dependency culture, *When the Levees Broke: A Requiem in Four Acts* recycles the images of Katrina to foster critical distance towards the ideological stance of the media as regards racial issues. Not only does Lee spotlight the experience of African-American homeowners to counter the prejudiced view, but he also endeavors to represent racial diversity among the residents he visits: the poor are either black or white whereas African Americans are homeowners or middle-class citizens.

Lee dwells on the controversy over the slanted portrayal of race on American television by inserting BBC news footage [*WTLB*, Act 1, 55:00; Act 2, 02:00], providing proof that foreign journalists were more daring when they investigated the devastation and recorded stories that never hit the American headlines. While the BBC highlighted the race and class issue when identifying the poor who were barred from entering Jefferson Parish as members of the underclass [*WTLB*, Act 2, 02:55], the situation hit American media headlines through the focus on uncontrolled crimes that were rumored to be going on—including alleged cases of rapes. The gap between the American presenters in search of breaking news and the BBC's on-the-spot reporting style becomes all the more cruel and shameful as the British crews of journalists are shown rescuing children whom nobody had visited since their mother died [*WTLB*, Act 1, 55:00] or taking part in a helicopter rescue operation [*WTLB*, Act 2, 07:00]. On the commentary soundtrack of the DVD, Lee overtly wonders "Why is this story on BBC? You weren't seeing this here in the States!" However, Lee explicitly chose not to mention the fact that American reporters also took part in rescue operations—as explained here by historian Douglas Brinkley in *The Great Deluge*, which provides a testimony about his experience of Katrina as a resident of the city where he was working at the time:

> Whether it was handing out pallets of water, rescuing people out of floodwaters, or finding rides out of New Orleans for the sick, reporters joined the effort to help. Not only did they bring international attention to the Great Deluge via newspaper dispatches and television reports, but they goaded city, state, and federal responders to do more.[16]

NBC news reporter Tony Zumbado was the first journalist to venture into the Convention Center, investigating a situation that had not yet been reported to any authority. Although his footage is incorporated in the film's narrative, its source is not identified. Tony Zumbado provided indicting statements against the authorities' incompetence while walking among the people whose desperate situation and tears of shame he brought to the television screens: "I can't put into words the amount of destruction that is in the city and how these people are coping. They are just left behind. There is nothing offered to them. No water, no ice, no C-ration, nothing for the last four days . . . Somebody needs to come down with a lot of food and water."[17] His comments however are cut from the film, which points to Lee's biases toward American media: Lee uses cross-editing to contrast the dramatized commitment of a British reporter who expresses dismay at the scene of chaos unfolding around him—police officers trying to arrest a looter block the road ahead whereas poor people sit in a derelict street waiting for help behind him [*WTLB*, Act 1, 01:00:00]—with the cold detachment conveyed by the staged interview of *Times-Picayune* journalist Brian Thevenot, pondering over the type of objects looters tried to steal, thus pushing the issue beyond the limits of a humanitarian crisis into the field of law and order. The sequences are juxtaposed so as to spotlight the biases of American television presenters and news programs.[18]

Not only does Lee aim to demonstrate through the compilation of various documents that the media misrepresented New Orleans African Americans, but he also argues that racism was behind the slow response of the government.[19] He hammers home this point by having rap singer Kanye West explain his sudden accusation that "George W. Bush doesn't care about black people," breaking with the bounds of decorum during a live television program [*WTLB*, Act 3, 10:00]. He also has CNN journalist Soledad O'Brien repeat and comment on what she told Michael Brown, director of the Federal Emergency Management Agency, during a television interview that is embedded in her own interview with Lee [*WTLB*, Act 2, 19:00]. Such a *mise-en-abyme* generates a critical distance with the events reported, pointing out Michael Brown's inefficiencies and contradictions in the interviews he gave to the press: the promises he made prior to Katrina [*WTLB*, Act 1, 05:00] are pitted against his mismanagement of the crisis when he publicly owned up to discovering the dire situation at the Convention Center, where as many as 20,000 people were stranded, five days after the levees' breach [*WTLB*, Act 2, 19:00]. Lee disrespectfully repeats the same images of George W. Bush congratulating Michael Brown for doing a "heck of a job" [*WTLB*, Act 2, 17:00], thereby conveying the shock he feels at the sense of self-satisfaction expressed by the nation's leader. The film shows the same three-second sequence three times in a row, thus accusing the president of wilfully misreading the facts. This was an embarrassing moment for Michael Brown as he confides in the sequel to the film.

Katrina was a traumatic event for African Americans who felt disempowered and disenfranchised as the days went by and no help was coming in. Lee allows the survivors to shape their own experiences in a collective narrative that helps them transcend the status of being a victim. Not only do they resist the media's commodifying gaze by bearing witness in front of the camera, but they also reclaim space by speaking out from New Orleans.[20] Editing provides the link between the testimonies delivered by the "talking heads" and the traumatic memories shattering their lives as the film cuts abruptly from outdoor images of the rain petering the deserted streets to close shots of witnesses embodying the ordeal of surviving Katrina and its aftermath. Fleeting images of flooding denote the enduring memories of fear that left most of them traumatized [Act 1, 21:00].

Sociologists Dynes and Rodriguez explain that "television constructed the frame of meaning to which audiences and decision makers came to understand Katrina."[21] The media framing of the crisis shocked many African-American viewers who felt that the television spectacle was imbued with racist overtones. Lee aims to convey their viewpoint as he lets Gina Montana recall the humiliation and the pain she vicariously endured when watching the news: she saw human beings "treated like animals" [*WTLB*, Act 2, 56:39] and for African Americans across the nation, the public display of neglect was rooted in racism. While African Americans were objectified in the gaze of the media, Lee's camera provides the attention needed to restore their humanity, allowing them to publicly express their feelings. The African-American survivors articulate a vision grounded in the dehumanizing experiences their ancestors had gone through. The psychological trauma of slavery was reactivated by a series of events that recalled past inhumanities in the antebellum South. Not only were African Americans deprived of their citizenship, but the treatment they received during evacuation also prompted parallels with the stories of oppression and struggle exposed by slave narratives. The director emphasizes the parallels between the management failures at every level of government, including the uncoordinated rescue effort in the face of an unprecedented humanitarian crisis, and the segregationist discriminatory practices of the past: the similarities between the African-American Diaspora experience and the treatment of African Americans in the wake of Katrina are illustrated by visuals that aim to shock the viewer.

Lee overtly compares the stranded victims of New Orleans with the slaves who had not fled the volcanic eruption of Mount Vesuvius in Pompeii [*WTLB*, Act 1, 40:00]. His use of montage is undergirded by arguments that lay bare racial prejudice and injustice: still shots depicting African Americans wading through the flood are contrastingly followed by the testimony of a white citizen (Charles McHale) uninterestedly stating that he heard of the devastation in New Orleans after he returned from visiting the ruins of Pompeii. Lee ironically cuts to photographs of ash-coated Pompeii corpses, whose rigid position further dramatizes the images of stray waterlogged bodies bespeaking vulnerability and trauma in New Orleans. In his book *Come Hell or High Water, Hurricane Katrina and the Color of Disaster*, culture critic Michael Eric Dyson also refers to Pompeii to underline the socioeconomic structure that both the archaeological site and flooded New Orleans symbolize. Rather than framing looting in terms of law and order, he suggests that the poor reacted like the Italian slaves who wanted to experience their owners' luxury before dying:

> The way it was for the poor of Pompeii is the way it was for the poor citizens of New Orleans. [. . .] The tragic replay in New Orleans on August 29 is unmistakable as city elites and the well to do fled without thought of their poor citizen-servants. And many of the slaves in Pompeii were found with grand and expensive items, things they wouldn't ordinarily possess but that they took nonetheless, knowing they couldn't make use of them during disaster but wanting to feel what it was like to have nice things, if only for a few fleeting, fatal hours.[22]

These comments prompt the viewers to take an analytical look at the images of despair they are watching as they arouse an awareness of desensitization through media exposure: Lee intimates that viewers are gazing at the suffering in New Orleans just as the tourists contemplate the plaster cast of the bodies of people buried alive by the Vesuvius ash fall. The news personalized the characters interviewed to cultivate emotion; neither did the short-term media focus on breaking news items allow the survivors to relate their complete story, not did it provide an overview of the events. The documentary includes an embedded television sequence about Katy, who was evacuated to Utah while her children were sent to another state; her story was shaped into public drama on television. The media footage introduced writes her tragic adventure with a happy ending, for Katy and her family were reunited in Pleasant Grove where they were invited to stay by the local community. The media spin on their story minimizes the trauma of displacement and echoes the president's mother's opinion that "this is working very well for them"—a comment she made when visiting evacuees in Reliant Park in Houston [*WTLB*, Act 3, 05:00]. Lee revisited

Katy five years later during the shooting of *If God Is Willing and Da Creek Don't Rise*: she had by then returned to New Orleans and retrospectively confessed that she had never felt part of the white community in Pleasant Grove. The experience even increased the trauma of displacement as she could relate to no familiar faces in the all-white neighborhood. Katy explains she felt estranged from the people around her and had to settle back in New Orleans to overcome her depression.[23] Like other displaced individuals in the wake of Katrina, Katy was deprived of all geographical and psychological landmarks, which annihilated her power to act and to decide for herself what she should do to recover from the shock of losing all her possessions. Displacement was therefore a trauma added to that of destruction, which the media made even worse by dubbing the displaced New Orleanians "refugees."

Lee calls attention to the impact of the word "refugee" that was used repeatedly across the media, thus once again identifying tropes of racism which many white viewers may have not noticed. The word fueled resentment among interviewees who vent their anger on screen: they were being discriminated against when treated as foreigners. The director underlines the polarizing use of language in the media through the interview of Gralen B. Banks which is intercut with extracts from news reports about the so-called "refugees," suggesting the images deprived him and other African Americans of a voice: "They were referring to people leaving New Orleans—they were refugees. Damn . . . When the storm came in, it blew away our citizenship too? [. . .] We weren't American citizens anymore? [. . .] I thought that was folks that didn't have a country, that didn't have anywhere" [Act 3, 21:08]. Spike Lee examines the vocabulary that cropped up in the media discourse; such words as "evacuees, victims, displaced, refugees, survivors" were recurrent, all of which resonate with racial overtones according to linguist Geoffrey Nunberg. The author famously compared the captions of two press photographs to pinpoint the racist bias of the mainstream media:

> One placed a young black man carrying a bag of food in chest-deep water with a caption that described him as looting; another showed a fair-skinned couple in identical circumstances and described them as "finding food at a local grocery store."[24]

The crisis was framed in moral terms, denying the fact that no other solution but looting was available to the people stranded in New Orleans without food or water. Much of the media highlighted the rate of crime in

New Orleans with an emphasis on violence [*WTLB*, Act 3, 06:00, 28:00], spreading out to the cities where the inhabitants had been dispersed. Many African Americans felt that their status as full-fledged American citizens was infringed upon during Katrina, which Lee enhances by confronting various types of archival footage.

Through the manipulation of archival footage drawn mainly from television news programs, Lee produces a politically reflexive documentary that levels criticism at the media spin on Katrina. Lee demonstrates that Katrina was a "media event" which media scholar John Fiske defines as:

> An indication that in a postmodern world we can no longer rely on a stable relationship or clear distinction between a "real" event and its mediated representation. Consequently, we can no longer work with the ideas that the "real" is more important, significant, or even "true" than the representation. A media event, then, is not a mere representation of what happened, but it has its own reality.[25]

Fiske suggests that a "media event" does not relate to the truth, for it produces its own images and discourse. African Americans did not connect to the images which portrayed them on screen. Lee calls attention to the distance between the media event and the African-American experience by confronting television extracts with the memories related by witnesses. Not only does he expose the racial bias that undergirded mainstream media reports, but his reframing of the events in the documentary makes visible his skewed perspective. While striving to convey the traumatizing experience of Katrina and its aftermath for African Americans trapped in the drowning city, Spike Lee recovers documents that provide supporting evidence to his version of Katrina.

Stereotyping Black Crime on Screen

When the Levees Broke: A Requiem in Four Acts presents Katrina as a television spectacle which reinforced racist stereotypes by spreading word that the city was rampaged by looters—all of them viewed as African American gangsters. Rather than focus on the reasons why some New Orleanians made the decision to withstand the hurricane, media discussion emphasized the wave of violent crime raging across the city, foregrounding the rumors of violence perpetrated by looters and isolated snipers. Lee's reflexive approach to media rhetoric implies a critique of television culture, which has become a staple of contemporary documentary[26]—including Robert Greenwald's *Outfoxed: Rupert Murdoch's War on Journalism* (2004). Greenwald interprets Fox footage through a statistical analysis that exposes the right-wing slant of the network's visual and oral discourse. Lee's selection of media footage recounting Katrina's devastation illustrates what Greenwald defines as the "Fox effect," which has reverberated throughout the American media that imitate "Fox's rhetoric of sensationalism, blurring news and political commentary, aggressive graphics and displays of patriotism."[27] Lee points to words and images that were chosen to sensationalize the events, shaping the humanitarian crisis into a crime story that generated fear. Whilst such words as looters amplified the impression of chaos conveyed by the scenes of disorder, public debates focused on the issue of law and order that caused havoc in the apocalyptic city. Governor Blanco authorized the military to take aim and shoot when necessary, thus exacerbating the tense atmosphere and the impression of danger that prevailed [*WTLB*, Act 2, 11:00]. When General Russel L. Honoré ordered the troops into New Orleans, he was hailed a hero by politicians and television presenters alike, who transformed the failures of local and federal authorities into public successes.

Nancy Boyd-Franklin underlines the embedded racism found in media reporting on Katrina and argues that the viewers' memories of Katrina have been shaped by distorted images that articulated and reproduced an enduring racial cleavage. The media contributed to misrepresenting the crisis by aggressively racializing poverty and crime:

> Although much of the reporting on snipers, gunfire, homicides, gangs of youth roaming the city, rapes, and so forth was later proven false, the images endured. Interestingly, coverage of predominantly white, middle-class areas did not include these stereotypic references to violence—it was only mentioned in the coverage of areas such as the Superdome and the Convention Center, which housed large numbers of African Americans.[28]

Lee pinpoints the conservative-leaning interpretation of the situation through the journalists' narrow field of reporting, which he visually expresses by inserting a series of close-ups on sensationalizing headlines. Lee criticizes the dramatic media angle by zooming in on such headlines as "Bullets kill another man in Central City," "No one admits to seeing anything," "Four killed in Slidell," while Mayor Ray Nagin can be heard

78 / The Spike Lee Brand

in voice-over blaming the poor educational system of the city with paving the way for rising criminality rates. According to him, the dysfunctional educational system produces the black youths' exclusion which gives them little option but to turn to gangster life.

If God Is Willing and Da Creek Don't Rise assesses the progress made in the fight against crime over a time span of five years through an interview with Tulane University criminologist Peter Scharf. Not only does the scholar cynically call New Orleans "the murder capital city of the United States," but he also presents the results of his on-field studies through statistics that connote a bleak picture:

> First of all, the numbers are staggering. In 2007, we had 210 murders which, according to new demographic statistics, puts us at over 100 per 100,000; New York is at 5.5. The tragedy is most of the murderers are African American young males and we're at 58 per 100,000—that puts us 20% higher than any city in the country. In the group class I work with at Booker T. Washington, half of the kids have seen somebody murdered. So you know, you get desensitized. During the study, 18% of the kids have carried a gun in the last 30 days. They kill because of circumstance and they kill because they think it's right to kill. [*IGIW*, Part 2, 22:00]

Lee cuts from the talking-head conversation to a mug shot of fifteen-year-old David Bonds, whose criminal record includes the murder of Dinerral "Dick" Shavers: the young man was shot in the back as he was driving through Tremé. *When the Levees Broke: A Requiem in Four Acts* presented Dinerral Shavers as a drum player in the Hot 8 Brass Band and the announcement of his death in the sequel provokes an emotional shock. Lee cuts to crime scene photographs when Peter Scharf argues that exposure to crime produces the desensitized youth of New Orleans. The camera zooms in and out of photographs showing the corpses of black men: one depicts a dead body lying in blood while the other captures a corpse covered with a black plastic sheet as it is being carted into an ambulance. The faces of the dead are hidden from view, conveying the reifying gaze of the murderers who see their victims as preys, and that of the photographers whose snapshots objectify the dead. The photographs also capture the faces of intrigued observers and upset loved ones in opposition to the cold-blooded professional emergency unit carrying the corpse away. The visuals evoke newsprint photographs that render murder a banal everyday event, which Lee opposes to footage of the victim's mourning family and friends—including Dinerral Shavers's son who honors his father's memory by playing the drums. The whole sequence suggests death is common sight and human life has little worth in New Orleans, conveying the sense of desensitization evoked by Peter Scharf. The corpses of the murdered victims also serve as visual reminders of Katrina's dead bodies conspicuously lying on the streets of New Orleans.

The testimony of Donnell Herrington provides a counterpoint to the media headline as he connects the crime situation in New Orleans to his personal story in a rap song that expresses an acute sense of helplessness. He was shot three times in the days that followed Katrina as he was struggling for his life. Three gunshots can be heard on the soundtrack, adding to the tense, rugged rhythmic style of his verse:

In August '05
That's when Hurricane Katrina came
1836 lives was claimed
Let's get down to the bottom like who really was to blame
You see 90% was man, the other 10 was rain
We looking all around like this shit kind of strange
While the waters keep rising
Fright gripping the heart, people starting to panic
No food no water, how are we going to manage? [one gunshot on the soundtrack]
Just when I thought it couldn't get much worse [one gunshot on the soundtrack]
I was shot in cold blood by some racist vigilantes [one gunshot on the soundtrack]
Wish I had armed myself
Meaning I wasn't strapped in, feeling like a crushed dummy without a seatbelt
And I'm surrounded by these white devils hunting black men
So a shotgun blast, I was lifted off my feet
And I fell on my ass, my vision blurry
Hearing shots all around me and the last thing I heard was "that black nigger down"
Now he's approaching with a gauge in his hand, trying to finish what he started
But God had a different plan
Through it all and with all of the frustration

> Never thought I'd be at gunpoint facing assassination
> By some bloody hand that was racist. [three gunshots on the soundtrack]
> [*IGIW*, Part 2, 23:39]

The recitation of this rap tune empowers Donnell Herrington as he relates his victimization to a larger cultural context, which allows him to transcend his status as a wounded black man into that of an accuser demanding for justice and speaking out against racial prejudice. The situation he relates could be an excerpt from a slave narrative or a reported case of lynching with "white devils hunting black men." Donnell Herrington takes into account the historical, racial backdrop of the city when telling his story, emphasizing the point that his aggressor wilfully made the decision to pull the trigger on him because he was a black man. His rap thus pursues the fight against discrimination and racial violence, turning him into a contemporary figure of the Civil Rights movement. However, he confesses he thought his attacker Roland Bourgeois would never be arrested for shooting at him in a desperate racist attempt to protect Algiers from black intrusion. Frontline investigative reporter AC Thompson explains that Donnell Herrington owned up to him that "it felt like my life didn't matter." His testimony conveys the idea that racial oppression devalues the worth of life among African Americans and that violence targeted at black people has all too often been normalized. Donnell does not express much self-esteem believing the police would never solve the case of his assault. Echoing his subjective remarks, Michael Eric Dyson draws on the history of crime and justice in American society when writing that "black life is at a low premium, and to hurt, maim, or murder a black person carried little punitive consequences or public concern."[29] The not-guilty verdict that allowed Emmett Till's white murderers Roy Bryant and J. W. Milam to walk out of the courtroom as free men is but one of the most notorious examples. The boy's mother published images of the brutalized black child as an accusation tool; Donnell displays the scars in his neck in front of the camera, exposing racial cruelty and politicizing his body as Emmett Till's mother did with her child's.[30] Through Donnell Herrington's story, Lee captures the psychological trauma which racist violence produces: Donnell Herrington felt deprived of his humanity and was objectified by the gunshots which a white man fired at him because of the color of his skin.[31] This story resonates with a series of other tales of racial violence, including the murder of Trayvon Martin in February 2012 and the shooting of Michael

Brown in August 2014. The space given to Herrington's testimony turns the film into an activist tool against racial violence, which Lee links to the disparaging images of black youths broadcast by the media.

Herrington was shot again a few years later and part of his leg had to be amputated, which he explains looking straight at the camera in *If God Is Willing and Da Creek Don't Rise*. Some black men wanted to rob him of his car and fired a round of bullets which hit him in the hip and in the leg. In the two films he is interviewed with New Orleans horizon in the far background, across what may be a canal or a lake, pinpointing a state of paralysis. Although five years had elapsed since the first interview, Donnell Herrington had to go through the same healing process after being shot again. He suffered two attempts on his life: one was an overtly racist crime whereas the other was a case of "black-on-black crime." Both, however, seem to originate from the same cultural climate of social and racial violence permeating the city. Criminologist Bernard Headly deems that black on black crime results from the economic conditions that push African Americans to the fringe of American society: "Crime is not the result of blackness (which is what the notion of 'black on black' crime implies), but rather of a complex of social and economic conditions—a negative 'situational matrix'—brought on by the capitalist mode of production, in which both the black victim and the black victimizer are intricately locked in a deadly game of survival."[32] He further argues that the connection between skin color and social status produces a deadlock situation, which may account for the high level of crime among the poor living in urban ghettoes that are clearly demarcated by race. His comments suggest that reconstruction may have provided an opportunity to challenge the city's racial divide. New Orleans education programs (including the promotion of charter schools) may have represented an attempt at dealing with inequality by improving school standards to "create new people for a new way of life"—in the words of education Professor Pauline Lipman.[33]

The media focus on crime and poverty does not construct a positive image of blackness which, Fred Johnson argues in the film, produces self-destructive violence: "A lot of black on black crime has to do with self-hatred. When you don't like yourself, when you look at yourself in the mirror and you don't like what you see, [. . .] you're prone to hurt that which looks like you" [*IGIW*, Part 2, 18:50]. These words express the weight of race on an individual who has internalized oppression, a feeling which Gloria Yamato links to systematic oppression:

> The oppressors are purported to have an innate inability to access economic resources, information, respect, etc., while the oppressed are believed to have a corresponding negative innate ability. The flip side of oppression is *internalized oppression.* Members of the target group are emotionally, physically, and spiritually battered to the point that they begin to actually believe that their oppression is deserved, is their lot in life, is natural and right, and that it doesn't even exist.[34]

Spike Lee prompts his interviewees to transcend the victimization which the media portray by giving them a voice in his documentaries and by endorsing their activist stance in *If God Is Willing and Da Creek Don't Rise*. Such endeavor undergirds the portrayal of Jim Brown, who became a paradoxical icon in American society, illustrating contradictory reactions to race, success, and scandal.

The Myth of the Black Athlete: From the Limelight to the Gutter

Jim Brown: All-American provides a close analysis of African-American athlete Jim Brown's emblematic career from the football fields to the Hollywood screen. Spike Lee spotlights the invisible prejudices that seep in the media's portrayal of African-American athletes and underlines the power of stereotypes to mold narratives of blackness through Brown's biography. The film begins with sports presenters commenting live on his football running tactics; their voices overlap and create a soundscape that enshrouds the viewer facing a dark screen. Exploiting the interstices between the visual and the aural tracks, Lee tries to dredge up memories of Jim Brown's record-breaking scores. The sports commentators enthusiastically depict the hectic races of the football player as he advances the ball into the opposite team's end zone without being tackled. Their voice-overs conjure up the suspense of the match, counting the meters as Brown rushes across the football field:

> Jim Brown gets the ball to the 30, to the 35, he fights away at the 40. Jim Brown gets to the 45, he's still fighting to midfield . . . [Voice overlap by the end of the second sentence] . . . hands the ball to Jim Brown outside left end to the 40 . . . He's to the 45, he's to midfield, he's to the 40, Jim Brown to the 30 . . . Jim Brown to the 20. [. . .] Jim Brown is going to score.

Jim Brown is identified by the figures of a two-digit number that looms on his back when his name appears on the screen, referring to his jersey number within the Cleveland Browns. From 1957 until 1965, Brown was associated with number 32, which metaphorically signifies the commodification of his name by sports presenters, whose excited remarks hint at the passion aroused by the spectacle he provided in a highly mediatized sports culture. They convey the thrill of winning, which the athlete inspired through "his power, speed, ability to change speeds and directions, stamina, leadership skills, and mental endurance" as summarized in the article dedicated to him in *African American Icons of Sport, Triumph, Courage and Excellence*.[35]

Figure 3.1. *Jim Brown: All American* includes archival footage that gives a glimpse into the past glory of the football player whose name became synonymous with number 32 among the Brown's fans. *Courtesy of Photofest*

The voices surrounding Brown create a myth that Lee strives to debunk by exposing the technical tools used by the media to turn the athlete into a star. The viewer is made to believe that s/he is watching a football match with Jim Brown as number 32: the camera follows a figure walking in the shade of a corridor from the changing-rooms to the football ground, whereas archival recordings create a soundscape that plunges the viewer into the mythical past of the football icon. When Brown walks out of the shade into the sunlight-bathed field, he is dressed in black and the stadium is empty. Yet we can still hear spectators screaming on the soundtrack as though a football match was really taking place. Viewers may have recognized Brown's gait because his body language fits the image a whole generation has memorized through watching his football deeds on television and his stunts in cinema. However, the man does not turn around to face the camera, frustrating the viewer's voyeuristic desire. The opening sequence exploits the discrepancy between the image and the soundtracks to posit that the icon being talked about does not reflect the man walking down the corridor. The character shaped by the media does not unveil Brown's true personality, which may have driven him to write his own autobiography in collaboration with Steve Desohn in a book published in 1989 whose title evokes his life beyond the field—*Out of Bounds*.[36] The opening sequence revives the legend built around Jim Brown, pointing to football as a spectacle that turns the players into popular heroes. The film underscores the semiotic elements which underlie the social construction of race and sports: the figure of the black athlete is reified by words and numbers that enhance his prowess on the field. Lee probes the discrepancy between the media portrayal of the football player and his self-image by allowing Jim Brown to speak about his own life. *Jim Brown: All-American* pinpoints the alienating power of images that isolated Brown from the people around him through fashioning a stereotypical racial narrative—which begs an analysis that will be developed further in this chapter. Lee offers a close examination of Brown's career, which he discusses with the character himself, both to rejuvenate his tarnished reputation and to study the power of media biases.

My approach to the film draws on cultural semiotics, which French philosopher Roland Barthes developed to decipher the ideological discourse that underpins mass media visuals, articulating a critical perspective on sports-as-spectacle in his *Mythologies*.[37] Barthes collaborated with Quebec writer Hubert Aquin on the production of a short documentary film entitled *Le Sport et les hommes*, which features a voice-over commentary written by Barthes, applying his notion of myth to five national sports: bullfighting, car races, the Tour de France bicycle race, ice hockey, soccer. Couched in a short essay entitled *What is Sport?* Barthes's remarks underline the social function of athletes in a culture that uses sports to perform ancient rituals purging violence from society. A few pages are devoted to soccer in England, which may be deemed as popular as American football in America:

> Why love sport? First, it must be remembered that everything happening to the player also happens to the spectator. But whereas in the theatre the spectator is only a voyeur, in sport he is a participant, an actor. And then, in sport, man does not confront man directly. There enters between them an intermediary, a stake, a machine, a puck, or a ball. And this thing is the very symbol of things: it is in order to possess it, to master it, that one is strong, adroit, courageous. To watch is not only to live, to suffer, to hope, to understand but also, and especially, to say so—by voice, by gesture, by facial expression. [. . .] In sport, man experiences life's fatal combat, but this combat is distanced by the spectacle, reduced to its forms, cleared of its effects, of its dangers, and of its shames: it loses its noxiousness, not its brilliance or its meaning.[38]

Barthes underscores the collective dimension of soccer: the spectator is invited to identify with the players running on the field in defiance of their opponents, living the games by proxy through the television screen. The focus on individual players mystifies athletic prowess, allowing the spectator to emotionally share in the fight that unfolds; s/he is metaphorically invited to withstand the test of combat. The first minutes of *Jim Brown: All-American* could be presented as a response to Barthes's question "Why love sport?" since the presenters' voices are able to arouse the spectator's desire to see the match commented on, appealing to the mystifying elements of sport through their detailed comments. Their focus on Brown makes every gesture a symbol, whereas their tone of voice carries emotions they probably wear on their faces. Missing from Barthes's analysis, however, is the racial dimension which impacts the ideological discourse shaped by sports-as-spectacle.

Following Barthes's theoretical demonstration, it may be argued that Brown *denotes* an African-American football player, yet his name *connotes* his commodification by the media and the sports industry. He was made an icon in the spectacle of media culture which, according to Guy

Debord, dramatizes society's dominant values.[39] Jim Brown was turned into a sport icon by the racial discourse crafted around his masculine athletic prowess. As illustrated by the voice-overs' observations in the title sequence, the media highlighted Jim Brown's physical qualities, giving rise to "stories of mental fortitude and gritty determination"[40] which made a legend of number 32. The public persona of Jim Brown is constructed by the interviews turning the man into an object being spoken about, shedding light on Brown's natural superiority rather than his intense practice. Art Modell, Cleveland Browns' owner from 1961 until 1995, typically understands Brown's accomplishments as hyper-masculine prowess. Sociologist Patrick D. Miller argues that racial prejudice undergirds the interpretation of sporting achievements: white accomplishments bespeak "diligence, forethought and application for the mind" whereas those of blacks are understood as a "natural" and "innate" predisposition.[41] The comments made on Jim Brown throughout the film illustrate this racist frame of interpretation. Cultural sociologist Ben Carrington argues that the media reinforce such arguments, relating the notion of race to an athletic predisposition while dramatizing each African-American achievement into a sensational plot:

> Black accomplishment in sport could not be understood as due to individual achievement, driven by dedication, hard work and perseverance in the contest of a deeply racist system that all but denied opportunities for self-actualization in most other areas. [. . .] In fact, with each sporting victory, each successful punch thrown, each finish line crossed, each broken record, 'race' was further consolidated and embedded as a demonstrable fact of ontological difference.[42]

In opposition to the deeply racist views which the media spectacle endorses, Lee focuses on the tactics Brown devised after studying the opposite teams' techniques, thereby anticipating the players' courses of actions to achieve victory. The second sequence starts on a football field with Jim Brown, Joe Frazier, and Hank Aaron addressing Baltimore Ravens during Final Practice before Super Bowl XXXV on January 26, 2001. Lee uses a dissolve to shift from the first to the second sequence, thus linking the icon of the past to the training that the media tend to overshadow when focusing on the athletes' noteworthy deeds only. Brown's advice to the team sheds light on the qualities he values to win: "intimidate them with your physicality and overwhelm them with your mentality" [05:18]. Lee highlights the ironic counterpoint between Jim Brown's comments and the statements made on him, aiming to reveal the weight of racial prejudice in the area of sports.

Jim Brown: All-American deconstructs Brown's public persona by allowing an older Jim Brown to look back at his own life story in a narrative that creates a dialogical space around the public memory of a younger Brown. Coaches and friends express their views and help piece together a multifaceted portrait of Brown, which demonstrates the impact of the media's racial framing on individual perceptions. The second sequence is interspersed with archival footage and a couple of interviews illustrating this point: Art Modell recalls Brown's exceptional physical qualities ("he did things I didn't think were possible" [03:53]) whereas Dr. Walter Beach III explains what Brown represented for himself and other teammates, stating that "he was one that represented what a man should be about [. . .]. He was at the forefront of standing up for his African maleness" [04:30]. The interviewees pinpoint the diverse and sometimes contradictory ideas Brown did arouse, disclosing as much information on themselves as on Brown: Art Modell evokes the pleasure of the gaze when depicting Brown's physical abilities whereas Dr. Walter Beach III underscores Brown's idealized maleness, expressing a model of masculinity other black players aspired to. These conversations reveal Brown's commodified body can be appropriated in various discourses, which may reflexively foreshadow that the sport biographical documentary will only produce another type of discourse and flesh out another fantasy character.[43] In a 1970 *Chicago Defender* interview, Brown himself admitted that "images are just that—shadows in the minds of people who don't even know you. A man and his image are seldom similar."[44] Lee tries to counter the media biases by allowing Brown to take part in the film so that he might give his version of events that repeatedly stained his reputation—which may appear as a shady prospect to some of Lee's detractors.

Not only does *Jim Brown: All-American* emphasize the athlete's obstinacy as a key to his success in sports, but it also underlines the role of an influential go-between that permitted him to breach the color line. Attorney Molloy played a pivotal role in Brown's career, negotiating his admission at Syracuse University by overriding institutional racism: Brown was not granted an athletic scholarship, a fact which could have turned him away from sports into street crime. The documentary intertwines snippets of interviews that address the relationship between race and sports, highlighting the various types of constraints that African-American students had to overcome during segregation. Although he excelled in basketball, track, lacrosse, football and even qualified for the Olympic Games as a decathlon athlete in 1956,[45] Brown was discriminated against at Syracuse

University (from 1953 until 1957). He recalls anecdotes that exemplify the humiliating, prejudiced situations he was confronted with, being either placed on the sidelines for most of the games or verbally dissuaded from pursuing a sport career. Brown voices the bitter disappointment he had to deal with: "If you were a person of color, it was very difficult to be accepted on any kind of equal level. They kept telling me I wouldn't be able to be a running back" [27:00]. Former basketball teammate Manny Breland explains that he "perceived a kind of unwritten quota as far as how many black athletes could start on a team" [28:40]. Brown eventually imposed himself by scoring the most points in a football game during which he was given a chance to play after two white players got injured [31:00]. As explained by sports historian Kathryn Jay, "the pressure to win" was what finally drove schools to integrate their football and basketball teams.[46] Lee cuts to original footage to indicate that the televised game against Maryland was a turning point, for Brown gained public recognition which compelled Syracuse football coach to make him play every game afterwards. Interestingly, the biographical focus on Jim Brown allows Lee to tackle an array of social and racial issues considering his life was molded by all the events that occurred in the 1960s' American society and threatened its conservative institutions.

Brown's achievements have contributed to the history of "muscular assimilationism," which historians Patrick B. Miller and David K. Wiggins define as "the slow and often wrenching process" to open mainstream American sport to the full participation of African Americans.[47] The documentary pinpoints the relationship between Brown's breakthroughs in sports at Syracuse University, where he encountered racism on a daily basis, and the larger civil rights crusade he personally endorsed in the 1960s, by having sports journalist Ralph Wiley speak about Brown's sport career as a fight against prejudice:

> As an American black man, an African American historically told to be docile, to be quiet, to be accepting of the abuse heaped upon you, Jim Brown said "I'm the best at this game and nobody can stop me" and nobody did stop him. And they tried all manner of things to stop him. Fighting, talking, cursing, kicking in very private areas, mentally affecting him, trying to dominate him. [32:00]

Brown himself does not mention the blows he received, calling attention to his achievements instead. He projected racial pride and assertiveness as his sport performances gained him respect, thus merging his black masculine identity with his sport image, foreshadowing the Black Power iconography of the 1960s. He relates that, during his senior year, he purchased a large red and white Pontiac Bonneville that he provocatively drove around campus. Lee ironically pans across an old advert of the Pontiac, suggesting that Brown appropriated a symbol of success in American white patriarchal society. He used the car to break the unwritten segregationist rules of Syracuse when he drove a white girlfriend to one of his home lacrosse games and kissed her mouth in public [31:30]. The sequence ends with a fade out that suggests the gap between college sports and going professional in so far as the change of status transformed Brown into a committed activist.

Kathryn Jay examines Brown's public success in relation to a change in the spectacle of sports as the athlete arrived in "the league just as it had begun to capture the imagination of American TV viewers."[48] Brown's athletic skills electrified spectators who were keen to watch National Football League Sunday afternoon games on television. Lee films football fans waiting and drinking outside a stadium to show the popularity of a sport that made Brown a hero. Fans sport their favorite teams' caps and tee shirts in opposition to Christians' appeals that they "worship Jesus not football" [34:10]. American football has become a moneymaking spectacle, with each team selling by-products emblazoned with its logo.[49] The marketing revolution that affected sports in the 1980s impacts the documentary: the editing connects different types of footage, opposing the lavish colored contemporary football ground [35:14] to the black and white archival material [37:00] whereas Brown's voice-over advertises the myth: "Each new Sunday meant a broad new challenge rich with new opportunities. A time for achievement. A time for glory." The dramatic musical score turns football into a spectacular drama, enlivening the game by enhancing individual skills and actions. Clicking cameras surround Brown even though he is no longer a player [35:00], suggesting that he became an entertainment figure before he was even given his first role by Hollywood. Not only did he provide the type of actions needed to entertain the viewers, but he also attracted further attention in public appearances after the games. Mike Freeman explains that Jim Brown was a celebrity whom people vied to be seen with:

> Each football accomplishment was also purposely punctuated by a public statement or appearance. Everyone wanted to speak to him, to be close to him. No one was exempt from

desiring to be in his presence, not the many women who courted him, not even American presidents. In December of 1963, after beating Washington, Jim and teammate Frank Ryan, the Browns quarterback, were invited to the White House by Lyndon B. Johnson.[50]

Lee reconstructs the life of Jim Brown in a documentary that sheds light on the making of his public image as both a hero and an antihero. Although Brown's sports career was perhaps a somewhat unique achievement for an African American athlete in the 1950s, the development of college sports as a commercial venture opened up opportunities that broadened the horizon of an increasing number of African-American athletes. Sports sociologist Michael A. Messner draws from his on-field studies to posit that college sports continue to attract youths from lower-status background, among them a majority of African Americans, only to limit their activities to sports.[51] Such was the walk of life followed by Jim Brown, who devoted most of his time to practicing and improving his athletic skills instead of studying for a degree. Lee does not completely challenge the stereotypical narrative since he does not mention Brown's academic achievements, relating the construction of his masculine identity to his athletic career instead. Brown received a Bachelor of Arts degree in Physical Education from the College of Liberal Arts of Syracuse University in 1957, which is not stated in the film.

Brown's football career soon conflicted with his film engagements: he missed the early 1966 football season when the production of Robert Aldrich's *The Dirty Dozen* got delayed, forcing Brown to remain in England while his team played the first games. Art Modell decided to suspend him, which entailed a fine that Brown refused to pay by anticipating his retirement from football. *The Dirty Dozen* was to become the box-office success of 1967, boosting his career in Hollywood where he was offered more opportunities. Lee highlights the transformation of Brown's image into a black icon of the Blaxploitation cycle, which was initiated by Melvin Van Peeble's *Sweet Sweetback's Baadasssss Song* (1971). The film provided the model emulated by the studios in the 1970s: Sweetback represents the African-American hyper-masculine hero who awakens to racial injustice and rebels against the authority of the white oppressor by flouting his laws: Sweetback kills a policeman, makes love to a white woman, and runs away to Mexico. Black audiences were invited to indulge in the pleasure of watching Blaxploitation films that incorporated sex, violence, and "super-cool" individualism.[52] From *Ice Station Zebra* (John Sturges, 1968) and *Riot* (Buzz Kulik, 1969) to *Slaughter* (Jack Starrett, 1972) and *Take a Hard Ride* (Antoni Margheriti, 1975), Brown established a new paradigm for black male actors, performing acts of violence that characterized his screen persona in stark contrast to Sidney Poitier, whose popularity with crossover audiences was linked to a weak racial identity and repressed sexuality.[53] Brown's screen persona challenged the Poitier character; his physical demeanor countered the emasculated figure of the integrationist hero who compromised his virility in such films as *Guess Who's Coming to Dinner?* (Stanley Kramer, 1967). Donald Bogle explains that Brown's arrogance touched "on the needs of the new younger black audience for more assertive, more aggressive, more powerful African American characters" [1:17:39].[54] Lee stitches together extracts from various films to reconstruct the screen persona of Brown, selecting passages that depict him as an action hero: he runs, fights, speaks his mind, makes love to white women. Brown radiated racial pride and acted out masculinity, capitalizing on the virile image developed in a sport which encouraged "rough play"[55] as Brown writes in his autobiography calling himself a "soldier of fortune"[56] on the field. Although he reflected "an emergent assertive, sometimes violent, black manhood," exuding "a sexual expressiveness long denied blacks on screen,"[57] the roles Brown interpreted did not subvert the ideological framework prevailing in Hollywood. Film critic Ed Guerrero underlines the limits of the hyper-sexualized iconography characterizing the representation of blackness on screen since Melvin Van Peebles's *Sweet Sweetback's Baadasssss Song* (1971):[58]

> For all the new potent force, sexuality, and assertiveness expressed in the images, bodies and portrayals of the *macho* men, their strength was almost always either at the service, or under the control, of white institutional power and authority. [. . .] In *The Dirty Dozen*, Jim Brown starts off as an incorrigible convict but ends up enthusiastically serving America's war effort. [. . .] The "football heroes" offered only superficial variations of older codes and themes, and the black film critic Donald Bogle goes so far as to call Brown's characters "nothing more than the black buck of old."[59]

The documentary includes an interview with Van Peebles, who considers Brown is another Sweetback. While Huey P. Newton extolled Sweetback's adventures in the context of an individual and collective rebellion against the oppressor,[60] Van Peebles fails to notice that Brown's character, including his sex appeal, was turned into a commodified asset of the Blaxploitation era. Brown may project male sexual power and virile masculinity like Sweetback; however, the representation of black sexuality and violence on screen became part of a commercial endeavor, repeatedly used as a promotion tool to entice African-American viewers into the cinemas. Blaxploitation created a special market niche, which Hollywood studios were keen to exploit in the 1970s. Sports sociologist Ben Carrington compares various African-American athletes who turned to an acting career in the 1930s, including heavyweight boxers Joe Jeanette and John Lester Johnson (*Wild Man from Borneo*, 1933; *Ali Baba Goes to Town*, 1937; *Tarzan's Revenge*, 1938) and remarks that most of them "were given roles that were defined by and limited to their physicality and that served to reproduce a superficial, sexualized and primitive representation of blackness."[61] Brown's film persona suggests that challenging as the 1960s might have been on the political level, they did not transform the "muscle roles" into round characters on screen.[62]

Jim Brown's life as an African-American cultural icon illustrates the ups and downs of a public career for an ex-athlete: while his talent at playing football drew admiration and opened him a second professional career in Hollywood, he was a vulnerable target to the rumors and accusations that questioned his morality and sexuality. Although the documentary enhances Brown's heroic deeds on the football fields, it also captures the ambiguities of representation that shattered his public image. Brown's name was dragged in the gutter when several major scandals erupted and precipitated his fall from the limelight. The film interprets this reversal of fate in the light of a racial subtext, which permeates media coverage on race and crime. When portraying Jim Brown, Spike Lee dwells on the accusations that repeatedly tainted the athlete's reputation—including a rape case in 1965, an assault and battery charge in 1966, driving without a license in the early 1960s and other misdemeanors which caused the FBI to collect and compile records and data on him.[63] Brown was entangled in affairs that made juicy press releases, yet they do not crop up until an hour and a half into Lee's documentary in reference to the moment when Brown was arrested on rape charges on February 21, 1985 [01:29:00]. Embedded footage shows that Brown's private life was brought into the limelight, disclosing a turbulent past that overturned the perception of him. The media headlines influenced public perception by highlighting his criminal record, erasing all the positive deeds he had accomplished as a committed celebrity. Brown was presented as a woman abuser, whose achievements either as an athlete or a social activist were simply forgotten.

Lee includes television footage to retrace how Brown's arrest was broadcast into breaking news: television presenters emphasized the descent of the star from his iconic status to the level of street crime by recalling incidents that marred his past ("1965—Paternity and sexual assault; 1968—Assault and resisting arrest; 1978—Assaulting a golf partner") [01:30:00]. They listed all the charges pressed on Brown before 1985, summarizing his police record in a few dates that were displayed beside a close-up of his face. The photograph resembled a police mug shot, thus visually expressing negative views and shaping biased public opinions on a man whose version of the story had not yet been heard. Brown was framed as a criminal in the news flash, which used Brown's celebrity status to increase audience rates.

Spike Lee demonstrates that the media exploited Jim Brown's criminal record to make it fit into a preexisting ideological framework. The media focus on the assault and battery charges reactivated primal fear of black male sexuality, echoing the treatment of the O. J Simpson case which provided a race spectacle that filled the television programs for weeks on end. Simpson's trial and tribulations after his ex-wife Nicole Brown and her friend Ronald Goldman were found dead on June 12, 1994, produced an entertaining drama. Film critic Linda Williams remarks that daily airings dramatized the case, for each new piece of information introduced a twist in the story, holding the viewers' attention from day in to day out.[64] Williams suggests that the charges leveled against Simpson were crafted by the media in a narrative that endorsed a traditional melodramatic line casting Simpson into a dual role as victim and/or villain. She points to this dichotomy when analyzing the television *mise en scène* of the case, enhancing the racial bias that seeped into the media's portrayal of Simpson. His public image was reversed to fit the stereotype of the "brutal black buck" (mentioned by Bogle), who could not stand his white wife's betrayal and was bound to be her killer.[65] Simpson's image as a criminal was based on a racist fantasy of blackness, which the media spread instead of seeking out the truth: Simpson's mug shot was used as an icon of his criminal behavior linked with skin color.[66] The former football player focused the attention of the "media spectacle," which marked a shift from journalism to infotainment according to Douglas Kellner, emphasizing the voyeuristic nature of the media dealing with a celebrity case.[67]

The narrative construction of *Jim Brown: All American* highlights the manipulation of images, which framed Brown into another "violent black man." Lee, however, counters the melodramatic spectacle conceived at the time by allowing Brown to respond and to comment on the events which cast him into a victim/villain. Through testifying in front of Lee's camera, he recovers a voice he was deprived of during the events, trapped by the on-going media spectacle around his alleged crime. Lee adopts an editing technique that he will further explore in subsequent documentaries, connecting various narrative strands that complicate the media story, raising suspicion against the veracity of the accusations leveled at Brown. A slow musical tune is edited over the extract from "Larry King Live" show, creating a sound layer that undermines the presenter's dramatic tone of voice as he demands Brown to defend himself in the face of an accusation: didn't he try to throw "a woman off a second-story balcony"? [1:39:00]. The added music weakens the shocking effect the presenter aimed to produce by having Brown confront live direct accusations. Lee cuts to an interview with Eva Maria Bohn-Chin, whose testimony does not clarify the episode of her fall off the balcony of her apartment, offering a confused version of the events that fails to convince. Lee cannot restore the dialogue between the two former lovers, whose stories he tries to connect by crosscutting from one interview to the other, thus rewriting the drama that occurred in 1968.

Spike Lee suggests that Jim Brown was tricked by the image of strong masculinity, which his sport career and his Blaxploitation films had shaped. The documentary includes an extract from *Fingers* (James Toback, 1978), which depicts him hitting two women's heads in a scene that evokes the possible confusion between his film persona and his individual character. Brown was punished for exhibiting his body muscles and baring his skin in Blaxploitation films' interracial love scenes.[68] Because Raquel Welch played a Mexican whose racial status historically differs from that of white Americans,[69] the big screen's first interracial love scene in *One Hundred Rifles* (Tom Gries, 1969) did not spark as much controversy as that of *Slaughter* (Jack Starrett, 1972). The latter film includes a nude love scene between Jim Brown and Stella Stevens, which overtly challenged the white supremacist notion of the "purity and sanctity of white womanhood" idealized in the plantation genre according to Ed Guerrero.[70] The blonde actress was the personification of an American stereotype of femininity, thus making the film's couple of interracial sex scenes more shocking to some white viewers, who accused Stella Stevens of misbehaving on screen. For film scholar Mikel J. Koven, *Slaughter* represents an example of "white-made Blaxploitation," the only African-American character in the film being Slaughter himself, played by Brown, "fulfilling a kind of James Bond role."[71] The author argues that the use of violence in the film is exploitative in so far as it does not convey the political subtext attached to Sweetback's rebellion:

> The most interesting subtextual strand of the film, again from a very white perspective, is its—and, one supposes, the audience's—fear of black masculine sexuality, particularly the black man's desire for the white woman. Black masculinity is displayed in a rather fetishistic way. We are supposed to want to be like Slaughter (the tough action man who is a hit with all the ladies) and yet he is rejected because he is different (i.e., black). This contradiction is demonstrated by the framing of Brown's muscular body, naked from the waist up, while that body is being humiliated and destroyed in scenes of violence and torture.[72]

While actress Stella Stevens testifies that she was insulted in public for her role in the film, Lee points out the aesthetic and political limits of Blaxploitation as he cuts to another extract from *Slaughter* depicting domestic violence: the betrayed husband kicks his unfaithful wife to the ground, vicariously avenging the white viewer's humiliation [1:15:00]. Ironically, the scene also foreshadows the moment when Brown himself hit the headlines for assault and battery.

Witnesses' comments also illustrate that they were confused by Brown's public image, as though his screen persona had merged with his true character. His wife Monique recalls that she phoned the police in a panic attack on June 15, 1999, because she was scared after Brown had vandalized her car in a fit of rage [01:34:00]. When sports talk radio host Mike Francesca speaks about Brown, he employs highly connoted words and metaphors that enhance the threat he represented as the "racial other": he first reports stories he heard on the grapevine ("that he was a very violent man, whether it was choking a guy on a golf course . . . I wasn't there so I don't know . . . or being very hard on women") and draws conclusions that betray his own fear of Brown ("You're always a step away from setting off that volcano in Jim Brown") [1:33:55].

Brown's running interviews widen the gap between himself and others and testify to the distance between the present (his evenly balanced speech) and the past (the public images recorded in dated films). Lee is interested in the cultural phenomenon which Brown represents, analyzing the tensions that bore on him as an icon of black masculinity and militancy. The film restores Brown's voice in opposition to his commodification by the media, which consistently framed him into negative stereotypes. Lee's documentary strives to counter the dramatization effect that underpins the media: the public persona of Jim Brown is given a human dimension through the interviews, which the film director exploits to debunk the stereotype of the "brutal black buck," laying bare the racist discourse that invisibly pervades the media's treatment of actuality. Through his portrayal of Jim Brown, Lee offers a racial analysis of the "black athlete" narrative, pointing to the ideological framework that undergirds the treatment of race on television. The filmmaker pursues the same endeavor when scrutinizing the Black Panthers' media representation through *A Huey P. Newton Story*.

The Media Story of the Panthers

Spike Lee confronts the media story of the Panthers to Roger Guenveur Smith's one-man show, developing a dual narrative strand in *A Huey P. Newton Story*: the media representation of the Panthers is measured up against Smith's interpretation. The film starts in the dark after the credits fade; Smith lights a cigarette in a cacophony of blinding flashes whereas shot-reverse shots oppose the single figure of the comedian to the black-and-white footage of a crowd of photographers aiming their cameras in the same direction. A frenzy of clicking camera shutters resounds like gunshots fired at the man's body. The flashes reveal the character of Newton as a weak figure, hiding his vulnerable body in the shade, his voice hardly piercing through the whistling sound of the microphone. The full shot isolates him in the middle of the stage in counterpoint to the viewers' silhouettes standing in line in the background, watching Newton from behind wire netting as though he was a dangerous animal in a cage. The square shape of the stage and the upper balconies create a prison-like setting, with the viewers waiting to visit a dear one in the corridors of a high-security penitentiary or attending an execution that is about to take place. Lee captures the backlit figures of onlookers wearing the Panthers' outfit, including the beret and the leather jacket, thus acknowledging the legacy of the party in the present and emphasizing the enduring power of the philosophy of the movement.

Instead of the wicker chair in which Newton had been photographed by Eldridge Cleaver for the promotional poster of the Party, used as an iconic prop in a 1968 rally to symbolize Newton's absence whilst in prison, the chair of the film/play is made of wood with a high back and straight legs, evoking the witness box in a courtroom, the setting of an interrogation room, and the electric chair. The film posits the distance between an older Newton (interpreted by Smith) and the "warrior hero of the famous poster"[73] by juxtaposing two visual discourses: the seated figure of Smith in the foreground counterpoints the strutting erect Panthers of the past, appearing in the archival footage projected in the background. The backdrop evokes a highly mediated environment, which Newton did not manage to control, constructing a false image of himself. Even though he joined Malcolm X, Bobby Seale, Stokely Carmichael, and H. Rap Brown, "who exuded manhood and potent masculine street bravado,"[74] he appears as an emasculated shadow in the film—sometimes even reduced to a blurred image [06:35]. Judith Newton argues that Newton ostensibly hated and "was terrified of having to live up to the idea that the famous poster projected."[75]

The character played by Roger Guenveur Smith visually shies away from the iconic image that defines Huey P. Newton in the public eye. Dressed in black from head to toe, the character impersonated by Smith strives to evade the pressure of a public role. He begins his soliloquy with an anecdote that minimizes the role of the political leader:

> I'm a rather shy individual. I wouldn't consider myself to be very charismatic; you know I never did anything hero-like, I just worked on some little community programs. I do have a role to play however—I'm a theorist of sorts—I work on theories. But I really do not enjoy discussing the details of my personal life except as it relates to the movement. I hate interviews, tape recorders, microphones stuck up in my face. To tell you the truth, I hate stages cause they expect you to entertain them.

The camera comes close to the microphone used as a visible prop during the show, recording the voice of the speaker and shedding light on his words rather than on his iconography. Newton is presented as someone who enjoys being listened to, narcissistically drawing attention to himself and not to the Party.

The film thus exposes the contradictions that characterized Newton: although he embodied the Panther Party for Self-Defense, proudly posing as its co-founder on the posters calling for financial support, he eschewed standing in the limelight. The film helps restore the Panthers' political agenda as Smith recites the Party's "Ten Points Program" on stage, didactically reflecting on the political issues that undergirded the conception of the platform in 1966. Smith's speech slows down as he focuses on the words that Newton engraved in each chapter of his program; a video projected in the background shows a secretary typing the words he is dictating, diverting attention from the figure of Newton to his ideas

Figure 3.2. Dressed in black from head to toe and chain smoking on stage, Roger Guenveur Smith embodies Huey P. Newton as an isolated character playing a role in front of mikes and cameras in *A Huey P. Newton Story. Courtesy of Photofest*

[09:00]. The film thus characterizes Newton as the philosophical leader of the Party, highlighting the theoretical underpinning of his political vision by explicitly quoting from Mao Tse-tung. Lee captures the dynamic relationship between Smith and an audience that responds enthusiastically to his statements, thereby hinting at the enduring popularity of Newton and his points among African Americans: some spectators in the audience repeat his words when he calls for "All power to the people."[76] Smith gives a philosophical background to Newton's promotion of violence, adopting Mao's motto "Power grows out of the barrel of a gun."[77] The film also includes a visual reference to Mao through the slogan painted on a sign hanging above the entrance of a Black Panther Party office indicating "We serve the people" [15:07]. Among the figures mentioned because they have shaped his political views appears Malcolm X; Smith borrows from his rhetoric to justify self-defense "by any means necessary."[78] Smith's play draws extensively on Newton's writing, some extracts of which the comedian incorporates in his performance.

The added archival footage provides a contextual backdrop to the play, creating a visual setting that calls attention to the popular image of the Panthers: they were framed as a menace by the media, which laid stress on their aggressive iconography and downplayed their political message. The memory of the Panthers is epitomized by a few iconic photographs that underscore the activists' clothing style: the black leather jacket connoted the tough urban ghettoes from which they emerged, highlighting the virility of hyper-masculine figures; the beret referred to the French resistance and testified to the Panthers' militancy, signalling their identification with the revolutionary programs of the Chicano Brown Berets;[79] the sunglasses provocatively defied the gaze of onlookers whilst instilling mystery and dread into their bold and provocative demeanor. Lee borrows from the media footage that emphasized the visual shock engendered by an imagery that frightened the audience. Cultural historian Jane Rhodes argues that the Panthers' confidence and defiance, embodied by Newton's bravado and arrogance, undermined the visibility of the party's political program while reviving racist stereotypes of blackness: "Although their platform was indistinct, what they represented was not. These visual and verbal images tapped into white Americans' primal fears of black male sexuality."[80] Newton's political views and the party's community activities were overshadowed by the iconic visuals that were circulated in the media, focusing on the parades organized in support of imprisoned Newton rather than on their free breakfast initiative. Although media visibility helped the Panthers build up the movement, attracting more and more young blacks into the party that embodied the Black Power slogan used by Stokely Carmichael in a 1966 rally in Greenwood, Mississippi, the media focus on the activists' paramilitary spectacle engendered fantasies of black violence that deflected attention away from their community programs and achievements.

The film allows Lee to retrieve a lost message among the abundant visuals used to discredit the Panthers. Newton's complex personality crops up through Smith's interpretation, challenging the visual stereotype which the Panthers had devised as a response to the media depiction of the Civil Rights movement. In *Seeing through Race*, art historian Martin A Berger examines press photographs of the 1960s and suggests that there was a deliberate intent on the part of the white press to publish photographs that curtailed the heroism of African-American rebellious characters. Rather than focalize on their bravery, the printed images showed men and women who subjected themselves to the authority of white counterparts. Berger illustrates his point by mentioning the photograph of Rosa

Parks being fingerprinted by the police after her arrest in 1956 or the black demonstrators being water hosed in Alabama. He explicitly accuses the mainstream media of downplaying the civil rights activists' political message by turning them into weak figures, which could be controlled and therefore posed no threat to the established order. Through a close analysis of many press photographs, he remarks:

> The determined efforts of the white press to frame the civil rights movement as nonthreatening had the collateral result of casting blacks in roles of limited power. With great regularity, iconic photographs show white actors exercising power over blacks.[81]

The mainstream media shaped the perception of the Civil Rights movement and fashioned the historical narrative of the period, subduing the voices and the courage of African-American activists who braved the segregationists.

The Panthers relinquished the nonviolent model of the early civil rights fighters and devised an empowering model of activism that, however, had a countereffect as it produced a backlash of fear. The media exposed Newton as a visual and oral trope for African-American militancy, stereotyping his political stance into a few clichés and catchphrases that neither reflected the content of his speeches nor hinted at the achievements of his community programs. Newton was one of the fiery orators in the Black Panther Party, coining the term "pig" in reference to the police, thus displaying his defiant behavior toward authority symbols.[82] He wrote a series of articles published in *Black Panther*, the party's weekly newspaper illustrated and designed by Emory Douglas, where he defined a pig as "a low natured beast that has no regard for law, justice, or the rights of people; a creature that bites the hands that feed it, a foul, depraved traducer, usually found masquerading as the victim of an unprovoked attack."[83]

Smith's long monologue in the film/play is based on a variety of interviews and writings, most of which were edited by Toni Morrison into a book entitled *To Die for the People*.[84] Words humanize the character of Newton, conveying his doubts and portraying him as a sensitive character in counterpoint to the visuals which reify his figure. The interplay of the visual and the verbal in the film is not balanced; the images projected in the background compete with Smith's speech delivered in the foreground. Stereotypes create a visual and imaginary barrier that separates the spoken words from the voice delivering them. Smith impersonates a fiery Newton who repeatedly levels criticism at a racist visual culture, which shapes the black people into stereotypes as exemplified by the character of Sambo, the "dimwitted, gullible, helpless African American boy, a stock character in much of nineteenth century literary tradition,"[85] whose image served to reinforce assumptions of white superiority in children's books. Smith draws on humor when retracing Newton's childhood memories: Newton "took his shoe off and threw it at the instructor" who was reading a book about Sambo in class, which had become an unbearable strain for the child. The anecdote triggers laughter among the audience, who are both amused and vicariously empowered by the memory of a child's rebellion. A few pages taken from an illustrated children's version of Helen Bannerman's *Story of Little Black Sambo* (1899) are enlarged and projected in the background, allowing the viewers to look at them through Newton's eyes and to feel the humiliation produced by the Sambo personality.

The one-man show adapted into a Spike Lee Joint transforms the message of Roger Guenveur Smith: while the comedian endeavors to portray Huey P. Newton as an ambiguous character, Spike Lee sheds light on the ideological power of stereotypes to control the political through the visual. Unlike the photographs studied by Hariman and Lucaites in *No Caption Needed*, which they argue contribute to enriching the democratic debate by nurturing civic identity in American society, the photographs of the Panthers engender a feeling of exclusion rather than inclusion, positing the color line informs the relationship between the spectator and the construction of blackness on screen. Berger refers to Dorothea Lange's "Migrant Mother" photograph to point out that the racial dimension needs be erased for visuals to reach an iconic status. He distinguishes "lessons of universal suffering (read from white bodies) [that] were not to be confused with racialized narratives of suffering (read from the bodies of nonwhites),"[86] which might account for the limited power of the civil rights photographs.

The Panthers obviously did not address crossover audiences while promoting a nationalist message, which often displayed Afrocentric cultural symbols. The photographs, which signified a betrayal from the dominant perspective articulated by the media, are interpreted as tools of empowerment when remediated by Spike Lee. The film captures the complicity between the comedian and his audience, which does not easily extend beyond the television screen. Newton embodies a radical stand that cannot be incorporated in a colorblind rhetoric—contrary to such figures as Rosa Parks and Martin Luther King, who represent "floating signifiers" that can be appropriated in various discourses.[87] Political scientist Andrew Hacker argues that Martin Luther King's nonviolent, integrationist stance made him an acceptable black figure in mainstream society and his memory is exploited in an array of contradictory narratives.[88] Conversely, the aggressive image of an armed Newton compromises his integration in America's visual democracy. Spike Lee, however, enhances the political and symbolical role he played for the African-American community through *A Huey P. Newton Story*. Newton provided an empowering figure for African Americans who looked at him as a model of resistance to the intricate and demeaning rules of white power. Through Smith's portrayal of Newton as an older figure, who is physically weakened by the use of drugs, Lee presents the fight he was engaged in as self-destructive. The dark stage and the prison-like setting of the play turn him into a martyr, whose memory Lee strives to recover.

Focusing on such controversial figures as Jim Brown and Huey P. Newton, the filmmaker strives to pinpoint the negative impact of the media, which frame the racial debate in moral terms as illustrated by the images of Katrina. Excluded from visual democracy are icons of Black Nationalism—unless they support a marketing strategy in a capitalist society.

CHAPTER 4

The Legacy of Black Nationalism

Culture and Politics

The commercial success of *She's Gotta Have it* (1986) permitted Spike Lee to found his own film production company—40 Acres and a Mule Filmworks, which partly ensures his economic and artistic independence. Lee further increased his financial clout by developing Spike DDB, an advertising agency dedicated to the production of promotional videos for the music industry and multinational corporations like Nike, PepsiCo, and General Motors. Film historian Andrew Dewaard contends that Lee has to negotiate the corporate logic of Hollywood to secure funding for his films. Using his celebrity status and his name as a brand which can be exploited both to target a specific audience and to impose his choices as an auteur, Lee's commercial endeavors pursue a "pragmatic method of African-American empowerment through free-enterprise economics" which Dewaard does not view in a negative light.[1] The scholar explains that the success of a film does not rely on its aesthetic qualities only; it also depends on its economic marketing. While this path of reasoning may be adapted to the constraints which the filmmaker has to face as a minority director in Hollywood, it nonetheless raises questions and doubts as to the sincerity of his political commitment to documentary filmmaking.

The 40 Acres and a Mule enterprise symbolizes Lee's viewpoint that African-American advancement relies on economic power and ownership, for the phrase itself refers to a policy brought in by General William Sherman in 1865, which granted land plots for newly freed slaves to cultivate. The order was revoked after Abraham Lincoln's assassination, putting an end to redistribution and fueling resentment among the emancipated slaves, who were thereby deprived of the means to self-reliance. The 40 Acres and a Mule phrase has since then signified the federal government's failure to pay compensation,[2] which Black Nationalists Marcus Garvey,

Malcolm X, Elijah Mohammed, and Louis Farrakhan interpreted as an icon of betrayal when calling for reparation.[3] African-American history scholar Manning Marable similarly associates compensation with the issue of reparation, which he yet defines more broadly when observing that "the demand for reparation is *not* fundamentally about the money,"[4] arguing instead that reparation requires the integration of black voices in the nation's historical narrative—"a history that more accurately presents the authentic story of black people from their own point of view, as they lived it."[5] The 40 Acres and a Mule phrase emphasizes both the historical underpinning of Spike Lee's filmmaking and his commitment to retrieving the message of Black Nationalism.

Malcolm X defined Black Nationalism in a speech he delivered in Cleveland, Ohio, on April 3, 1963, which is referred to as "The Ballot or the Bullet." Viewing American democracy as "disguised hypocrisy" which did not offer the same opportunities to blacks and whites, Malcolm X considered it was necessary for African-American communities to exert political control at a local level to thrive economically. As the leader of Black Power, he drew attention to the interwoven notions of self-reliance and self-determination, which should be developed in relation to a program of economic advancement positioning African Americans as active consumers and producers within their neighborhoods. He advocated the empowerment of African Americans through economic initiatives that would permit self-reliance to blossom on individual and collective levels:

> The economic philosophy of Black Nationalism is pure and simple. It only means that we should control the economy of our community. Why should white people be running all the stores in our community? Why should white people be running the banks of our community? Why should the economy of our community be in the hands of the white man? Why? If a black man can't move his store into a white community, you tell me why a white man should move his store into a black community. The philosophy of Black Nationalism involves a re-education program in the black community in regards to economics. Our people have to be made to see that any time you take your dollar out of your community and spend it in a community where you don't live, the community where you live will get poorer and poorer, and the community where you spend your money will get richer and richer.[6]

In this extract, Malcolm X accuses the white power structure of maintaining a system of exploitation that victimizes blacks, denying them equal opportunities in all fields—from education to jobs and politics. His goal was to empower African-American communities economically to liberate them from white domination, which subjected African Americans to abuse and intimidation. Drawing on the theoretical underpinning of decolonization, including Frantz Fanon's *The Wretched of the Earth*, which opposes capitalist imperialism to socialism while advocating a "new humanism,"[7] Malcolm X called for a black cultural revolution to transform individual consciousness. After he returned from his 1964 tour in West Africa, the leader gave his first speech on behalf of the new Organization of Afro-American Unity (OAAU) which he had founded in Ghana. His address fostered awareness of a distinct black culture developed through a common racial history: "We must recapture our heritage and our identity if we are ever to liberate ourselves from the bonds of white supremacy [. . .] We must launch a cultural revolution to unbrainwash an entire people."[8]

References to icons of the black revolutionary tradition are sprinkled throughout Spike Lee's films, which articulate a politics of identity that foregrounds the assertion of self-pride and economic empowerment. His films are imbued with black power sentiment, which he puts forth when plumbing the past in search of hidden stories that testify to the African-Americans' active role in shaping American society and culture. His documentaries unfold a biographical vein, galvanizing tales of resilience about African Americans fighting injustice. Rather than focus on Martin Luther King, Jr., whose legacy of nonviolence has been hailed by white America, Spike Lee sheds light on the revolutionary voices of nationalist figures Malcolm X and Huey P. Newton, whose radical message continues to be subdued and distorted. When making biographical films that underscore the struggles the two leaders went through in order to gain a political voice in American society, the filmmaker broaches the race problem and pinpoints continuities between present and past discriminatory practices.

Lee endeavors to have the Black Nationalists' legacy acknowledged by recounting the political fights their leaders carried on, foregrounding their economic views and the sense of cultural pride they radiated with. Through a study of the ideological impact of integration on black middle-class culture, Charles T. Banner-Haley is able to demonstrate that Lee's public recognition was linked to the specific context of the 1980s and

90s, marked by a conservative shift on the political level and a revival of racial consciousness in the fields of arts and culture: "The absorption by the black middle-class of cultural nationalism and black pride coexisted reasonably with America's increased awareness of and willingness to accept ethnic culture."[9] Neither did the nationalist creed permeating the semiotic discourse of Lee's films conflict with the integrationist stance of the African-American middle-class audience, nor did the cultural identity celebrated by Black Nationalist icons betray the rising black bourgeoisie values. The African-American audience endorsed Lee's engagement with racial politics, which suggests that his pragmatic approach to economic empowerment was in line with the popular view.

Whether he recounts the exceptional sport career of Jim Brown or retraces the music and business adventures of Michael Jackson, Spike Lee extols the skills and achievements of the characters he portrays. The filmmaker turns ordinary individuals into heroes of daily life by giving prominence to their exceptional stories and unknown talents in *If God Is Willing and Da Creek Don't Rise*. Watching his documentaries turns out to be empowering viewing experiences insofar as they spotlight the success of resilient African-American figures whose portrayal is inspiring. However, the focus on notable African Americans who have become billionaires in the entertainment industry or in the corporate sector (like Lee himself) produces a skewed vision, for the accomplishments of a few have neither lessened the levels of poverty nor tempered inequality among African Americans.[10] Social and economic injustice continues to prevail over everyday life inside the United States, marginalizing African Americans from the mainstream. In an attempt to redress the negative stereotypes embedded in the media representations of blackness, Lee would rather shed light on the positive aspects of black culture than examine the role of structured race and class inequalities in hampering social progress.

Musical Resilience and Creativity

Malcolm X was concerned with raising awareness of a distinct cultural heritage among African Americans by lauding the unique achievements of writers and musicians whose creativity testifies to the richness of black culture. In the 1960s, the emergence of soul music reflected the mood of resistance and self-determination that permeated Black Nationalism with James Brown singing lyrics of defiance—"We'd rather die on our feet, than keep livin' on our knees."[11] Spike Lee draws on the black musical heritage to transform the spectator's viewing experience into empowerment, using jazz songs to create a sense of solidarity beyond screen space at the beginning of *When the Levees Broke: A Requiem in Four Acts*. Quite significantly, the series begins with African drumbeats preceding a montage of images rummaging through the past of New Orleans, with Louis Armstrong's voice nostalgically asking "Do You Know What it is to Miss New Orleans?" Lee offers a path to transcend the traumatizing experience of Katrina, which the government's mishandling only made worse, by reviving New Orleans' energizing cultural life. The film's musical score further dramatizes the documentary as it arouses empathy and sympathy, allowing the viewers "to feel the feelings of others."[12]

Spike Lee's New Orleans documentaries convey the attachment that the city inspires to most African Americans across the United States. New Orleans has retained an ethnic character that pervades its cultural life because ancestral cultural traditions survived there,[13] which Lee emphasizes by lingering on such symbolic sites of memory as Congo Square. The filmmaker identifies the square where the slaves could practice their bambula beats as central to the development of African-American musical forms. The bambula beats are evocative of the African heartbeats, highlighting that New Orleans occupies a special place in the history of African-American culture, for the city's local customs permitted the slaves to develop and to preserve some rituals [*WTLB*, Act 3, 37:00]. African-American music and dance traditions betray the influence of their ancestors' original practices. Historian Michael E. Crutcher, Jr., recalls that the Congo Circus became the setting of a seasonal attraction around 1812. The slaves were allowed to gather and perform their languages, dances, and instruments there, which made it "a place of active resistance to the dominant slave society."[14] Spike Lee dwells on Congo Square as a site of memory, which should instil pride and confidence among the members of the African-American community in New Orleans and beyond. Lee cuts from Congo Square to paintings that illustrate what Congo Square might have looked like, inviting African Americans to look back at the past to project themselves into the future.

The documentarian uses music to design a path for regeneration amidst the debris. Lee symbolically offers his film as a tribute to the dead of New Orleans, allowing the viewers to share in the mourning process through the ceremonies recorded by the handheld cameras and broadcast on television. The fourth and final act of *When the Levees Broke: A Requiem in Four Acts* opens with the Hot 8 Brass Band walking in front of a horse-drawn hearse carrying a coffin labeled "Katrina" through

Figure 4.1. Spike Lee marks his engagement visually by accompanying his characters in the derelict city, which Terrence Blanchard dramatizes by filling the abandoned streets with the music of his trumpet in *When the Levees Broke: A Requiem in Four Acts*. Courtesy of Photofest

a landscape of debris. The slow music of the beginning turns into an upbeat, joyful composition by the end of the act—as is the tradition in New Orleans funeral parades that celebrate the departure of the dead and the happy memories of the past. Historian Richard Mizelle, Jr., comments on the funeral tradition in New Orleans as a metaphor and a ritual that help understand the culture of resilience that characterizes its inhabitants:

> The history and culture of New Orleans is also closely linked with the jazz funeral, a unique and ritualized ceremony of mourning and celebration. The process of celebration and rejuvenation in a jazz funeral is called the "second line," and I use this term as a model for how we can apply the lessons of Katrina to bring change. The jazz funeral is both a metaphor for dealing with the losses caused by Katrina and a window into the culture of New Orleans. Jazz funerals offer

a way of understanding the psychological and physical pain of bereavement in New Orleans and provide a model for the regeneration of the city.[15]

Lee revives New Orleans' energizing cultural life through the funeral processions he follows, using the colorful and musical images of the local tradition to connote the possibilities of a new start.[16] The filmmaker exploits the viewing experience offered by the documentary to provide comfort and to recreate the community bond among African Americans whose roots are symbolized by local musical traditions. By filming the processions surrounding a coffin called Katrina, Lee invites a community of viewers to gather and to identify with the mourners. He explores the cultural web of the city to reconstruct a broken community bond among African Americans who sometimes decided never to return to the city that abandoned them [*WTLB*, Act 3, 47:00]—either they had no home to go back to and the city's reconstruction was too slow to welcome them back, or they discovered new horizons for themselves and their children after evacuation.

The third act of *When the Levees Broke: A Requiem in Four Acts* starts with a prayer by Audrey Mason, indicating that the film endeavors to find a path of healing. Sitting with her eyes closed in the middle of the wood frame used to characterize her as a Madonna in a painted portrait, she thanks the Lord for leading her through the troubled water, recalling faith supported her as it did her ancestors: "Father, as we waded through the waters, my mind thought about the song that my ancestors used, what I was raised upon. [. . .] I want to thank you for bringing us through that water." She performs her prayer in front of the camera, sharing an intimate and private moment with the audience whom she addresses. Her comforting words and soft tone of voice provide solace that contrast with the dramatic violence of the media coverage cited in the documentary. After telling the stories of the dead in the first two episodes of *When the Levees Broke: A Requiem in Four Acts*, Lee offers testimonies about individual survival in New Orleans, connecting the present plight to that of the past. Lee envisions the rebirth of New Orleans through its ties with the musical culture that thrived there, allowing African-American singers and jazz players to become renowned across the world. Music helped them resist subjugation and conquer space, which Lee tries to pursue when filming the bands playing through the streets and filling the city with their musical thrills.

Although Lee conveys solace through the musical score and the funeral processions he follows with a handheld camera, Douglas Brinkley suggests that he might be misleading when contending that New Orleans could be reborn through clinching to its jazz traditions, which social historians trace to the large percentage of poor African Americans trying to scrape a living in the city. Brinkley explains that the past of the city should not be romanticized because it does not help New Orleanians project a different future, "except as a means of keeping things, right or wrong, the same."[17] By reviving the musical culture and the racial history of New Orleans, Lee imparts to the film a "powerfully local flavour,"[18] a hint of exoticism and nostalgia that may sound counterproductive, putting forth "images of unending oppression and poverty amid ameliorative musical innovations."[19] Although he returns to New Orleans history and culture to rebuild a positive image of African Americans whom the media stereotyped negatively as looters, he also romanticizes the conditions under which the poor survived in the city. It seems that the pull of the Big Easy creates a mythological framework that challenges the political consciousness he strives to awaken. Lee views the past of New Orleans through rose-tinted glasses, prompting New Orleans residents to return to the city that saw the birth of African-American jazz music before its growth into a worldwide phenomenon.

Music is integrated into the fabric of Lee's films, which is further illustrated by the music videos he directed for African-American singers, underlining the Black Nationalist roots of Tracy Chapman's political and musical engagement in the "Born to Fight" video: the short film cuts from a boxing ring, where the woman sings her song and plays the guitar, to archival footage of the Civil Rights movement—including marches, speeches by Malcolm X, pictures of Rosa Parks and black-and-white footage of boxing matches. The visuals thereby transform the activist singer into an icon of collective fight, the spirit of which she captures through the lyrics of her song. The video made for the rap band Public Enemy uses the streets of Brooklyn as a setting for a crowd of marchers demonstrating to the motto of "Fight the Power." The film starts with archival footage of the 1963 march on Washington, drawing a political link between the original Civil Rights movement and its radicalization through Black Power. Dancers are dressed in black, visually echoing the outfit of the Panthers, whereas the singers stand among the crowd, posing as urban icons of ghetto culture and modern civil rights fighters.

The music videos are conceived so as to promote the songs and their interpreters, which makes Lee less critical in his latest documentary dedicated to Michael Jackson. *Bad 25* resembles a music video rather than a documentary insofar as it is devoted to reconstructing the public persona of Michael Jackson. The film celebrates Jackson's musical and artistic creativity by dwelling on the conception of the songs and the visuals elaborated with them: Lee invites choreographers to analyze Jackson's dance moves and urges director Martin Scorsese to comment on the technical details of his making the promotional video for "Bad." Eschewing all the controversies the singer was implied in, Lee draws an idealized figure of the pop star. According to the film's narrative, the persecuting media victimized Michael Jackson and deprived him of a voice to defend himself. His success was sacrificed for the scandals that boosted the sales of tabloids. Delving into the stories behind the songs, which his interviewees nostalgically relate, Lee romanticizes the singer's career, trying to capture the mystifying power of the star. Quite significantly, Michael Jackson's growing talent among the Jackson Five is summarized in an embedded sequence, which allows Lee to pinpoint Michael's original dance steps. Lee presented the film as "a love letter" to Michael Jackson, celebrating the 25th anniversary of the "Bad" album (1987).[20] Spike Lee's paradoxical stance as to the legacy of Black Nationalism becomes obvious when he claims that Michael Jackson was and remains an icon of African-American culture. Although the star became a billionaire in the entertainment industry through sheer hard work, clearly posing as an African-American singer with an Afro haircut in the 1970s, Michael Jackson claimed neither his African roots nor his masculinity as a star. Had Lee started the film with the "Thriller" album (1982), which was an even bigger hit on the front of pop music, he would have spotlighted Jackson's physical transformation and tarnished the portrayal of him as an icon of black pride.

The Expression of Black Pride

Spike Lee's documentaries shed light on individual paths of resistance through biographical narratives that pinpoint qualities building up a sense of black pride. Not only does *A Huey P. Newton Story* represent an example of cultural creativity which can be shared and promoted through the film based on Roger Guenveur Smith's one-man show, but the double narrative strand (film/show) allows the Panthers' message to be remediated and transmitted to another generation. Spike Lee and Roger Guenveur Smith combine their arts to help spread the political message of Huey P. Newton: the live performance is embedded in the film's narrative, which strengthens the political discourse fashioned by the Black Panthers' leader. The actor sits at the center of the stage, drawing attention to the complicity between himself and the audience, whom he addresses directly when interpreting the birth of "The Ten Points" program.[21] The *mise en scène* enhances the central role of Newton in the history of the party, reflecting the Panthers' vital function within the African-American community. The political and economic theoretical framework of the Panthers' project is embodied by the character of Newton in the play and given more power by the visuals associated with the words he utters. As he expands on the Marxist-Leninist line of the Party, pondering on the meaning of the words he manipulates, the footage projected behind his back depicts a female secretary typing up the revisions he demands, replacing the phrase "the white man" by "the capitalist."[22] The words selected underline the link between racial oppression and capitalism, which pinpoints the ideological legacy of Malcolm X on the Panthers. *A Huey P. Newton Story* does not silence the Panthers' revolutionary message and defiant rhetoric, which echoes Stokely Carmichael and Charles V. Hamilton's *Black Power, The Politics of Liberation in America*. The book provided the political framework behind the struggle that aimed at liberating black people from white oppression in America and throughout the world; the authors argued that racism was deeply linked to the capitalist economic model and to America's political institutions.[23] Calling for revolution when interpreting Newton on stage, Smith reactualizes this political discourse.

Lee includes a few outside shots of homeless people when the character defines point number 4 as a call for "decent housing," thereby indicating that Newton's theories are inspired by the experience of African Americans on the street. As the film cuts to footage of anti-war demonstrations, hinting at the involvement of the Panthers along with peace activists, Smith introduces point number 6 demanding "exemption from military service." His voice mixes with the hissing and booming sounds of bombs dropped in Vietnam whereas archival footage depicts the violence perpetrated by American soldiers carrying out their "search-and-find" missions. Lee reinforces Newton's message through the insertion of visuals that compare the Vietnamese to the African Americans, suggesting they are facing the same enemy: be they soldiers in Vietnam or police officers on the domestic front, Americans in uniform use brutality in order to impose their domination. Quite interestingly, the audience applauds when the character accuses the police of murdering African Americans, which Lee illustrates with a still photograph of a coffin carried by five Panthers [11:00]. The camera zooms out of the shot, which once again disrupts the visual flow of the show: Lee cuts from Smith's figure to the records of the past as though he was digging up repressed memories. It is quite difficult to know whether the audience claps in response to the denunciations of police brutality against the Panthers, including the murders of Bobby Hutton (1968) and Fred Hampton (1969), or whether they react to a situation which they feel still affects them.

Smith ends the enumeration of the program with a pun on the word justice, which he distorts into "just us," to argue that a penitentiary is a symbol for the African-Americans' martyrdom.[24] Such jokes continuously crop up in the show, toning down the tragic overtones of the recounted stories and conveying a sense of black humor. Laughter is used a form of resistance to counter the ideological slant of the "white oppressor." Through the use of puns and anecdotes, the speaker unveils the ideological framework linking language and power.[25] For example, he criticizes the recurrent use of the word "infiltration" by J. Edgar Hoover in the thousand-page FBI files devoted to his name, explaining that the Black Panthers' activists could not really "infiltrate" the black neighborhoods from which they originated. To Russian philosopher Mikhail Bakhtin, laughter has a social significance in so far as it is "directed toward something higher—toward a shift of authorities and truths, a shift of world orders."[26] Smith and Lee exacerbate the incipient irony of Newton's writings, using laughter as a strategy of resistance "in the process of becoming free."[27] They endeavor to recover Newton's original voice in dry remarks, using sports as an example of racial discrimination:

> I was reading a news item just the other day about this guy, Jimmy the Greek, sports broadcaster, on one of these television networks. And he was fired from his network position because allegedly he said that black people are intellectually inferior because we are athletically superior. But he did not say that. What he said was that black people, if given the chance, can do anything we want in this society, even play golf and tennis. [28:00]

The character of Newton is framed by a medley of voices emerging from the past, heard in voice-over or speaking in archival television footage, drawing a contradictory portrait of him as either a hero or a villain. Smith remains quiet during the sequence, yet his body moves as though each word was like a knife thrust in his body and torturing his mind [58:30]. The film frames Newton as a martyr, intensifying the gap between an isolated man on stage and the public portrayal of him in the archival footage: Smith's physical portrayal of Newton as a fidgety character, whose chain-smoking betrays an addiction to drugs, suggests the destructive elements of the fight he physically and mentally committed himself to. The archival material included in the film creates a dialogic exchange around the figure of Newton, introducing complexity into his shady characterization.

Spike Lee uses Smith's show to recover Huey P. Newton's political message, which had been distorted into a threat by J. Edgar Hoover, who launched COINTELPRO in 1967, a secret program of political repression, the purpose of which was "to expose, disrupt, misdirect, discredit, or otherwise neutralize the activities of black nationalists, hate-type organizations and groupings, their leadership, spokesmen, membership and supporters."[28] The FBI's campaign intensified in 1969, sending numerous Black Panthers into jail, forcing some into exile and causing others to be killed.[29] Lee enhances Newton's views on revolution by projecting an enlargement of the iconic photograph that depicted him as a modern-day African-American warrior, posing with Zulu shields, rifle, and spear. The fundraiser poster appears in the background as the character comments on the notion of revolution, drawing attention to the African tools used to symbolize the Panthers' fight:

> Black Panther Party for Self Defense was just the vanguard of the revolution. We're like the tip of the spear, we make the first impact but the real damage is done by the people cause they're the ones that make the revolution—they're like the butt of the spear, they make the real penetration. See, without the butt penetration there's no more danger than with a toothpick.[30]

The film creates a link between the words and the visuals associated with them: the spear stands for the violence of the war to be waged by African Americans if they want true and lasting social change in America. Although he repudiated cultural nationalists, including U.S. Black People's leader Maulana Karenga,[31] Newton himself took advantage of the appeal generated by African symbols, yet openly criticizing an attitude which he branded "pork chop nationalism,"[32] for he considered the Afrocentric trend was counterrevolutionary.[33] The portrait showing Newton dressed in Panther regalia, armed and seated in a wicker chair, illustrates the contradictory nature of the man: even though he did not endorse Afrocentric views, he borrowed from Afrocentric imagery and symbolism to visually define the Panthers.

A Huey P. Newton Story testifies to Spike Lee's commitment to Black Nationalism, for he tries to magnify the message embodied by the Panthers rather than discredit it. However, the filmmaker also directed television commercials for the U.S. Navy when recruits fell short of 7,000 men in 1999.[34] No doubt the U.S. Navy capitalized on Lee's popularity to draw more young African-American males in its ranks. According to political scientist Melissa T. Brown, the five commercials Lee directed for the U.S. Navy promoted different aspects of military life as indicated by their respective titles ("Travel," "Homecoming," "Seals," "Education," "Band").[35] Ironically enough, these short films were broadcast on television at about the same time as *A Huey P. Newton Story* (2001), which leads us to question Lee's commitment to Black Nationalism. The documentary and the commercials cannot be reconciled since they endorse antithetical messages. Lee has managed to straddle the oppositions between his commercial works and his committed films by separating his artistic activities from his advertising contracts through the creation of two distinct companies: 40 Acres and a Mule and Spike DDB are not dedicated to the same purposes. However, the twofold career of the filmmaker blurs and compromises the racial consciousness he strives to awaken in his films, reducing Black Nationalism to an economic stance promoting the values of the black bourgeoisie.

Lee's advertising company's website features a promotional video using Martin Luther King's "I have a dream" speech as a voice-over in a General Motors and Chevrolet campaign,[36] comprising a four-city tour organized to celebrate the unveiling of the Martin Luther King, Jr., National Memorial in Washington DC on August 28, 2011. The campaign espouses Martin Luther King's narrative of a beloved community, gathering black and white people from all walks of life as "brothers and sisters" around a table that stretches from the Atlantic beaches to Washington DC. The table spreads across the national landscape, weaving its way through the ruined quarters of broken houses in New Orleans, the rural communities of the countryside, the peace and quiet of suburbs outside the city centers and the main street in the capital city. The visuals connote an idealized view of American society, where the American dream has become reality for all.

While Lee's films attempt to recuperate the legacy of Black Nationalist figures like Malcolm X and Huey P. Newton, whose subversive revolutionary discourse he endeavors to have acknowledged in the history of the nation, his contribution to the General Motors and Chevrolet campaigns reinforces the "Great Man" myth theorized by Clayborne Carson, which underlines the key role of great historical figures such as Martin Luther King while overshadowing local community involvement in bringing forth change.[37] *Four Little Girls* and *A Huey P. Newton Story* offer insight into the ideological discursive framework of the civil rights fight whereas the "table of brotherhood project" initiated by the automobile industry reinforces the myth of a colorblind nation, which does not measure up to the facts mentioned in *When the Levees Broke: A Requiem in Four Acts*.

Spike Lee remorselessly sells African-American culture in his advertising spots, promoting the image and the values of the black bourgeoisie when shooting promotional videos for Jaguar to widen the appeal of the brand. The short film he directed for Jaguar explicitly taps African-American customers—dubbed the "new jag generation,"[38] embodied by a young man who travels by taxi from London airport to Jaguar headquarters to place an order for the new X-type Jaguar car. Dolly shots convey Spike Lee's signature, enhancing the proud composure of the man who is then delivered the brand new car by the English engineers outside his brownstone apartment in trendy Harlem. Flattering though the portrait might be, it produces mystification while dressing up American society into a multicultural environment which fits the idealized world of corporate advertising. Cultural critic Paul Gilroy argues that corporations exploit "the perfected, invulnerable male body that has become the standard currency of black popular culture"[39] and contends that Lee himself contributed to shaping this climate. The beautiful black bodies of athletes and actors are displayed as signifiers of prestige, blurring the historical boundaries between race and class. The Jaguar promotional video uses an ironic voice-over, which prompts the viewer to "imagine" he was in the shoes of actor Preston Greenwood, ironically avowing most African Americans do not have the money to buy Jaguar luxury cars. The short film depicts an idealized version of multiculturalism, reinforcing the raciological constructions of blackness. The glamourized male body draws on the aura of black physical prowess, which Gilroy traces to Leni Riefenstahl's filmic aestheticized look at Jesse Owens's body in *Olympia* (1938).[40]

Lee's commercial engagements conflict with the political stance he advocates through his committed documentaries insofar as they explicitly deny the race problematic. The speech he gave at Morehouse College at the launch of the Chevrolet sponsored "Table of Brotherhood Tour" conveys his belief in education as the great equalizer, denying the differences he nonetheless observed when focusing on education and crime in New Orleans during the making of *If God Is Willing and Da Creek Don't Rise*:

> I am happy to be here at Morehouse [College]. We should remember that Dr. King was a Morehouse man and so was his

father, Daddy King. We are talking about a great tradition of education. We as black people have gotten away from education. Our ancestors worked from can't see in the morning to can't see at night knowing that one day education would be the way to get us out of the bondage of slavery. We knew [then] education was the vehicle to get us to where we need to be. We have gone wayward. We live in a world today where if you are an intelligent young black kid, who speaks 'correct' English, that you were chastised as a white girl, white boy, Oreo [or] sellout. I think hope has a lot to do with this. We live in the world where education is not something to be proud of. We have to include hip-hop, not all hip-hop, the music video and the lyrics . . . all of this stuff is crazy. We have a lot of black folks who pray before the pulpit of the almighty dollar and will put their mother on the corner for a dollar bill. All they care about is making money, no matter who it hurts. That's the kind of thinking that will be our deaths.[41]

Lee's comments are surprising as they deny the existing structural barriers on the way to self-accomplishment. In *If God Is Willing and Da Creek Don't Rise*, Lee examines the school system and weaves critical distance into the presentation made by Paul Vallas, superintendent of the Recovery School District of Louisiana, as he expresses in a face-to-face discussion his views of education and the purposes of the reforms he enforced to rescue the school system of New Orleans.[42] The film first exposes the political reasoning behind the reforms by introducing the authorities' arguments: Paul Vallas associates such words as "superior," "best," "brightest," "elite" with the notion of "charter schools," which obviously represent the path he and Governor Kathleen Babineaux Blanco chose to rejuvenate the school system.[43] During Vallas's interview, the film cuts to snapshots taken in the classroom and focusing on students and their teachers, illustrating the gap between them. Dynamic and bright as they might be, the young teachers hired by the school boards may find it hard to connect with students whom Eddie Compass characterizes as "traumatized by Katrina." The bright picture conveyed by Paul Vallas's words does not seem to translate into convincing photographs—some students hold their head in their hands and are photographed from behind a grid that connotes imprisonment; the white teachers speak from a dominating position, towering over their group of black students. Pauline Lipman analyzes the teachers' "ideological dispositions" as a barrier which may be erected on the path to educational success for African-American students who feel alienated from these young teachers coming from outside the city and representing a social status they are not familiar with.[44]

Spike Lee confronts the theoretical model to its impact on the community by focusing on the only school that reopened in the Lower Ninth Ward—the Dr. Martin Luther King Jr. Charter School, which stands as a symbol of the enduring civil rights fight. Lee recounts how the school was reopened through a dual interview with school principal Dr. Roche-Hicks and community organizer Tanya Harris, whose success is presented as the result of community action, with photographs depicting citizens' collective actions and solidarity among the debris which they helped to clean. Tanya Harris explains that Mrs Doris Roche-Hicks "had" to go charter to be able to re-open the school, which suggests that the money made available to go charter created forced choice; parents and community members were pressured to reopen the schools as charters. The film cuts to archival footage of Barack Obama's visit to the Dr. Martin Luther King Jr. Charter School; while his presence may be flattering and supportive, it does not question the long-term effect of the experiment. The citizens interviewed voice a critical perspective, which Lee edits together into a didactic demonstration pinpointing the shortcomings of the reform. Working as a researcher in sociology, the filmmaker examines whose interests these policies serve, their social implications, and their meanings for students in New Orleans. The ideological stance he embodies through the New Orleans nonfiction series strikingly contrasts with the economic strategies he adopts in the business of making films.

The discrepancy between Lee's political and economic discourse is all the more disturbing, for he explicitly contributes to celebrating the "almighty dollar" by designing sneakers and watches for corporations that exploit his name to boost their sales. He takes part in the development of a consumer culture by targeting the young generation through brand sneakers, which he promotes by exploiting the popularity of African-American celebrities.[45] Charles T. Banner-Haley examines Spike Lee's Nike and Levis commercials as creative works that were somewhat "subversive, deconstructing the whole world of advertising in an attempt to reach the black masses while also promoting images of cultural pluralism."[46] Assuming the role of a go-between that has access to corporate money and to the African-American consumers, the filmmaker was and is still able to negotiate profitable contrasts with brands and corporations that tap into the niche market. The ads may be seen as provocative and challenging since they depict African-American figures in positions of power; however, the consumerist message they put across is hardly subversive. A case in point is the reference to basketball, which has marked Spike Lee's advertising debuts.

Sports: The Path to Success

Lee created his own advertising company Spike DDB in 1997 after he released several commercials staging Michael Jordan for the promotion of Nike shoes.[47] According to sociologists Brian Wilson and Robert Sparks, the association of the increasingly popular filmmaker with the basketball star played a key role in developing the commercial overtones of sports culture:

> While early Nike ads (mid-late 1980s) showed the young "Air" Jordan as a gravity-defying slam dunk artist in more conventional (but still effective) athletic apparel commercial formats, it was his 1991 association with filmmaker Spike Lee that launched Jordan and Nike well beyond the sport and into mainstream culture. [. . .] It was Spike Lee's elevation of "style" within and deriving from his films such as *Do the Right Thing* [. . .] that confirmed the marketing genius of Jordan-Lee ads for Nike.[48]

Not only was the relationship profitable to Spike Lee and Michael Jordan, but it also helped the brand gain worldwide appeal, influencing patterns of consumption and behavior among the youth. *Do the Right Thing* depicts a consumer culture that spread to the streets and shaped both dress codes and styles of behavior. Lee's advertisements contributed to the development of commercial sporting culture, which turned basketball into a commodity spectacle dominated by a profit-driven corporatization of sports. His Nike commercials were accused of promoting consumer values instead of self-esteem and hard work, reducing athletic abilities to the consumer's power to purchase trendy Jordan sneakers and equating the athlete's image with the commodities that he markets.[49]

Lee directed seven original commercial films in the early 1990s promoting Nike as an innovative brand endorsed by sport stars; the ads' appealing visual and oral comic effect derives from the opposition between the short filmmaker, who appears in the guise of Mars Blackmon from *She's Gotta Have it* (1986), a character who parodies the look and style of urban black youths by wearing oversized glasses and a gold necklace in the shape of capital letters spelling his name around his neck, and the tall, towering figure of Michael Jordan. Blackmon's loquaciousness contrasts with Jordan's laconic style, whose athletic performing body may be *"in motion* but *speechless"* as noticed by Carrington.[50] A close reading of *African American Icons of Sport, Triumph, Courage and Excellence*,[51] which sheds light on the lives and legacies of highly successful and influential African-American athletes and teams, reveals that many of these iconic athletes used their popularity to become spokespeople for ideas that extend beyond the sports arena. Despite nationally acclaimed performances, the names of Mike Tyson, Tiger Woods, Muhammad Ali, Tommie Smith, and John Carlos were discredited after the athletes delivered controversial statements and made public commitments that were not deemed in line with the values they were expected to endorse as public figures representing the colors of the nation. Muhammad Ali's conversion to the Nation of Islam as well as his overt stance against the Vietnam War, in which he refused to serve by rejecting military conscription, eroded his popularity.[52] When victorious sprinters Tommie Smith and John Carlos raised their clenched black-gloved fists in a Black Power salute during the 1968 Mexico Olympic Games, they were booed off the podium and out of the stadium. Both faced harassment on their return to the United States, experiencing stressful unemployment.[53] Although scholars and historians often hail committed athletes, the media nonetheless interpret their activist commitment unfavorably.[54] Douglas Kellner observes that African-American athletes who use their visibility to put forward racial issues run the risk of a backlash, which underlines the enduring weight of racist prejudice:

> [S]uch are the negative representations and connotations of Blacks in American culture and such is the power of the media to define and refine images that even the greater black icons and spectacle can be denigrated to embody negative connotations. As Michael Jackson, O. J. Simpson, and Mike Tyson have discovered, those who live by the media can die by the media, and overnight their positive representations and signification can become negative. Media culture is only too happy to use black figures to represent transgressive behavior and to project society's sins onto black figures.[55]

Jim Brown: All-American illustrates this reversal of fate, portraying Jim Brown as a vocal icon of Black Nationalism. His life spans some of the most tumultuous decades of the twentieth century, ranging from the Civil Rights movement of the 1960s to the Blaxploitation trend which launched the professional football player's film career in the 1970s. Jim Brown shaped a public persona that stirred controversy, disrupting the status quo in every aspect of his life. From his college years where he excelled in several sports to his experience in Cleveland's National Football League team, Jim Brown ran up against a host of restraints imposed on colored athletes by the racial divide that permeated sports culture, especially in the southern states. Through the construction of his persona Lee discusses the events that bore on African Americans at a time of heavy political and social unrest.

The notion of race is a prevailing theme in the narrative of Brown's life, molding both his view of himself and of American society. When he mentions his roots on St. Simons to account for the will and determination he developed as an athlete and an activist, Brown recounts the story of his west-African ancestors abducted to the islands: the Ebos would rather march "into the ocean to their deaths"[56] than accept the fate of slavery. The close-up on his face suggests that this episode of collective memory has become part of his personal story, symbolizing the link that ties him both to the place and to the black community in St. Simons. Brown grew up in a segregated community, whose collective memory derived from the experience of slavery and the spirit of resistance it nurtured with its focus on family as a protective unit from outside aggression.[57] Brown wishes to preserve and transmit the past by speaking in front of the camera and by helping his children to remain property owners in an area that is progressively gentrified.[58] The sequence on St. Simons recreates an incomplete family around Jim Brown, whose role as a father figure is emphasized through the portrait introduced, which however excludes his own father and his children's mothers, indirectly alluding to his unstable relationships with women [09:00].

The filmmaker focuses on Jim Brown as a committed athlete, who co-founded with John Wooten the Negro Industrial and Economic Union (NIEU) in Cleveland while still playing with the Browns, thus using his sports fame as a platform to engage in the civil rights fight. Winning empowered Brown and aroused a spirit of challenge at a time when "sports and social change were on a collision course" according to historian Kathryn Jay who explains:

> In turn, sporting events and black athletes provided the civil rights movement with visible role models and spokespeople

for social change. In the 1960s, sports and politics became increasingly difficult to separate. The desire to succeed and the will to win remained as potent as ever for athletes, but the social unrest of the 1960s meant that, for some, new layers of meaning emerged. Many athletes challenged traditional ideas during the decade. Sometimes this manifested itself as active protest against injustices within sports and in the larger society. At other times, it appeared in new clothing styles and hair lengths or as rebellion against coaching authority.[59]

Brown requested help from other professional black athletes to advance economic development and self-determination through the creation of African-American-run businesses, thus promoting a nationalist stance that resonated with the message of Malcolm X. Brown can be heard in the film recalling that "the Negro Industrial and Economic Union (NIEU) was started to remind black people and entice black people and help black people get into economic development" [57:50]. The activist succeeded in gathering the support of a community of athletes who used their influence to voice dissent while advocating racial equality and justice by creating the NIEU, which provided loans to help start and develop small businesses. The program was innovative at the time, making Brown and the NIEU the forerunners of today's micro-loan system.

When Muhammad Ali relinquished his slave name Cassius and converted to the Nation of Islam [59:57], Brown and other athletes openly expressed their support for a gesture that was deemed highly controversial. Their public declarations demonstrated that African-American athletes were conscious of the power they had developed as celebrities. Instead of feeling restrained by their image, some of the best-known sports figures felt empowered by their popularity at a time when "black was beautiful." They defied the commodification of their names by speaking up on the racial issue, using their visibility in sports to proclaim their political beliefs. Brown did not shy away from criticizing the government for its treatment of blacks and was dubbed "the most controversial athlete of the year" by *Time* magazine in 1965 even after being given his first role in *Rio Conchos*, a Hollywood western released in 1964.[60]

The legacy of Jim Brown and the message endorsed by Spike Lee need to be questioned in light of his subsequent sport documentaries, which include such commercial works as *Kobe Doin' Work*. Kobe Bryant may well embody the economic success Jim Brown strove for through the creation of the Negro Industrial and Economic Union (NIEU); nonetheless, the documentary reinforces the myth of sports as a "mobility route" by focusing on the basketball star, epitomizing a model which leads many young black men astray according to Margaret L. Andersen and Patricia Hill Collins:

> For young black men growing in communities with few opportunities, sports are perceived as an attractive mobility route. [. . .] Of the 40,000 African American boys playing high school basketball, only thirty-five will make it to the NBA (National Basketball Association) and only seven of those will be started. This makes the odds of success 0.000175![61]

Rather than interrogate the relationship between sports and business, the documentary deflects attention from the industry around basketball and conveys the filmmaker's fascination for the figure of Kobe Bryant, restoring the myth of sports as "a democratic force." The documentary highlights the blending of white and black players, positing that sports play a political and social role in a democracy as argued by Kathryn Jay: "The playing field, with its emphasis on teamwork, taught the lessons of pluralistic democracy, in other words, and sticking up for a teammate required that players ignore differences in class, race, and ethnicity."[62] The Lakers appear as a multicultural team in the film, with Kobe Bryant blending into the melting pot of sport. Produced by the sport channel network ESPN, *Kobe Doin' Work* serves a commercial purpose which leads Lee to revise and even silence his critical, controversial views.

The documentary tackles none of the moral dilemmas posed by a professional career that drives young African-American athletes away from their family and social roots into the corrupt world of money basketball. Conversely, Lee questions the power of individual ethics over the financial clout of professional teams through the tense son and father relationship in in his fiction film *He Got Game*. Film critic Thomas McLaughlin compares *He Got Game* to the documentary *Hoop Dreams* (Steve James, Frederick Marx, Peter Gilbert, 1994), for both films unveil the darker sides of basketball: the documentary filmmakers followed five years in the lives of Arthur Agee and William Gate, two teenagers whose talent in basketball fostered dreams of a professional career, which the film depicts as a "false hope for ghetto black kids" who are easily deceived by "hypocritical coaches, unscrupulous agents, and hustling recruiters."[63] Spike Lee himself appears in the documentary, warning the young players attending the Nike-sponsored ABCD camp (the acronym stands for

"Academic Betterment, Career Development") against misconceptions about their roles: he reminds them that they are seen as commodities and their value will be of importance as long as they manage to win. He bluntly declares: "Nobody cares about you. You're black, you're male, all you're supposed to do is deal drugs and mug women. The only reason you're here is you can make their team win. If their team wins, these schools get a lot of money. This whole thing is revolving around money." Lee develops a critical stance toward recruiters whose fictional counterparts prey on Jesus in *He Got Game*; Jesus is offered tantalizing promises of money and other grand prizes, including a Ferrari car and a billionaire's high-tech mansion, provided he accepts becoming a puppet in the hands of an agent who will manage his profitable career. The film also revises the basketball rags-to-riches stories that the media have shaped into a national mythology, evoking instead the corrupt institutions that surround the games. In their study about *Race, Class, and Gender: An Anthology*, Margaret L. Andersen and Patricia Hill Collins examine college basketball and posit that "the companies and organizations that profit the most—whether schools, product manufacturers, advertisers—are part of a class system where there are differential benefits depending on your "rank" within that system."[64] Players may get scholarships and be offered a chance to earn college degrees; however, they are forbidden to take any payment for their skills. They are not those who really benefit from a system which, as the authors quoted above explain, reproduces race and class. In a book published with the collaboration of sportswriter Ralph Wiley and entitled *The Best Seat in the House: A Basketball Memoir*, Lee criticizes the evolution of basketball from a sports competition to an entertainment industry, suggesting money has corrupted the game and mollified the players' desire to win.[65] He deems the system is organized like a "racket."[66]

Sports writer Jeffrey Lane remarks that a purely moneymaking orientation separates Michael Jordan "from black athlete-activists such as Jim Brown and Arthur Ashe, who used their fame to expose social ills."[67] Money has limited rather than expanded the power of athletes, who have relinquished their predecessors' political commitments to take an active part in corporate marketing strategies. Mary G. McDonald argues that Michael Jordan embodies a new generation of athletes:

> Jordan's political voice did not imitate those of predecessors such as Tommie Smith, John Carlos, or Muhammad Ali. In many ways, he was a willing corporate pitchman as much as he was a star athlete. His participation in advertisements for Nike

and the NBA stands in stark contrast to the vision of African American athletes as outspoken critics of the white establishment. Jordan certainly had myriad reasons to work with these institutions, preferring to serve as a role model for the ideas of racial tolerance, dedication, hard work, and achievement.[68]

Rather than blame Jordan for complying with the demands of an expanding sporting market, the author contends that the conservative 1980s created a different cultural atmosphere to the 1960s, producing new attitudes among African-American athletes. "They narrow themselves down to the game" declares Brown himself, alluding to those athletes whose life in sports is dedicated to making money and earning prestige [01:07:00].

Although Lee criticizes the business of sports, the filmmaker's career advanced thanks to the contracts he signed with Nike and Michael Jordan. As the original creator of the Jordan Spiz'ikes, a pair of sneakers which he designed for Nike with Michael Jordan in 2006, Spike Lee seems too involved in the corporate system to represent the radical streak of "Black Nationalism." Costing more than $200 a pair, Jordan Spiz'ikes do not really symbolize black empowerment. The firm's contentious practices, including its child labor policy and low wages in production facilities in Indonesia,[69] which spurred scandals after Lee made his first Nike promotional videos in 1987, have not urged the filmmaker to relinquish lucrative contracts to spearhead global fair trade. His latest NBA commercials[70] (including *Royalty is Big*)[71] and his most recent Nike ad (*The Chance Nike Sportswear*)[72] suggest that he continues to make profits from them. The filmmaker makes a cameo appearance at the beginning of the Nike video, addressing the viewer directly by looking straight at the camera. His voice-over commentary does not mention Nike, for Lee makes a very personal statement about drive as the fuel behind practice:

> Drive is the fuel that makes you want to succeed. If you're dedicated to your craft, that's going to permeate your entire being. When you have a drive, you have a goal and when you're focused you're not going to anything that's going to hinder where that goal is . . . That's what drive is for me, it's the fuel.

The video focuses on a teenager whose life centers on running, which he practices both at night and in the daytime when he is not in class or playing football. The video lays stress on individual performance, moralizing the practice of sports, which provides the drive to achieve success.

The urban setting denotes the ghettoes, a bleak environment which does not hamper the drive to run and to climb up the social ladder. While criticizing the media in his documentaries, Spike Lee's promotional videos indiscriminately reproduce the media rhetoric regarding sports, enhancing a discourse about individual and collective ethics. Kathryn Jay posits that sports connote positive values, which overshadow the ethical problems associated with performance:

> We celebrate athletes as national heroes and regard sports as a place that teaches all the best qualities of citizenship, especially integrity, reliability, and a sense of responsibility. In the next breath, however, the problems of sports—cheating, drugs, violence, and an overweening emphasis on financial gains—are bemoaned as representing the decline of the nation itself, with sports serving as a sort of public barometer of ethical values and decency.[73]

Whenever they break records and draw attention to their sports, African-American athletes are drawn into the limelight. The media add dramatic overtones to their stories, used to exemplify the individualist mythology mentioned above and to further the interests of those corporations whose business is centered on sports. Lee's adverts are imbued with a naïve optimism, which does not permeate such film as *Hoop Dreams*—which the filmmaker yet evoked as his favorite sports film in an interview given to ESPN.[74]

Rarely mentioned is the fact that Lee's documentary *Jim Brown: All-American* was partly financed by the adverts for which Nike CEO Phil Knight gave him a check.[75] Such information seems to imply that Lee may have compromised his ethical stance to be able to finance committed works—including his two New Orleans pieces.

Exposing the Racial Politics of Neoliberal New Orleans

When Lee revisits the Lower Ninth Ward five years after the quarter was devastated by the floods that followed the failures of the levees, his camera dwells on a number of ragged lots dotted by the concrete foundations upon which houses used to sit. *If God Is Willing and Da Creek Don't Rise* [*IGIW*, Part 1, 46:08] conveys the sense of desolation generated by the sight of "the white, irregularly spaced rectangles unnervingly calling to mind tombstones,"[76] which literary critic Evie Shockley depicts as an eerie spectacle: the voids in the landscape reveal the haunting presence of those who have either died or been unable to return. The silent, empty streets also bring up the absence of former New Orleans residents to Harry "Swamp Thang" Cook who recalls playing with the Hot 8 Brass Band in the quarter, enjoying himself with the people who ran out of their houses and joined the procession. *If God Is Willing and Da Creek Don't Rise* analyzes the relationship between the city and its residents, weaving the filmed visual landscape into the witnesses' oral narrative: the combination produces either a sense of belonging or a feeling of estrangement. The film assesses the lingering impact of Katrina through the visual traces left on the landscape, which in a sense express the traumatic experiences that have not been recounted—be they linked to Katrina's destructions or to the city's programs of demolition and reconstruction. Some places have been refurbished, others have been demolished, transforming the relationship of residents to their city.

Lee investigates the city's geography and architecture through the viewfinder of his camera, enhancing the transformation of New Orleans's landscape, as the city is being reborn from urban planning. He uses editing to oppose its flamboyant reconstructions (such as the Superdome) and contested programs of demolition (concerning the city's housing projects), expressing the loss of population as a physical and cultural wound which is not tackled. The visual landscape changes and testifies to political decisions that do not put forth solidarity across race and class.[77] After he was re-elected in 2006, Mayor Ray Nagin indeed openly declared that the city would not focus help on the Lower Ninth Ward and New Orleans East: "I've been saying this publicly, and people are starting to hear it: low-lying areas of New Orleans east, stay away from . . . Move closer to the river."[78] Try as they might, many New Orleans residents could not return to their home city, which did not provide the facilities needed to make everyday life an easy task. The film conveys feelings of resentment and isolation, experienced by individuals who could not cope with the gap between their expectations as ordinary citizens and the quest of prestige that lay behind the choices of the Bringing New Orleans Back (BNOB) urban planning commission founded in September 2005 by Mayor Ray Nagin and chaired by local real estate developer Joseph Canizaro. The plan explicitly stated that "in rebuilding New Orleans the goal must be more than recovery, it must be a transformation . . . a reconstruction that takes the city of New Orleans to a new level."[79] The plan of transformation was conceived from an ideological stance, which is given a vivid metaphor through the reopening of the Superdome in Lee's documentary.

Lee calls attention to the Superdome as an iconic element of New Orleans cityscape and to the organization of the Super Bowl as an event illustrating the commodification of a building used for a spectacular *mise en scène*.[80] Rather than focus on the football match which is summarized in a few decisive actions, the filmmaker captures the spectacle of brash colors used to signify the aestheticization of social life: the orange seats of the Superdome, the Saints' golden trousers and the lively tones of the Lombardi Gras Super Bowl Champs Parade testify to the regeneration of New Orleans. The first sequence of the documentary begins inside the renovated Superdome just before the XLIV Super Bowl Final was launched on August 7, 2010 [*IGIW*, Part 1, 05:05]: the camera tilts down the brand new seats and upgraded turf of the refurbished stadium, captures the looming National Football League (NFL) logo in a long shot of the field, which expresses the financial and moral support brought by the League that encouraged the Saints to return to New Orleans in 2006 after moving to the San Antonio Alamadome for the 2005 season.[81]

The emphasis on the Superdome allows Lee to visually summarize the policies enforced to reconstruct New Orleans. Historian Kathryn Jay contends that hosting a local team proves a city's "big-league" status and nurtures local pride and identity among fans, sometimes leading cities to overpay to claim the prestige of major-league teams.[82] Such concern undergirded the local authorities' decision to promote the rapid reconstruction of the Superdome after the National Football League announced that the New Orleans Saints would remain in Louisiana for the 2006 season, contesting team owner Tom Benson's wish to relocate in another city. Repairs of the Superdome were financed by public and private investments: FEMA contributed $116 million to the first phase, $294 million were financed through bonds issued by the state government and the NFL provided $20 million more after securing local business supports through the creation of the Saints Business Council—"an affiliation of 27 local business leaders who pledged to support the Saints by buying suites, tickets and sponsorship."[83]

Remembered as the familiar backdrop to the portrayal of stranded citizens during Katrina, the notorious stadium was renovated in time for the return of the Saints to the city in September 2006, which Mayor Ray Nagin indicated was an important economic and political symbol, demonstrating to the nation as a whole that the city was on the road to recovery.[84] The amount of attention paid to the Superdome at the beginning of *If God Is Willing and Da Creek Don't Rise* points to the psychological impact of its reconstruction on New Orleans residents: the upbeat music of "Who dat say they're gonna beat dem Saints . . . who dat? who dat?" accompanies the filmic discovery of the renovated Superdome, conveying the enthusiasm of football fans and New Orleanians who felt that their city was symbolically being reborn. The Super Bowl drew thousands of spectators from neighbor states and the largest viewership ever in U.S. television history, suggesting New Orleans had recovered its pre-Katrina place as a national attraction.

The film highlights the social and economic function of the Superdome, reflecting an imagery that helps shape the tourists' gaze on New Orleans: the traumatic memories of Katrina were supplanted by a picture of social harmony as the media spotlighted the festive gathering around the sport event. The "Louisiana Superdome" was completed as early as September 2006, restoring the structure to its 1975 status. Geographer Peirce F. Lewis asserts that the Superdome was originally "symbolic of the new New Orleans—an attempt to outdo Texas in bigness, shininess, and the size of its color TV screens."[85] The reconstruction of the Superdome suggests that the same economic concerns prevailed in 2005: the building was originally expected to spur business and enliven the Central Business District, which had developed around the Rivergate Convention Center completed in 1968.[86] When filming the activities taking place around the Superdome, including the football fans' celebrations and the Mardi Gras Parades, Lee sheds light on the social function of the Superdome, which contributed to turning New Orleans into a "tourist city" in the 1980s under the guidance of a new breed of businessmen—among whom the name of Joseph Canizaro appears.[87]

Local authorities made the reopening of the Superdome a top priority in the months that followed Katrina, which demonstrated that the development of tourism would take precedence over housing reconstruction in the new New Orleans. Although Lee takes part in the festivities of the Saints' victory, he enhances the estrangement some New Orleans residents feel when witnessing the gay parades flowing into the streets of the French quarter while other areas have not been rehabilitated yet. The tradition of Mardi Gras is explicitly compared to the media spectacle orchestrated around the Super Bowl: rituals and sports are transformed into commodities, designed to revive the economy rather than the community. Quite interestingly, the lively Super Bowl sequence in *If God Is Willing and Da Creek Don't Rise* deceivingly leads to frustrations and disappointments after the Saints' victory. The tone of the whole documentary darkens as the film unfolds, shattering the budding optimism expressed by the people who rejoiced after the game.

Documentary filmmaking highlights the indexical quality of cityscapes,[88] registering the imprints of the city's geographical development in relation to its economic and ethnic evolution. According to sociolinguists Adam Jaworski and Crispin Thurlow, "the city can be read as a text, a festival of signs—an 'iconosphere,'"[89] which Lee's nonfiction series emphasizes by presenting the city as a symbolical landscape for the viewer to decipher. Lee points to architectural designs like the Superdome as icons of economic choices that changed the city's outlook. Interviewing football fans who dressed up to attend the Super Bowl, Lee depicts the spectacle which the local authorities and the media orchestrated to modify New Orleans's public image: the city that had failed to support its community in the face of Katrina is portrayed as a melting-pot of people [*IGIW*, Part 1, 10:45].

The credit sequence of *If God Is Willing and Da Creek Don't Rise* is built on a dichotomy that encapsulates Spike Lee's documentary project: appearances are misleading and one should look below the surface to grasp truth. Lee first places the viewer in an attitude of contemplation by filming the city from afar; but he forfeits physical and critical distance to look at the city from the street level and to experience it actively, revealing the Super Bowl festivities as a simulacrum. While the characters interviewed confide their faith in the rebirth of the city, the eclectic montage of handheld camerawork and studio footage spotlights the fragile hopes aroused by the Saints' victory. The first images of post-Katrina New Orleans bespeak what Julia Hell and Andreas Schönle define as "a culture obsessed with its self-image, struggling to determine what defines its underlying reality once the layers of its self-representation are peeled away."[90] *If God Is Willing and Da Creek Don't Rise* captures an act of representation: the Super Bowl gave New Orleans national exposure, which the city's authorities took advantage of to shape public perception and overturn negative stereotypes. According to Professor of urban design and planning Laurence J. Vale, the emphasis on symbolic milestones is a common theme in post-disaster recovery, which ranges "from efforts to restore architectural landmarks (such as the plan to repair the New Orleans Superdome in time for the Saints to begin the fall 2006 football season) to the resumption of signal events (such as Mardi Gras, just six months after the hurricane)."[91] Although four and half years had elapsed since Katrina when Lee started shooting the second season of his series, the traumatic images that circulated on the Internet and in the media continued to haunt public memory of New Orleans. All the interviewees speak about the past and revisit New Orleans with these memories in mind, illustrating the notion of dark tourism which attracts new visitors to the Lower Ninth Ward and to the Superdome.[92] Evie Shockley notes that the traces of Katrina provide a spectacle for "tourists [who] are particularly interested in seeing the Lower Ninth Ward, where they snap pictures through the windows of their vehicles as former residents of the area search for salvageable possessions, cut up fallen trees, and gut the houses in which they had lived for long years."[93] While Lee's camera travels around the city, recording the spectacle provided by the surreal landscape of broken houses, he strives to counter the tourist's voyeuristic gaze by associating the sight of smashed buildings with the individual stories they signify. Rather than adopt an external point of view that would impose his view of the city, Lee expresses his support to the characters he accompanies through the streets by walking beside them with a handheld camera, striving to understand and to convey their relationship to the city.

When the Super Bowl celebrations end, Spike Lee discovers a landscape of ruins that connotes past and present discriminations: Endesha Juakali criticizes the programs that focus on entertainment instead of improving access to everyday facilities: "We're broke, we're poor, we're suffering, we have nothing. We need to focus on struggle, not entertainment." As a former resident of the demolished St. Bernard housing project, he expresses the first discordant view in the documentary, refusing to buy the "Who Dat" spirit as he sits in bright daylight in front of a house whose barred window signifies both the visual and geographical distance between the touristic attractions of the city center and the derelict landscape in other parts of the city [*IGIW*, Part 1, 15:06]. Sitting still in front of the camera, he compares New Orleans with a "plantation" which he is "trying to run away" from [*IGIW*, Part 1, 18:48]. The attention paid to such symbolic sites as the Superdome both reveals and conceals the plans that guided reconstruction. Using his camera to give voice to such characters as Endesha Juakali, who emerged as a vocal critic of city politics, Lee turns his film into a civil rights tool and thereby continues the struggles of the activists he follows in the city.

The Civil Rights Fight in New Orleans

The comparison of *When the Levees Broke: A Requiem in Four Acts* with *If God Is Willing and Da Creek Don't Rise* highlights an evolution as to Spike Lee's political framing of the situation. Literature scholar Anna Hartnell contends that the filmmaker's ideological message was rather ambiguous in the first documentary, which highlighted the difficulties of African-American homeowners whose rights were blatantly ignored by insurance companies. Lee's visit to middle-class Gentilly enhanced the plight of African-American homeowners, allowing individuals to voice their discontent at the local and federal lack of initiative. However, this perspective simultaneously discarded the case of African Americans whose needs were not provided for because they lived in rental housing, especially public housing. In his attempt to undermine the racist discourse that permeated the media, Lee focalized on the predicament of African-American homeowners:

> This rhetoric rightly rejects a racist discourse that links blackness and dependence on the state, but it also plays into a rhetoric that privileges property rights—one that nonetheless founders on the fact that these rights are left unprotected by insurance companies and a federal government that claim to guarantee them. As this particular witness indicates, a number of the property owners that appear in the film are clearly members of a black middle class, whose success and savings are encapsulated in the homes they've lost to the storm. Most poignant perhaps is the trip made by Terence Blanchard—composer of the documentary's elegiac score—and his mother to the wreckage of the family home in Act III. But the emphasis placed on the fact that insurance companies are busy wriggling out of their obligations by claiming to cover the effects of wind and not water testifies to a dream of home ownership bankrupt from the outset by its connections to corporate America.[94]

Missing from Lee's portrayal of homeowners in the Lower Ninth Ward is a sociological background which Evie Shockley gives us when she observes that "they owed relatively little or nothing at all—homes that, in some cases, they had built with their own hands—was what made it possible for them to live comfortable lives on relatively little money."[95] Lee eschews portraying the African-American poor, laying stress instead on the plight of homeowners who cannot have their houses rebuilt without the necessary support from local government.

The situation he discovers in 2010 prompts the filmmaker to revise his views and to endorse an activist stance in opposition to the politics of reconstruction enforced as part of the urban renewal plans. Rather than promote a more equitable city, these development schemes further exposed race and class differences, which *If God Is Willing and Da Creek Don't Rise* spotlights through the controversy aroused by the demolition of the housing projects. The city council called for the replacement of low-income housing developments with mixed-income housing, thus denying poor black residents the possibility to return and to integrate many white areas of the city. When filming the housing projects, Lee conveys the sense of absence that pervades the empty buildings, whose barred windows metaphorically suggest that the residents were given no voice in the process. Low-income residents were strongly discouraged from going back to New Orleans by the loss of affordable housing combined with a shortage of construction materials, the prohibitive price of which acted as a deterrent to rebuilding. Hazel Denhart states that money became the key to returning to New Orleans, where unemployment rates were high:

> Since the majority of low-income housing was destroyed (and very little of it was back in place 2 years later), those returning to the city in the early years after the storm were those who had the money to return. Large numbers of low-income residents were threatened with being priced out of the rebuilding effort. [. . .] Before the Hurricane, the Housing Authority of New Orleans (HANO) operated 5100 low-income units in four sites. By late spring, 2008 only 880 families had been allowed to return to this low-income housing.[96]

Although the projects belong to the Housing Authority of New Orleans (HANO), placed under federal control through the Department of Housing and Urban Development (HUD), the city council has the final say concerning the policies to be enforced as part of city planning. On December 20, 2007, the city council unanimously voted in favor of demolition: four housing projects were concerned, which made it impossible for former tenants to return.[97] The decision to tear down a series of housing projects was interpreted as merely another sign of racial discrimination, which Attorney at Law Advocates for Environmental Human Rights Monique Harden shockingly qualifies as "ethnic cleansing" [*IGIW*, Part 1, 38:00] in front of Lee's camera. Musicologist Ned Sublette blames the cynical attitude of local and federal authorities, which he believes seized Katrina as an opportunity to have the Housing Projects erased from New Orleans map:

> The sudden evacuation of the city, the mandatory evacuation of everyone in the city provided a unique opportunity to move

all the people out and close the projects down—a process that would have taken years. So that the projects were not just boarded up, but the windows were sealed with lead shields. People who had left quickly found themselves locked out and they never got to come back. [*IGIW*, Part 1, 35:00]

Such is the view endorsed by many African Americans interviewed in the film, expressing they felt deprived of their voice as citizens when the police blocked access to the public meeting of New Orleans City Council on December 20, 2007. The photographs interspersed in the archival footage of the meeting emphasize the shocking brutality of repression: African-American protesters were tasered to silence when the city council members were expected to vote for or against demolition. A line of policemen blocked the entrance to the council, recalling the segregation practices of the past.

If God Is Willing and Da Creek Don't Rise is pervaded by gloom and a keen sense of loss as reconstruction efforts promoted demolition instead of renovation. Evie Shockley goes as far as positing that demolition was conceived as a plan to get rid of the Lower Ninth Ward residents, considering that "the urgency of the demolition plans was intended to demoralize those who are committed to returning and rebuilding the Lower Ninth."[98] Lee presents the housing projects in a nostalgic light, using editing to underscore the opposition between the present and the past. Black-and-white still photographs visually depict the original projects as pleasant communities whereas colored footage conveys their progressive degradation. The photographs incorporated in the film narrative may be promotional shots as their harmonious spatial composition creates a sense of happy innocence with children playing about in the open green areas. The black-and-white photographs of St. Thomas (1941), Magnolia (1958), Lafitte (1953), and Iberville (1952) produce a visual rupture in the film, idealizing the housing projects which originally symbolized the concern of Rooseveltian liberals for social justice and cohesion. Peirce F. Lewis suggests that the housings were icons of the New Deal, which adds a highly symbolic dimension to their demolition. While the progressive city disappears in the new New Orleans, sacrificing traces of its past,[99] the photographs capture the sense of community that prevailed in the projects: one of them depicts a teacher addressing her class of attentive black children on the Lafitte well-tended lawn [*IGIW*, Part 1, 35:13]. This idyllic atmosphere pervades the archival stills which, however, strongly contrast with the colored footage of the Desire Projects dating back to

1978. The rosy picture is replaced with a bleak prospect: garbage litters the foreground while indistinct human figures loom in the background, generating an atmosphere of gloom and danger [Part 1, 36:00]. Although they were originally segregated, the housing projects became predominantly black in the 1960s: the white flight to the suburbs and the scaling back of social services caused the projects to deteriorate and they "acquired a fearsome reputation" according to Ned Sublette [*IGIW*, Part 1, 36:00]. The film traces the slow degradation of the projects which grew more and more segregated after integration was made compulsory, prompting the middle-class whites to move to the new suburbs that impinged on the surrounding wetlands converted into residential areas.[100] Only the poor remained in the projects—most of them being African Americans suffering from discrimination. Peirce F. Lewis notes the "close correlation between poverty and black population, especially in public housing" in opposition to "the low incidence of poverty in suburban areas which developed after 1950 and in fashionable areas of the city—Vieux Carré, Garden District, and the university district."[101]

The documentary endorses the political message of the filmed participants who perceive the closure of the housing projects as a measure designed to get rid of the poor in New Orleans. It conveys the emotion produced by images of demolition that destroyed individuals' sense of place by focusing on the image of a child standing behind wire netting gazing at a bulldozer that tears down the walls of the B. W. Cooper projects (December 12, 2007). The boy's still figure in the foreground contrasts with the mechanical, repeated moves of the bulldozer in the background. A close-up shows his hands clutch at the wire netting, expressing the powerlessness of former residents whose point of view was never taken into account by the city council [*IGIW*, Part 1, 39:48]. The bulldozer's blade rips through the houses and tears a community apart, thereby destroying the possibility of returning for those who wished to recover their former lives. The figure of the child adds emotion to the scene, evoking the trauma of displacement and destruction, for the demolition of the housing projects signified total loss for the former inhabitants. The figure of the child clasping at the wire netting suggests his up-rootedness as he is reduced to being a silent observer. The emotion that pervades the shot does not transpire in Mayor Ray Nagin's voice when he retrospectively justifies the political choices made:

> I think that prior to Katrina, public housing in the city of New Orleans was atrocious. I think it got worse after Katrina. I'm

> not convinced that other than one public housing development being the Lafitte, all the rest of them were beyond repair. In my humble opinion Lafitte probably could have been saved but it would have been astronomical as far as the cost. The shell was solid but all the internal wire, all the internal plumbing. Everything would have to be done from scratch. [*IGIW*, Part 1, 40:51]

Although Mayor Ray Nagin makes an exception of the Lafitte Housing Projects, he never fought to keep them open. Lee uses editing to spotlight the lack of dialogue between the authorities and the citizens, who regain a voice through the film.

By confronting images of the past with present footage, the documentary relates urban iconography to the dominant political and socioeconomic ideologies. The projects testified to the federal government's support to the poor in the Roosevelt era whereas their demolition was determined by private market ideology. Lee underlines the opposition between Ray Nagin and Annise Parker, the mayor of Houston, who helped welcome New Orleanians after Katrina even on a long-term basis [*IGIW*, Part 1, 25:10]. Lee weaves together Annise Parker's comments with interviewees' testimonies, illustrating the impact of political commitments on an individual level. Pastor R. C. Blakes, Jr., states that Houston "changed his world view" as he saw "white upper middle class Republican people reach out in tangible ways to lower class impoverished black people" [*IGIW*, Act 1, 24:55]. Such statement tends to reaffirm New Orleans's difference to the rest of the United States, emphasizing its alien status within the nation, suggesting that no positive change can emerge from Katrina.

While the constructed landscape of New Orleans exemplifies historical race and class barriers that contributed to shaping ethnic diversity into a unique cultural fabric, the new New Orleans appears as a project dedicated to maximize profits. Many citizens viewed the plan established for reconstruction as an attempt to eliminate concentrated poverty without introducing long-term reforms. As member of New Orleans City Council, Cynthia Hedge-Morrell publicly argued that she favored demolition to put an end to the cycle of poverty in the projects: "I'm voting for demolition because I believe in my heart that the replacement of the Saint Bernard Housing Development with the mixed-income community will do more for the development and the improvement of District D than any other single step we might take" [37:00]. This analysis exposes a bias against poverty which also pervaded HUD secretary Alphonso Jackson's national stance on the Housing Projects when he stated on June 4, 2007: "We should not put them back in the drug-infested, killing-infested environment they came out of" [*IGIW*, Part 1, 41:42]. Underlying this view was also an economic argument in favor of contractors and developers who targeted the markets for more profit.

Lee's interviewees voice their awareness of institutional discrimination, which pervaded urban planning during reconstruction. In this section of the film, talking heads are identified as activists who are committed at a local level: Endesha Juakali stands for the residents of the St. Bernard housing projects; Jeanne Nathan represents the quarter of Tremé through the Creative Alliance of New Orleans; Monique Harden blends her personal and professional commitments as Attorney for Environmental Human Rights; Krystal Muhammad speaks up for all the members of a displaced community during the meeting of New Orleans City Council. *If God Is Willing and Da Creek Don't Rise* calls attention to the activist initiatives led by citizen groups which, however, had very little impact on the policies of reconstruction, illustrating the failure of participative democracy in the face of corporations whose money flow acted as a determining factor. The demolition of the projects built in the days of the New Deal was as symbolical an event as the opening of the Superdome: the traces of the Roosevelt era were wiped out from the city which Mayor Nagin wished to rejuvenate by getting rid of all social ills related to poverty. Quite significantly, the houses built in replacement to the St. Bernard Housing Projects are part of the "Columbia Park at the Bayou District"—a name that connotes local gentrification. Lee only shows the façades of units that resemble each other, with immigrant gardeners planting rows of green plants to create harmonious designs that will enliven the place. For Tracy L. Washington, the whole plan of reconstruction is based on a lie, for low-income and middle-income residents will not mix as imagined. She dubs the project a "utopian community" [*IGIW*, Part 1, 44:00] which echoes the plans presented for the construction of a brand new hospital that "includes abandoning the landmark Charity Hospital along with its historical medical district and clearing 27 city blocks" [*IGIW*, Part 1, 01:42:00]. The film cuts to a television news program that presents the project as a modern facility through futuristic images which convey an idealized view of the future hospital in stark contrast to the footage of the allegedly outdated Charity Hospital. Contradictory accounts about the damage undergone by the buildings produce the same effects as conspiracy theories in *When the Levees Broke: A Requiem in Four Acts*. Jacques Morrial contends there was a "myth out there that Katrina and the floods destroyed Charity Hospital but the truth is only the basement flooded" [*IGIW*, Part 1, 01:42:00]. Even though opinions diverge as to the extent of damage that affected the building structure, Mitch Landrieu unveils the economic aspect of the negotiations that allowed New Orleans to obtain $127 million from FEMA. Sandra Stokes from the Foundation of Historic Louisiana explains that 70 neighborhood organizations opposed the project which would cause 243 houses and businesses to be demolished—including some 125-year-old houses representing historical heritage buildings.

Spike Lee's political stance seems to evolve from a belief in self-enterprise, embodied by the figures of Jim Brown and Kobe Bryant in his sports documentaries, to a more progressive stance, highlighting the responsibilities of the government to its constituents in *If God Is Willing and Da Creek Don't Rise*. The struggles that underlie reconstruction in New Orleans led many people to assume active roles as citizens, fighting to preserve their environment or their jobs in the face of corporations and politicians whose priority was to rejuvenate the city through the promotion of private ventures even if it meant sacrificing the community fabric. A variety of citizen organizations sprung up in the wake of Katrina, gathering citizens beyond class and race to put forth the identity of their quarter which they felt was threatened by demolition programs. The crisis was made even worse by the British Petroleum oil spill caused by the explosion of its Deepwater Horizon rig on April 20, 2010. The cameras' insistence on landscape testifies to the visual shocks provoked first by Katrina, second by the oil slick, which ruined the region's natural assets. Douglas Brinkley cynically comments on New Orleans as a city plagued by its past, which undermines any dream of progress [*IGIW*, Part 1, 17:34]:

> There is no new New Orleans. Cities have one straight line history. This is a city, if you look at the history of New Orleans, that's had yellow fever plagues where everybody dies, typhoid, dysentery, civil war, burnings, slavery, Katrina is just part of a continuum. So it's still the same city, just struggling in many ways with the same problems. Where I'm concerned it cannot go back to its kneejerk boosterism. "We're amazing. We're the best." There's deep down a kind of weird inferiority complex that goes in New Orleans. The one thing that unites everybody is both the feeling that they're spending their whole life telling everyone how great things are but secretly they know they're not and that creates a kind of weird schizophrenic attitude.

The historian does not distinguish the traditional parades from the Super Bowl media event, suggesting both are no more than rituals that help communities cope with a history of injustice. He points to a state of denial that has led to "schizophrenic attitudes" which may even have impeded progress. Interestingly, Douglas Brinkley adopts a more committed stance through his renewed collaboration with Spike lee, delivering overtly controversial statements that caused him to "catch some heat" according to the filmmaker's remarks on the commentary soundtrack. As the American scholar draws a psychological portrait of the city, Lee ironically cuts to images of Mardi Gras which vanish in the blinding sunshine; the city residents are in disguise when parading on the streets.

While demolition programs provoked fierce reactions among New Orleanians whose houses the government decided to have bulldozed when damage was estimated at beyond 51 percent of their fair market value,[102] reconstruction projects led by Brad Pitt and other organizations in the Lower Ninth Ward offer a glimpse of hope for a number of residents. In counterpoint to Clovina "Rita" McCoy, who keeps repeating that she hates Texas where she was compelled to move, Lee portrays several New Orleans homeowners who pose proudly in front of the houses that Brad Pitt had a team of architects design for them in the Lower Ninth Ward. Conceived as safe, energy efficient, affordable "green constructions," the houses were built with the support of the Make It Right Foundation which the actor created and launched on December 3, 2007.[103] The place exhibits a different atmosphere to Humble: homeowners planted small shrubs that demonstrate the new relationship they are experiencing with an environment they no longer fear; children are playing outside, progressively appropriating a site that had been devastated and abandoned; the families interviewed or photographed stand smiling in front of their new houses which symbolize the change in their life. The development of the new Lower Ninth Ward pinpoints what can be achieved in terms of "green construction." Brad Pitt comments on the collaboration that allowed the quarter to be reborn, involving both homeowners and architects in the process. The environment-friendly houses have been built on pillars with an open access to the roof, which ironically suggests the levees may not be trusted in case of another huge storm. The camera follows Brad Pitt as he walks through the Lower Ninth Ward, relates to the homeowners the Make It Right Foundation supported, depicting his commitment on the ground in opposition to the distance that keeps members of the city council away from the housing projects they decided to have demolished. The new Lower Ninth Ward exemplifies the vision that was expressed in the United New Orleans Plan drafted by the New Orleans Community

Support Foundation, incorporating the work of many agencies and neighborhood associations that had devised "recovery." The plan delivered in April 2007 stated that "all citizens, business and investors in our great city have a right to a safer, smarter, stronger city that enable a substantially higher quality of life, greater economic opportunity, and greater security against hurricanes than New Orleans had in the past."[104] Part of these objectives were achieved in the Lower Ninth Ward, whose residents were homeowners determined to return to their roots in a quarter they were deeply attached to.

The families filmed in the reconstructed area radiate fulfillment despite the remaining physical traces of Katrina around them, including the concrete remnants of houses that were swept away by the floods [*IGIW*, Part 1, 46:00]. Lee uses a series of still shots to capture the landscape of desolation conveyed by the concrete blocks where the houses used to sit, exposing the lack of progress in reconstruction and the feeling of abandonment that has kept haunting the present since the storm. The modern houses built by the Make It Right Foundation herald the rebirth of the Lower Ninth Ward as a community, for they have helped residents overcome the trauma of Katrina, linked to the shock of seeing dead bodies as well as to the experience of displacement.[105] This example illustrates how reconstruction can be devised to help individuals heal from the trauma of Katrina and improve quality of life in the city. The sequence devoted to reconstruction provides a source of comfort after the narrative retraces the desperate attempts at preventing the demolition of New Orleans housing projects. It also makes the documentary a more militant piece, presenting alternative paths of action to be followed. The film actively supports the struggles of the speakers whose arguments Lee develops into powerful visuals.

The Documentaries' Ethical and Political Stance

While Bill Nichols argues that ethical issues are key to documentary filmmaking,[106] he is also keen to observe that no set of fixed principles should be applied to define an only rule. In other words, "an open-ended or situated ethical standard—one rooted in the concrete contingencies of time and place" should prevail.[107] Depending on the situation investigated—whether it implies powerful characters who have access to representation or people without a voice in society, the responsibility and accountability of the man or the woman behind the camera varies. Questions of ethics may prompt a filmmaker to intervene in the course of action s/he is documenting—either to undermine deception on the part of his interviewees or to help them express themselves. This intrusion disrupts the belief that "spontaneous, uncontrolled cinematic recordings"[108] would allow unmediated truth to emerge, which undergirded the notion of Direct Cinema developed by American filmmakers Robert Drew, Richard Leacock, and Donn Alan Pennebaker.[109] Documentary scholar Michael Renov contends that filmmakers no longer shy away from displaying markers of subjectivity—"the filter through which the Real enters discourse as well as a kind of experiential compass guiding the work toward its goal as embodied knowledge."[110] The ethics of documentary filmmaking are unstable: while the uncontrolled aesthetic of Direct Cinema was to testify to minimal tampering with the events recorded, the obtrusive presence of Michael Moore's on-screen persona serves to signify his engagement with the issues he documents and the people he encounters, self-reflexively pointing to his films as constructions expressing a subjective perspective. The documentaries produced exemplify opposite ethical stances: Pennebaker deemed he was accountable to his audience whereas Moore foregrounds his responsibility to lower-class characters, whom he makes sure gain a voice in the process of his filmmaking.[111]

Judging from *When the Levees Broke: A Requiem in Four Acts*, Lee's ethics prompts him to side with his interviewees. The situation in New Orleans led the filmmaker to discuss many issues that did not crop up in his previous work. African Americans faced problems that hit the whole American working class and middle class, which drove Lee to adopt an activist stance that could be compared to Michael Moore's or Robert Greenwald's. Opposition to corporation greed seems to be the mantra of these documentary filmmakers who use their films to call for more justice. In an interview delivered to the *LA Times* on August 23, 2010, Spike Lee reacted to the ongoing oil spill in the Mississippi Gulf Coast by calling for justice: "It's about justice, it's about right and wrong. I love this country, and these people are just screwing it up over greed. It's a disgrace. What we stress is that eleven people died on that oil rig over a company's decision to cut corners."[112] These words do resonate with Robert Greenwald's activist filmmaking as defined on the website of his company Brave New Films,[113] for Lee allows his interviewees to make their opinions heard by using the screen space which the film director's name can open up on television. Not unlike Greenwald, Spike Lee's documentary contributes to democratizing screen space by incorporating amateur footage shot by Dr. Ben Marble, a resident of Gulf Port on the Mississippi Gulf Coast who made videos to record the devastation in this area which seemed "to go unnoticed by the media" [*WTLB*, Act 3, 12:30]. The young man was shocked to discover a line of policemen blocking the road to his destroyed house because Vice-president Dick Cheney was being interviewed a few blocks from there; Marble approached Cheney and notoriously told him to "go and fuck himself." Ben Marble recalls the event in front of Lee's camera, taking full responsibility for his slander. The anecdote evokes an act of subversion that Lee endorses by appropriating the filmed footage in his documentary.

Although working within the media system through HBO, Lee challenges the "propaganda model" which manufactures consent according to Edward S. Herman and Noam Chomsky. His documentaries may contribute to promote social change by educating viewers and fostering democratic debate, which Herman and Chomsky argue should be the purpose of free, independent media:

> The organization and self-education of groups in the community and workplace, and their networking and activism, continue to be the fundamental elements in steps toward the democratization of our social life and any meaningful social change. Only to the extent that such developments succeed can we hope to see media that are free and independent.[114]

This didactic concern actually widens the scope of Lee's filmmaking in *If God Is Willing and Da Creek Don't Rise*, which addresses a crossover audience by tackling environment concerns that affect all the coastal communities. The color line disappears in the face of such disasters as the Deepwater Horizon oil spill. Rather than use his interviewees as mouthpieces, Lee's documentary endorses his interlocutors' commitments to fighting against injustice in the new New Orleans.

Contrary to *When the Levees Broke: A Requiem in Four Acts* which was based on a series of interviews with many ordinary citizens, *If God Is Willing and Da Creek Don't Rise* touches on specific issues that require the knowledge of specialists in the field. These experts, however, speak on behalf of New Orleans citizens whom they represent through their status within the community. The individuals interviewed offer crisscrossing perspectives: local fishermen (Albert Andry III, Dustin King, Vietnamese American fishermen), scholars (Douglas Brinkley), journalists (David Shammer, Anderson Cooper), musicians (Dr. John), environmentalist activists (Lisa Margonelli, Fred Krupp), local attorneys (Scott Bickford,

Joseph Bruno), local associations (William Nungesser, Fred Johnson) and official representatives (Ahn "Joseph" Cao) express an array of opinions that bring considerable insight into the local consequences of a national state of affairs. Lee thus highlights the dynamics of associations of concerned citizens determined to have their views and opinions listened to by local authorities during the reconstruction process after Katrina and the 2010 oil slick. While the 2006 documentary series relied on a diversity of participants, who voiced their individual experiences of Katrina with the purpose to bearing witness to history, its sequel broaches the subject of reconstruction in New Orleans through the activist citizens' commitment to recovering their place in a city undergoing a rejuvenating process. During his Mayoral Inauguration speech delivered on May 3, 2010, Mitch Landrieu presented the oil slick as a twofold danger, enhancing the intertwined environmental and economic crises looming ahead: "The spill threatens the wildlife and the wetlands, the fisheries that feed our nation. In fact, it threatens the economy and the very way of life on the mend" [*IGIW*, Part 2, 53:00]. The documentary offers a medley of voices in response to this statement, expressing individual reactions that extend beyond the economic concerns to convey environmental worries.

The committed stance of this documentary goes beyond race and class issues when tackling the environmental crisis wrought by British Petroleum's explosion on its oil-drilling platform located fifty miles off the coast of Louisiana on April 20, 2010. Although Lee emphasizes the local threat by interviewing all the people affected by the spill, whether on a personal or a professional level, he also broadens the subject by defining the environmental catastrophe in moral and political terms. Interestingly, the film creates a community of opponents across the class and race divide; wherever they live in New Orleans, whatever their social status, the participants question the political and economic roots behind the crisis. They identify a set of issues unveiled by the British Petroleum spill, pointing out the failure of the state and federal governments to deal with the immoral, excessive economic and environmentally unsafe practices of the British multinational oil and gas company, BP. All of the participants are representatives of the civil society, whose dissenting voices seem, however, to bear very little on the situation. President of Plaquemines Parish William Nungesser confesses he was in disarray when he was told no one was allowed to fly over the Gulf Coast to assess the extent of the spill: "When the first crews went out to take pictures, the coast guards turned them around and said: 'BP has the canal closed.' How could BP have the canal closed? How can the FAA [the Federal Aviation Administration] sit in BP's office in Houna and tell our local airport they can't fly?" [*IGIW*, Part 2, 57:20] Lee depicts a group of citizens who articulate critical views of the collusion between private industry and local, state as well as federal governments. Cedric Johnson's book entitled *The Neoliberal Deluge* posits that the American neoliberal economic model has produced the conditions that made Katrina and the oil spill possible. He analyzes the ideological underpinning of policies that have created a favorable climate to corporations' growth and profits, promoting a culture of profit that values "private property over life, liberty, and the common good that had been a guiding principle of American ruling elites long before Hurricane Katrina made landfall."[115] He also compares Barack Obama to George W. Bush, underlining that the British Petroleum spill was referred to as "Obama's Katrina":

> Those who described the BP disaster as "Obama's Katrina" captured a core truth—the two disasters are related not merely by common geography and the population impacted, but, more fundamentally, both disasters share common roots in neoliberal restructuring. White the catastrophic inundation deaths in New Orleans were consequences of state divestment in social services and physical infrastructure, the BP oil disaster stemmed from a deregulatory environment that was crafted by Congressional Democrats and Republicans alike.[116]

If God Is Willing and Da Creek Don't Rise evokes Barack Obama's response to the oil spill through archival footage depicting the moment when the president visited local fishermen and announced his determination to have BP pay for the damage. He publicly declared on May 2, 2010: "BP is responsible for this leak. BP will be paying the bill" [*IGIW*, Part 2, 01:04:45].

The documentary's reference to the oil slick disaster underlines the parallel with Katrina, implicitly comparing the presidents' weak response to the two crises. Lee's compilation montage emphasizes the contrast between the citizens' commitment and their elected representatives' aloofness. Although Obama visited the Gulf Coast instead of flying over the area as George W. Bush did in 2005, the pictures do not grasp a more committed stance. Archival footage shows him walking on the beach, inspecting the traces of oil on the sand with a hand in his pocket, displaying what Douglas Brinkley calls a "Dr Spock-like kind of cool collected control" (in reference to *New York Times* journalist Maureen Dowd's characterization of the president) which seemed out of place to most observers [*IGIW*, Part 2, 01:19:41]. Cedric Johnson contends that Barack Obama's political convictions do not represent an ideological rupture with George W. Bush's, which was revealed by his attitude to the crisis on the Gulf Coast.[117] The author evokes Franklin D. Roosevelt's New Deal policies, including the creation of "a state-funded and state-managed public works project"[118] providing temporary jobs to displaced residents, to suggest what could have been done to counter BP's abuses of power—including the use of Corexyl dispersant chemicals which are banned in Great Britain due to their toxicity and deleterious effects on the environment.

Lee's environmental concern is conveyed by his interviewees, among whom features Lisa Margonelli who retraces the path of oil from the Niger Delta to America's gas stations in her book *Oil on the Brain*,[119] addressing a wake-up call to Americans whose oil consumption growth has increased the country's dependence on regions of the world viewed as politically unstable.[120] As founder of New America Foundation Energy Policy Initiative, she addresses a warning against BP slogan "Beyond Petroleum" which urges the consumer to think of oil as clean energy instead of the pollution in the Niger Delta: "If you go to Nigeria, the oil comes out of a place called the Niger Delta and it's about the size of England. And basically every year since 1969, they've had the equivalent of the Exxon Valdez spill." [*IGIW*, Part 2, 01:03:00] Lee cuts to images of the Niger Delta illustrating Margonelli's statement, which serve to reinforce her arguments.

The various types of footage interwoven in the narrative, shifting from television news archive to original filming material, display the gap between the official records of the situation which tend to downplay the crisis and the subjective responses among witnesses who feel overwhelmed. The film includes a two-minute sequence composed of grainy footage of the Deepwater Horizon leak, representing each day passing by from April 30, 2010, until July 15, 2010, when the hole was eventually capped [*IGIW*, Part 2, 01:37:00]. The repetitive musical tune creates a stifling atmosphere, which contrasts with the reassuring tone of BP's public service announcement presented by Tony Hayward who puts forth the rapid deployment of exceptional resources "to protect the shoreline" [*IGIW*, Part 2, 01:17:10]. The inserted BP promotional sequence uses sleek images of the coast in counterpoint to a soundtrack of waves booming and seagulls shrieking, suggesting BP's technologies will protect the wildlife from the danger of the spill. The BP announcement sequence creates a rupture within the documentary; it shows no sign of the spill apart from the cleanup teams ready to deploy their efforts; nor does it mention the eleven men who died when the rig exploded. When Lee accompanies William Nungesser as he investigates the impact of the spill on the marshes, lamenting about the lack of urgency he witnesses, one can only be struck by the deadly silence around him: no BP team has started the clean-up, no seagull can be heard around [*IGIW*, Part 2, 01:25:00]. As suggested through this example, the filmmaker's ethics of engagement urges him to side with his interviewees in the face of injustice. Lee downplays his voice to allow his filmed subjects to speak up.

Just as he repeated the same sequence three times when George W. Bush congratulated Michael Brown for doing a "heck of a job" with FEMA in *When The Levees Broke*, Lee repeats the same images of Tony Hayward's infamous declaration: "I want my life back" three times [*IGIW*, Part 2, 01:13:00]. The device highlights the cynical and insensitive character of Tony Hayward, who took time off to attend a yacht race as oil gushed into the Gulf.[121] In opposition to his self-complaining and detached comments, Lee honors the memory of the eleven dead victims by introducing their portraits along with personal details, thus outlining the dangers of offshore drilling. Bloomberg news reporters Stanley Reed and Alison Fitzgerald explain that BP's corporate culture "depends on and even celebrates calculated risk-taking,"[122] valuing the profits generated over the safety of complex and dangerous operations.[123] Although BP laid stress on individual safety, standards were repeatedly laid down in process safety—which was revealed by a series of accidents staining the company's image in the last ten years. Douglas Brinkley draws a list of accidents which should have prompted BP to take precautionary measures and the Minerals Management Service (known as the MMS) to enforce stronger regulatory measures: "BP, in 2005, they had a blow-up in Texas City and were sued. 14 men lost their lives. In 2006 in Alaska, up in the North Slope they were taking oil out spilling it over all the tundra which is an incredibly environmentally sensitive area. The blow-up of the Deepwater Horizon was their third major industrial accident in the U.S. on a five-year period. It is pure negligence." [*IGSW*, Part 2, 54:10] The media focus on Tony Hayward's statement divested attention from the political context that made it possible for BP to drill off the shore of Louisiana which, however, Lee's interviewees are keen to examine.

This part of the documentary widens the appeal of Spike Lee's militant piece to a larger audience than his previous films. The environmental concern of the film's participants is no longer tied to race; they evoke a situation that impacts all levels of society. Scientist Ivor Van Heerden compares the Gulf Coast spill to the incident that caused the deaths of coal miners in West Virginia on April 7, 2010, for both illustrate the criminal practices of corporate governance: "It is my understanding from the coal mining incident in West Virginia that safety regulations were ignored. It is my understanding from what is happening in the Gulf of Mexico right now that potential safety issues could have been brought into play into the regulations but were ignored." [*IGIW*, Part 2, 01:03:00] Not only do the interviewees blame the corporation's greed, but they also point to notorious cases of corruption within the Minerals Management Service ("scandals involving gifts and sex" [*IGIW*, Part 2, 01:02:00]), which regulates environment and labor safety in the oil and gas industry. Spike Lee's film echoes the environmental documentary produced by David Guggenheim and Al Gore, *An Inconvenient Truth* (2005), in so far as the environmental crisis is presented in terms of economic and political choices. At a time when George W. Bush was still denying the effect of climate change, Al Gore discussed the existing scientific evidence about global warming in a film that unexpectedly brought him the Nobel Peace Prize in 2007.

Lee's interviewees expose the moral and political contradictions of local and national governance while underlining the president's retreat from public responsibility for the general welfare of American citizenry. Such disasters as Katrina provided a golden opportunity to neoliberal advocates who took advantage of the chaos to privatize former public services. Spike Lee's portrayal of New Orleans reconstruction illustrates this analysis: housing projects have been replaced by mixed-income housing, built by contractors whose employees are low-paid immigrants; the new hospital project which is to replace Charity Hospital will introduce more private medical practice; FEMA trailers were mass-produced and built by subcontractors with substandard materials, including formaldehyde which caused many residents to fall ill [*IGIW*, Part 1, 01:11:00]; state money was made available for the opening of casinos, not for libraries [*IGIW*, Part 1, 01:36:00]. The opening of charter schools provides another interesting example of neoliberalism which, Cedric Johnson further argues, "is a form of world-making predicated on the abatement of labor rights, social provision, public amenities, environment regulations, and other artifacts of social democracy deemed impediments to capital accumulation."[124]

By endorsing the anti-corporation stance of his participants, Lee joins a fight that allows him to reach out to a larger crowd of viewers than the racial angle advocated in his former committed filmmaking. Serge Halimi referred to the variety of characters Robert Greenwald interviewed for the making of *Wal-Mart: The High Cost of Low Price* (2005) as "American patriots,"[125] considering that the fight against Wal-Mart was able to gather both Republicans and Democrats: small businessmen and Wal-Mart employees, be they male or female, black or white, may speak from various standpoints, all of them suffer from the discriminatory policies and the marketing strategies that define the corporation's ethics. The film investigates the dramatic consequences of Wal-Mart's industrial, environmental, and labor practices on the lives of Americans who either compete with the corporation or work for it. The corporation's excessive practices undermine the ethos of self-enterprise in America's free trade economy, which allows Robert Greenwald to widen his audience beyond the progressive base. The approach to reconstruction in New Orleans has been underpinned by a commitment to neoliberal, free market principles which have neither alleviated racial tension nor promoted social equality, thus leaving lingering issues of crime and corruption unsettled.

Lee's documentaries on New Orleans articulate a highly subjective version of the truth, which can be illustrated by a comparison with Luisa Dantas's five-year-long investigation of reconstruction in New Orleans in *Land of Opportunity* (2010–2011).[126] Serving as creative mentor for her project and using some of her footage in his own documentary series, Lee tries to put a positive spin on the African-American experience of reconstruction by underlining the actions of activists between 2005 and 2010, whereas Dantas gives voice to all the victims of neoliberal policies, including low-paid Latino workers and lower-class African Americans, proposing an even darker view of the new New Orleans. *Land of Opportunity* encompasses a web platform that was developed to further the viewing experience of the documentary, inviting browsers to probe other Internet sources that broaden their perspectives on the issues addressed by the filmed participants.[127] The title of the whole project ironically suggests that New Orleans turned into a *Land of Opportunity* after Hurricane Katrina washed over the city, creating a sort of *tabula rasa* on which new projects could be experimented unhindered by the past. The documentary, however, points to the legacy of a geography of class as the camera captures the power relations that are ingrained in the landscape of a city divided along racial lines. Making herself invisible behind the camera, Luisa Dantas offers her footage as raw documents that provide evidence of an ongoing process of gentrification—which Lee also condemned in a recent public address in Brooklyn.[128]

Conclusion

From made-for-television documentaries to big-budget blockbusters, the sheer variety of Spike Lee's films reflects his struggle to combine art and commerce, prompting us to explore the tension between profit and creativity which characterizes his career. Unlike Oscar Micheaux with whom he is sometimes compared,[1] Lee will not content himself with a shoestring budget that would confine his filmmaking to the margins of the film industry. He is an impassioned entrepreneur, who diversified his production into several businesses (40 Acres and a Mule, Spike DDB), dealing with independent (Island Pictures), mini-major (New Line, HBO, Searchlight), and major studios (Universal, Warner Brothers, Sony).[2] Spike Lee embodies the businessman as artist who makes creativity happen,[3] overriding the limits between art and commerce when turning his characters into consumers promoting brands and his advertising videos into artistic short films. His models are African-American cultural icons, whose careers illustrate a reversal of power between blacks and whites. Spike Lee actively promoted his latest documentary *Bad 25*, giving enthusiastic interviews about Michael Jackson, whose musical and artistic creativity he endeavored to spotlight after scandals deflected attention away from his achievement. While the aggressive marketing strategies developed behind such blockbusters as *Malcolm X* (1992) and *Inside Man* (2006) may partially account for their box-office success, the persona of Spike Lee as a "sellebrity" allows the studios to capitalize on his auteurist reputation.[4] Lee sells his name like a brand that signifies aesthetic characteristics and commercial ethics, which is best defined by his pragmatic approach to the business of making films. His longevity is related to his ability to navigate the constraints of production,[5] which he more often than not manages to circumvent in order to leave his creative imprint on the films that bear his signature. Identified as products of his own company 40 Acres and a Mule, his nonfiction "joints" also exhibit his trademark shots—including the dolly camera movements that are associated with his fiction filmmaking.

Lee assumes the position of a go-between (echoing the role of Mookie played by Lee himself in *Do the Right Thing*), wilfully accepting to direct advertising campaigns for the corporations that wish to tap into the African-American community. His latest promotional videos depict a world in which African Americans buy luxury cars like the trendy Chevrolet and Jaguar models, offering the audience an idealized image of a multicultural society in which African Americans have climbed up the social ladder. While the firms he works for use his name to target a niche market, Lee exploits these advertising opportunities to portray inspiring models of success, ironically selling the American dream as a fantasy world. As a filmmaker whose art depends on the money he is able to garner, Lee defends his market share by advancing the African Americans' consumers' rights. Although documentaries usually require a lesser budget than fiction films, involving neither professional actors nor constructed setting, they do not represent an especially distinct approach to the business of filmmaking for the director. Lee's thematic and economic concerns straddle his fiction and nonfiction projects, combining his fascination with such subjects as basketball with the need to make profitable films. Thus such films as *Kobe Doin' Work* (2009), produced by and for the Entertainment and Sports Programming Network (ESPN), demonstrate that documentaries can serve moneymaking goals. However, Lee's documentaries are based on investigations that more often than not challenge his commercial ethics, pointing to the distance between the filmmaker's middle class values and the real-life problems his interlocutors testify about. *When The Levees Broke: A Requiem in Four Acts* exposed race and class inequalities by revealing the plight of the African-American poor who could not flee New Orleans before Hurricane Katrina struck whereas *If God Is Willing and Da Creek Don't Rise* captured the enduring geographical traces of segregation on the landscape, pinpointing the race and class dynamics of policymaking.

Lee's political commitment prompts him to spotlight African Americans' active roles in the historical narrative of the nation: whether he retraces the ideological and psychological path of the Black Panthers' leader Huey P. Newton or focuses on a tragic history of racist violence and oppression through *Four Little Girls*, Lee highlights positive role models among African Americans. Rather than depict black history as a tale of victimization, his nonfiction films emphasize the resilience of individuals whose lives intertwine with the civil rights fight against racial prejudice and socio-economic discrimination. *If God Is Willing and Da Creek Don't Rise* appears as a turning point in Lee's documentary filmography, considering that it clearly endorses leftist politics when analyzing the devastating impact of the 2010 oil slick. The documentary addresses race and class issues from a larger perspective than his previous works: Lee develops what could be dubbed a "citizens' documentary" articulating the concerns of those who were affected by the neoliberal choices underpinning reconstruction in New Orleans—most of them being African Americans. The film is divided into two parts which gather a group of citizen activists among the interviewees who, while addressing such issues as education, housing, labor and crime on a local level, testify to broader national and international economic dynamics. Interestingly, Spike Lee takes advantage of his own position within the media spectrum to produce an alternative historical, social, and racial discourse.

Lee has joined other "engaged celebrities" who use their fame to assume a public critical voice in the context of protest, defining their "civic role as the result of a direct relation with a public: the symbolic coup at work is based on the equivalence state between 'having audiences' and 'having constituencies,' justifying the self-assignation of an ability/legitimacy to speak for others, especially for voiceless people."[6] French sociologist Violaine Roussel analyzed the commitment of artists at the beginning of the Iraq War (2003) and posited that the professionals' position of stabilized success and great renown placed them "out of reach" as regards the potential harmful professional outcomes of their political involvement.[7] These artists demanded a political voice and asserted their civic roles both through their art and outside of their professional activities. Lee's commitment also extends beyond the screen: he attended protests over the death of black youth Ammadou Diallo, who was shot dead by police officers outside his home in the Bronx; he regularly took part in anti-war rallies in 2003 and never failed to criticize George W. Bush's policies—including in his Hollywood-produced *Inside Man* which incorporates a scene evoking the excesses of the Patriot Act. Krin Gabbard suggests that Lee has willingly assumed the role of spokesperson for African Americans after directing political advertisements for Jesse Jackson in 1988:

> Lee has accepted this advocate's role by appearing frequently on news and talk shows and consenting to regular interviews. He may still be the only black filmmaker to make this transition: it is difficult to imagine Mario van Peebles, Charles Burnett, or the artist formerly known as Prince (the auteur of two films in his own right) discussing race relations with Ted Koppel on *Nightline*.[8]

Lee's activist voice is vicariously embodied on screen by such public figures as Douglas Brinkley, who personifies the "engaged intellectual," and well-known personalities who have become icons of social and civic performances in contemporary Hollywood. Brad Pitt has financially contributed to rebuilding the Lower Ninth Ward by investing time and money in the Make It Right Foundation whereas Sean Penn took physical risks by visiting New Orleans in the days that followed Katrina when people were still waiting to be evacuated. *If God Is Willing and Da Creek Don't Rise* incorporates footage of Sean Penn running aid operations in Haiti, highlighting the practical actions that define his activist commitment.[9]

While other filmmakers have been able to capitalize on their political commitments, even when they gave rise to polemics and criticism,[10] Lee's engagement with issues of race has often been questioned in the light of commercial productions that make him an icon of late capitalism.[11] *Kobe Doin' Work* represents a flagrant example of corruption of Lee's activist stance given that the documentary unquestioningly contributes to the mythification of the basketball star and to the commodification of sports. Although one may posit that Kobe Bryant's voice-over conveys his alienation from the world around basketball, including his audience, thus stimulating the schizophrenic atmosphere of playing as a professional for the NBA, the film celebrates his stereotypical masculinity as an African-American athlete whose fetishistic commodification is absolute. Contrary to such film directors as Haile Gerima and Charles Burnett, Lee has chosen to integrate the system which (re)produces the racial dynamics he endeavors to overturn. It is however a controversial stance: Lee gained more visibility thanks to a compromised political stance, which forces him to navigate between business deals and personal engagements. Cultural critic George Nelson contends that his political commitment is not tarnished by his commercial career:

> There is a nationalist underpinning to his financial and creative activities, yet Spike has no problem doing business with corporate America. His entrepreneurial integration has led him into ongoing business relationships with Nike, Universal, Barneys, the Gap, Levi Strauss, and Simon & Shuster. *She's* (sic) was very much a guerrilla enterprise that was distributed by Island, then a maverick studio. Ever since, Spike has worked with major studios and national advertisers. Is there a contradiction in this? In the face of modern corporate infotainment monoliths, the most realpolitik counterstrategy is to be in business with as

many as possible. Diversifying protects you against co-optation by any single corporate entity and industry.[12]

The scholar emphasizes Lee's practical approach to filmmaking: had he not developed his own production company and increased his financial resources, his commitment would have been confined to the margins of minority filmmaking. Because his name connotes a share of the film market, Lee has been able to overcome the limits imposed on minority directors in Hollywood. Drawing on a series of interviews conducted with filmmakers working in the film industry, Jack Rothman points out the specific issues African-American directors have to contend with: "Some directors lamented that once classified a minority filmmaker, a director is marginalized, since studios assume that minority-themed films will only appeal to minority audience. The studios make relatively few of these ethnic-themed films, believing that mainstream audiences will stay away—which results in tightly confined opportunities for these directors."[13] Minority filmmakers' careers are constrained by the ethnic perspective they are expected to endorse. In other words, their creativity is restrained by their being labelled as minority filmmakers.

The path Lee has chosen is not open to all minority filmmakers:[14] he has managed to broaden his audience by straddling entertainment and commitment while engaging with the commercial and the not-for-profit. In his 1993 study entitled *Framing Blackness, The African American Image in Film*, Ed Guerrero hailed Lee's engagement to representing the authentic experience of African Americans, which he qualified as auteurism, and simultaneously feared a "drift toward a contained, mainstream sensibility."[15] Lee's documentaries demonstrate the opposite: he has been able to bank on the financial success of his films when incorporating the mainstream of commercial cinema to advance issues of race. Not only do his nonfiction films contribute to the struggle for representation that undergirds African-American filmmaking, but his latest filmic investigation into the reconstruction of New Orleans also suggests that Lee's activism has not weakened. Lee interrogates the media-framed images of Katrina by juxtaposing television extracts with interview snippets, creating a dialectical search for truth through the interplay of oral and visual narratives.

The filmmaker has adopted an increasingly pragmatic stance by broadening the civil rights fight beyond the color line, allowing a community of citizens to find a voice in his films. However, he will not relinquish lucrative contracts as suggested by *Kobe Doin' Work*, accepting the compromise between money and engagement as the only path to garner sufficient influence in Hollywood to remain a politically committed filmmaker.

As he agreed to follow the genealogical guidelines adopted in the television program "Who Do You Think You Are" on NBC (April 30, 2010), Lee offered to investigate into his mother's slavery roots. After the genealogical journey made him travel from the Georgia State Archives to Twiggs County, where he was able to step on the land that once belonged to his great-great-grandfather, he discovered that his grandmother's mother Lucinda was born into slavery to Matilda Griswold. Identified as a mulatto in the archival records, Matilda has Lee mull over his possible family connection with the white slave-owner (Samuel Griswold) who might have fathered her. The mulatto woman was registered as working for the slaveholder's daughter (Eliza Grier), whose descendent (Guinevere Grier) may therefore be related to him as a third cousin. The genealogical research leads to the encounter between Spike Lee and Guinevere Grier, which provides an emotional climax in the program: as the two sit on a couch discussing ancestors they may have in common, they raise awareness to the complexities of American history and to the enduring power of repressed family stories.

The Spike Lee brand defines both the limits and the scope of the filmmaker's work, signifying Lee's commitment to exploring racial issues while making financially profitable films. "Who Do You Think You Are" reveals striking similarities between Spike Lee's commercial commitment and his great-great-grandfather's, whose name (Mars Jackson) ironically refers to the character *She's Gotta Have it* and Nike commercials made famous (Mars Blackmon). Mars Jackson exploited more than eighty acres of land as a farmer who became a landowner in the wake of the 40 Acres and a Mule order, thus reflecting Lee's belief in economic empowerment. The television program sheds light on a hidden story in Lee's own past, which may unconsciously bear on his view of the world as expressed in his film endeavors.

Notes

Foreword

1. Nelson George, "The Foreword to He's Gotta Have It" in Spike Lee, *Spike Lee's Gotta Have It: Inside Guerrilla Filmmaking* (New York: Simon & Schuster, Inc., 1987), 15.

Introduction

1. R. Colin Tait, "Politics, Class and Allegory in Spike Lee's *Inside Man*" in ed. Mark A. Reid, *Spike Lee's Do the Right Thing* (New York: Cambridge University Press, 1997), 41–60.
2. Janet K. Cutler and Phyllis R. Klotman, "Introduction," eds. Phyllis R. Klotman and Janet K. Cutler, *Struggles for Representation* (Bloomington, IN: Indiana University Press, 1999), xvii.
3. Clyde Taylor, "Paths of Enlightenment: Heroes, Rebels and Thinkers," Ibid., 142.
4. PBS co-produced the film, along with the African American Center, and has developed several resource pages on its website: <http://www.pbs.org/hueypnewton/huey.html> (accessed on February 8, 2014).
5. Bill Nichols, *Introduction to Documentary* (Bloomington, IN: Indiana University Press, 2001, 2010), xiii.
6. Matt Singer, review of *Bad 25*. See <http://blogs.indiewire.com/criticwire/did-spike-lee-make-two-movies-this-year-about-michael-jackson#comments> (accessed on February 11, 2014).
7. David Sterritt, *Spike Lee's America* (Cambridge, UK/Malden USA: Polity Press, 2013), 171.
8. Bill Nichols, *Introduction to Documentary*, 1.
9. Gary Crowdus and Dan Georgakas, "Thinking about the Power of Images: An Interview with Spike Lee," *Cineaste* 26, 2 (2001), 9.

10. The duties of the griot "included those of historian, reporter, adviser and story-teller." Sheila Curran Bernard, *Documentary Storytelling, Making Stronger and More Dramatic Nonfiction Films* (Burlington, MA: Elsevier Inc., 2007), 13.

11. Jean-Louis Comolli, *Voir et pouvoir, L'innocence perdue: cinéma, télévision, fiction, documentaire* (Paris: Editions Verdier, 2004), 153.

12. Marc Ferro, *Cinema and History*, translated by Naomi Greene (Detroit: Wayne State University Press, 1988), 29.

13. Ibid.

14. Mark P. Orbe and A. Elizabeth Lyons, "Spike Lee as Entrepreneur: Leveraging 40 Acres and a Mule" in eds. Janice D. Hamlet and Robin R. Means Coleman, *Fight the Power, The Spike Lee Reader* (New York: Peter Lang, 2009), 378.

15. "While Lee's project is thus under the sign of history, it seeks a certain relief from the burden of history and the weight of memory via his logo, 'a Spike Lee Joint,' which signals the sightlessness and memoryless floating realm of commodity and sign production of late 20th century America." Laleen Jayamanne, *Toward Cinema and its Double: Cross-Cultural Mimesis* (Bloomington, IN: Indiana University Press, 2001), 241.

Chapter 1

1. Bill Nichols, *Introduction to Documentary*, 6.

2. Ibid., 42.

3. Ibid., 65.

4. Ibid., 60. Bill Nichols borrows the terms "social actors" from sociologist Ervin Goffman's *The Presentation of Self in Everyday Life* (1959) to point out the self-conscious pose of the documentary participants. I will use the same term in this text, considering like Nichols that: "People are treated as social actors rather than professional actors. [. . .] Their value resides not in the ways in which they disguise or transform their everyday behaviour and personality but in ways in which their everyday behaviour and personality serve the needs of the filmmaker." Ibid., 8.

5. "The film is dedicated to the families of victims of police brutality: Eleanor Bumpurs, an old black woman who was evicted from her apartment; Michael Steward, strangled like Radio Raheem by a choke hold; Arthur Miller, a black entrepreneur who was the victim of mistaken identities, unjustly arrested and beaten up, and in 1978, died as a result of the beating." Catherine Pouzoulet, "The Cinema of Spike Lee: Images of a Mosaic City" in ed. Mark A. Reid, *Spike Lee's Do the Right Thing* (New York: Cambridge University Press, 1997), 36.

6. Catherine Pouzoulet, "The Cinema of Spike Lee: Images of a Mosaic City" in Ibid., 36.

7. Catherine Pouzoulet comments on the highly stylized representation of Bed-Stuy which she depicts as "a warped vision of the actual social scene in the 1990s." Ibid., 34.

8. Keith M. Harris, "*Clockers* (Spike Lee, 1995): Adaptation in Black" in ed. Paula Massood, *The Spike Lee Reader* (Philadelphia, PA: Temple University Press, 2007).133.

9. Bill Nichols, *Introduction to Documentary*, 162.

10. Errol Morris explains that his documentaries involve the type of research he could had done as a private-eye investigator in his youth: "Finding truth involves some kind of activity. As I like to point out, truth isn't handed to you on a platter. It's not something that you get at a cafeteria, where they just put it on your plate. It's a search, a quest, an investigation, a continual process of looking at and looking for evidence, trying to figure out what the evidence means." Errol Morris, Interview with *The Believer*, April 2004. <http://www.errolmorris.com/content/interview/believer0404.html> (accessed on March 18, 2014).

11. "New modes signal less a better way to represent the historical world than a new way to organize a film, a new perspective on our relation to reality, and a new set of issues and desires to preoccupy an audience." Bill Nichols, *Introduction to Documentary*, 162.

12. In 1968, Fred Hampton founded the Chicago chapter of the Black Panther Party. He developed community service programs such as a free breakfast for children program and free medical services clinic. On December 4, 1969, while everyone was asleep at party headquarters, he was murdered in a police raid that also killed Mark Clark. The sequence includes footage of his coffin.

13. Jeff Ferrel, *Crimes of Style: Urban Graffiti and the Politics of Criminality* (New York: Garland Publishing, 1993), 183.

14. Michael Renov, "Introduction: The Truth About NonFiction" in ed. Michael Renov, *Theorizing Documentary* (New York & London: Routledge, 1993), 2.

15. Lee borrows the musical score of *Inside Man* for the soundtrack of *When the Levees Broke: A Requiem in Four Acts*, ironically commenting on his twofold career: the two films were made at the same time (2006), yet they represent two parallel tracks. Paula J. Massood opposes the commercial entertainment venture to the made-for-television documentary about Katrina's destruction and reconstruction of New Orleans, thereby trying to account for the controversies surrounding the filmmaker: "Lee's fiction films upset the compact between Hollywood and spectators because they ask uncomfortable questions of their audience (both black and white) rather than entertain them; in this sense, they are difficult. His non-fiction films, by contrast, are expected to be historical and informative, and therefore visibility is a virtue rather than a limitation." Paula J. Massood, "Introduction" *in* ed. Paula J. Massood, *The Spike Lee Reader,* xxv–xxvi.

16. "Joseph Michael Gratale on Jane Chapman's *Issues in Contemporary Documentary*," *European journal of American studies*, Reviews 2010–11. <http://ejas.revues.org/7817> (accessed on February 1, 2014).

17. "This form of documentary is founded on participants' stories, and it is the fact that viewers are given access to the real world through the narratives of social actor that makes the authorial voice more the product of a partnership with the filmmaker, although control of the message still ultimately resides with

the latter in the selection and arrangement of the actors, what they say, and how long they are given to say it, even if participants are provided with the space to tell their stories at their own pace." Jane Chapman, *Issues in Contemporary Documentary* (Cambridge and Malden, UK: Polity Press, 2009), 104.

18. Bill Nichols, *Introduction to Documentary*, 203.

19. Phyllis Montana-Leblanc and Spike Lee, *Not Just the Levees Broke: My Story During and After Hurricane Katrina* (New York: Atria Books, 2009).

20. J. Steven Picou and Brent K. Marshall, "Introduction: Katrina as Paradigm Shift: Reflections on Disaster Research in the 21st Century" in David L. Brunsma, David Overfelt, J. Steven Picou, *The Sociology of Katrina: Perspectives on a Modern Catastrophe*, 16.

21. Douglas Kellner presents Michael Moore as: "A unique character in popular culture, himself, and a unique genre of filmmaking, the personal witnessing, questing and agit-prop interventionist film that explores issues, takes strong critical point of view, and targets villains and evils in U.S. society." Douglas Kellner, "Michael Moore and the Aesthetic and Politics of Contemporary Documentary Film" in ed. Matthew H. Bernstein, *Michael Moore: Filmmaker, Newsmaker, Cultural Icon* (Ann Arbor, MI: University of Michigan Press, 2010), 100.

22. Sheila Curran Bernard, *Documentary Storytelling, Making Stronger and More Dramatic Nonfiction Films*, 130.

23. Bill Nichols, *Introduction to Documentary*, 30.

24. Sociology assistant Professor Gary Perry questions H.U.D's spending and politics: "The Department of Housing and Urban Development has spent around $500.000 to board up and demolish public housing units, preventing working-class residents—largely Black women and children from reclaiming their homes." Garry Perry, "New Orleans Survivors: a People Without a Home" in *Freedom Socialist*, August 2007. <http://www.socialism.com/drupal-6.8/?q=node/513> (accessed on February 3, 2014).

25. The city appears to be segregated by income more than by race since Lee interviews many Whites among the victims. However the archive footage of the Superdome and the Convention Center show a majority of blacks.

26. Jasmine Nichole Cobb and John L. Jackson, "They Hate Me, Spike Lee, Documentary Filmmaking and Hollywood's 'Savage Slot,'" in eds. Janice D. Hamlet and Robin R. Means Coleman, *Fight the Power, The Spike Lee Reader*, (New York: Peter Lang, 2009), 264.

27. Janet Walker, "Rights and return: perils and fantasies of situated testimony after Katrina" in eds. Bhaskar Sarkar and Janet Walker, *Documentary Testimonies, Global Archives of Suffering* (New York/Oxon: Routledge, 2010), 84–86.

28. Jane Chapman, *Issues in Contemporary Documentary*, 106.

29. Ellen C. Scott, "Sounding Black, Cultural Identification, Sound, and the Films of Spike Lee" in eds. Janice D. Hamlet and Robin R. Means Coleman, *Fight the Power, The Spike Lee Reader*, 227.

30. Bill Nichols, *Introduction to Documentary*, 158–159.

31. Quoted in Peter Rubie, *The Elements of Narrative Nonfiction, How to Write and Sell the Novel of True Events* (Fresno, California: Quill Driver Books, 2003, 2009), 2–3.

32. Peter Marks, "A Huey P. Newton Story" in the *New York Times*, Theater Reviews, February 13, 1997.

33. Bill Nichols, *Introduction to Documentary*, 199.

34. The opening sequence epitomizes the film's use of archive material. Roger Guenveur Smith comments on the collaborative effort behind the editing choice: researcher Leanne Clifton provided hours of documentary material, from which we might choose imagery to strategically accompany the performance. Spike respected the integrity of the play and didn't want the archive shots to be distracting, but including a very carefully selected number of them would layer the project with a cinematic and historical nuance. Disembodied voices from the original sound design became reunited with their talking heads, Richard Pryor, William F. Buckley, and Huey's mother among them. Obvious choices such as *Black Orpheus*, Huey's favorite film, were included, as well as odd cameos from Marlon Brando, speaking at Little Bobby Hutton's funeral, and Orson Welles, making himself up to play Macbeth, whom he describes as "a gangster with a conscience." <http://www.ahueypnewtonstory.com/revolution/revolution_journey.html> (accessed on February 12, 2014).

35. Lee qualifies basketball as an "art form" when recalling the style of such players as Alcindor and Tiny who made it "an entertainment spectacle, whose athletic artistry and creativity lifted pro hoop from the distant outpost of its origins and ethnic urban subculture base into the world-wide consciousness today." Spike Lee and Ralph Wiley, *The Best Seat in the House: A Basketball Memoir* (New York: Random House Inc., 1998), 23.

36. Douglas Kellner, *Media Spectacle* (London and New York: Routledge, 2003), 68.

37. Douglas Kellner, "The Sports Spectacle, Michael Jordan, and Nike" in eds. Patrick B. Miller and David K. Wiggins, *Sport and the Color Line, Black Athletes and Race Relations in Twentieth-Century America* (New York & London: Routledge, 2004), 307.

38. Ben Carrington, *Race, Sports and Politics: the Sporting Black Diaspora* (London: Sage Publications Inc., 2010), 86.

39. Cheryl L. Cole, "America Jordan: P.L.A.Y., Consensus, and Punishment," *Sociology of Sport Journal*, 13, 4 (1996), 366–397.

40. "Whereas drama-documentary attempts to align itself with documentary in order to validate its claims to truth, mock-documentary utilizes the aesthetics of documentary to undermine such claims to truth. [. . .] In general terms, the mock-documentary filmmaker seeks to construct a particular relationship with factual discourse which often involves a reflexive stance with regard to the documentary genre." Jane Roscoe and Craig Hight, *Faking it, Mock Documentary and the Subversion of Factuality*, (Manchester: Manchester University Press, 2011), 46–47.

41. "A conspiracy theory creates and ties together a series of events in relations of cause and effect. Conspiracy is predicated on uncovering a specific form of order and structure." Martin Parker, "Human science as conspiracy theory" in eds. Jane Paris and Martin Parker, *The Age of Anxiety: Conspiracy Theory and the Human Sciences* (Oxford: Blackwell Publishers, 2001), 193.

42. *When the Levees Broke* explores the "performative mode" of the documentary, in which "a key focus becomes the prioritization of the subjective aspects of documentary accounts of reality. These texts are heavily stylized and quite consciously blur the boundaries between fact and fiction." Jane Roscoe and Craig Hight, *Faking it, Mock Documentary and the Subversion of Factuality*, 46–47.

43. Sheila Curran Bernard, *Documentary Storytelling, Making Stronger and More Dramatic Nonfiction Films*, 3.

44. Bill Nichols, *Introduction to Documentary*, 30.

Chapter 2

1. Marc Ferro, *Cinema and History*, 29.

2. Amiri Baraka, "Malcolm as Ideology" in ed. Joe Wood, *Malcolm X: In Our Own Image* (New York: St. Martin's, 1992), 21.

3. Pierre Nora, "Between Memory and History: Les Lieux de Mémoire" in eds. Geneviève Fabre and Robert O' Meally, *History and Memory in African-American Culture* (New York: Oxford University Press, 1994), 290.

4. "Mass culture makes particular memories more widely available, so that people who have no 'natural' claim to them might nevertheless incorporate them into their own archive of experience." Alison Landsberg, *Prosthetic Memory, The Transformation of American Remembrance in the Age of Mass Culture* (New York: Columbia University Press, 2004), 9.

5. Ibid., 2–3.

6. Paul Ricœur, *Temps et récit, Tome 1: L'intrigue et le récit historique* (Paris: Le Seuil, 1983).

7. "The strategies of forgetting are directly grafted upon this work of configuration: one can always recount, by eliminating, by shifting the emphasis, by recasting the protagonists of the action in a different light along with the outlines of the action. [. . .] The resource of narrative then becomes the trap, when higher powers take over the emplotment and impose a canonical narrative by means of intimidation or seduction, fear or flattery. A devious form of forgetting is at work here, resulting from stripping the social actors of their original power to recount their actions themselves." Paul Ricœur, *Memory, History, Forgetting*, translated by Kathleen Blamey and David Pellauer (Chicago: University of Chicago Press, 2004, 2006), 448.

8. Ibid., 648.

9. Maurice Halbwachs, *On Collective Memory* (1941), edited, translated by Lewis A. Coser (Chicago: University of Chicago, 1992), 60.

10. Ibid., 64.

11. James L. Baggett, "Sixteenth Street Baptist Church" in eds. Leslie M. Alexander and Walter C. Rucker, *Encyclopedia of African American History, Volume 1* (Santa Barbara, CA: ABC-CLIO, LLC, 2010), 1027–1029.

12. Renee C. Romano notices that "the Justice Department [. . .] moved to restart their investigation of the bombing shortly after the release of Spike Lee's documentary. The film helped put the bombing case back on the national agenda and it created pressure to bring the bombers to justice." Renee C. Romano, "Narratives of Redemption, The Birmingham Church Bombing Trials and the Construction of Civil Rights Memory" in eds. Renee C. Romano and Leigh Raiford, *The Civil Rights Movement in American Memory*, (Athens, GA: The University of Georgia Press, 2006), 109.

13. Walter Benjamin, "The Work of Art in the Age of Mechanical Reproduction," in *Illuminations*, trans. Harry Zohn (New York: Schocken Books, 1968), 236.

14. Susan Sontag, *On Photography* (London: Penguin Books, 1979), 15.

15. Ibid., 16.

16. Siegfried Kracauer, *The Mass Ornament*, translated by Thomas Y. Levin (Cambridge, MA: Harvard University Press, 1995), 51. First edition: Suhrkamp Verlag, 1963.

17. Roland Barthes, *Camera Lucida*, translated by Richard Howard (New York: Hill and Wang, 1981), 64.

18. Ibid., 109.

19. Roland Barthes, *Image, Music, Text* (New York: Hill and Wang, 1977), 44.

20. Barthes, *Camera Lucida*, 71.

21. Valerie Smith, "Remembering Birmingham Sunday, Spike Lee's *4 Little Girls*" in eds. Deborah E. Barker and Kathryn McKee, *American Cinema and the Southern Imaginary*, 187.

22. Susan Sontag, *On Photography*, (Athens, GA: The University of Georgia Press, 2011), 15.

23. Stanley Cavell, *The World Viewed, Reflections of the Ontology of Film* (Cambridge, MA; London, England: Harvard University Press, 1971, 1974, 1979), 200.

24. Martin A. Berger, *Seeing Through Race: A Reinterpretation of Civil Rights Photography* (Berkeley and Los Angeles: University of Berkeley Press, 2011), 141. The author adds: "The white media showed greater interest and sympathy for black victims who were female (and presumably less politically active and physically threatening) but that coverage managed to generate white emotion by downplaying the motivations for the crime." Ibid.

25. Valerie Smith, "Remembering Birmingham Sunday, Spike Lee's *4 Little Girls*" in eds. Deborah E. Barker and Kathryn McKee, *American Cinema and the Southern Imaginary* (Athens, GA: The University of Georgia Press, 2011), 189–190.

26. Ibid., 191.

27. Michael Frisch, *A Shared Authority: Essays on the Craft and Meaning of Oral and Public History* (Albany, NY: State University of New York Press, 1990), 293.

28. "I recalled having to explain to my Professors and to my friends every single day that all of Birmingham hadn't erupted in violence and in fact it was awfully hard to explain how I didn't really think that fire hoses wasn't the worst thing that could have happened compared to firearms, certainly compared to killing and beating."

29. "For hundreds of years white men in America positioned themselves as the only "true" men in this country. They attempted to emasculate (both literally and metaphorically) men of color by stripping them of the economic wherewithal and social standing to support and protect their families." Steve Estes, *I am a Man! Race, Manhood, and the Civil Rights Movement* (Chapel Hill and London: The University of North Carolina Press, 2005), 186.

30. Marc Bloch, translated by Peter Putnam, *The Historian's Craft* (Manchester: Manchester University Press, 1992; first edition: Alfred A. Knopf, 1954), 160. Marc Bloch gives the following example to illustrate his point: "The virus of the Black Death was the prime cause of the depopulation of Europe. But the epidemic spread so rapidly only by virtue of certain social—and, therefore, in their underlying nature, mental—conditions, and its moral effects are to be explained only by the peculiar propensities of collective sensibility." Ibid., 160.

31. Owen J. Dwyer gives the example of Kelly Ingram Park, which was converted from a once-segregated park into a 'Place of Revolution and Reconciliation' in 1992. Owen J. Dwyer, "Interpreting the Civil Rights Movement: Contradiction, confirmation, and the Cultural Landscape" in eds. Renee C. Romano and Leigh Raiford, *The Civil Rights Movement in American Memory*, 7.

32. James Edward Young, *Writing and Rewriting the Holocaust: Narrative and the Consequences of Interpretation*, 161.

33. Susannah Radstone, *Memory: Histories, Theories, Debates* (New York: Fordham University Press, 2010), 236.

34. George Lipsitz, *Time Passages: Collective Memory and American Popular Culture* (Minneapolis: University of Minnesota Press, 1990), 213.

35. Janet Walker, "Rights and return: perils and fantasies of situated testimony after Katrina," in eds. Bhaskar Sarkar and Janet Walker, *Documentary Testimonies, Global Archives of Suffering* (New York/Oxon: Routledge, 2010), 95.

36. "A powerful discriminatory tendency in planning is for environmentally vulnerable low-income neighborhoods to be deemed dispensable, whereas equally vulnerable high-income neighborhoods are deemed indispensable because they are more valuable." Reilly Morse, "Environmental Justice Through the Eye of Hurricane Katrina" (Washington DC, Joint Center for Political and Economic Studies, Inc., 2008). The document can be accessed online at <http://www.jointcenter.org/hpi/sites/all/files/EnvironmentalJustice.pdf> (accessed on February 2, 2014).

37. R. W. Kates, C. E. Colten, S. Laska, and S. P. Leatherman, "Reconstruction of New Orleans after Hurricane Katrina: A Research Perspective" in

PNAS October 3, 2006, vol. 103 no. 40, 14653–14654. <http://www.pnas.org/content/103/40/14653.full.pdf+html> (accessed on January 31, 2014).

38. John M. Barry comments: "I think there are too many similarities between the 1927 flood and Katrina. For one thing, the levee policy of the federal government—the flood protection policy of the federal government—was directly responsible. I mean it was deeply flawed in 1927 and had been widely criticized. The city of New Orleans had exercised its political muscle, and dynamited the levee outside the city, flooded out its neighbors. And this wasn't about race: it was about money."

39. John M. Barry, *Rising Tide, The Great Mississippi Flood of 1927 and How it Changed America* (New York: Simon and Schuster Paperback, 1998), 238–258.

40. The expository documentary offers "an economy of analysis, allowing points to be made succinctly and emphatically, partly by eliminating reference to the process by which knowledge is produced, organized, and regulated so that it, too, is subject to the historical and ideological processes of which the film speaks." Bill Nichols, *Representing Reality: Issues and Concepts in Documentary* (Bloomington, IN: Indiana University Press, 1994), 35.

41. Lee uses the documentary to allow his interviewees to regain some kind of agency as they voice their theories of conspiracy: "The conspiracy narrative foregrounds the cognitive act of interpretation as performed by both protagonist and audience and suggests that the protagonist is able to re-establish his agency—which, like that of everyone else, has been lost to the conspiracy—through cognition." Mark Fenster, *Conspiracy Theories, Secrecy and Power in American Culture,* Minneapolis, University of Minnesota Press, 2008 (First edition: 1999), 126.

42. The destruction of the levees was negotiated and reparation was planned as part of the resolution presented by the governor on April 25, 1927: "The governor signed first, followed by the mayor and the president of the Orleans Levee Board; then Butler, president of the Canal Bank; Hecht, president of the Hibernia Bank; then the presidents of the other banks. Fifty-seven men signed their names to the pledge. Only six—the governor, the mayor, two councilmen, and two levee board members—were public officials." John M. Barry, *Rising Tide, The Great Mississippi Flood of 1927 and How it Changed America*, 247–248.

43. Noam Chomsky defines conspiracy as the process of decision-making among people who hold power: "There are doubtless cases in which people get together; in fact, every example of planning decisions is a case where people got together and used their power, or the power that they could draw from to try to achieve a result. If you like that's a conspiracy. With that definition, everything that happens is a conspiracy." This statement comes from an interview with Michael Albert in *Z Magazine*, quoted by Alasdair Spark, "Conjuring order: the new world order and conspiracy theories of globalization" in eds. Jane Parish and Martin Parker, *The Age of Anxiety: Conspiracy Theory and the Human Sciences*, 53.

44. Mark Fenster, *Conspiracy Theories, Secrecy and Power in American Culture*, (Minneapolis: University of Minnesota Press, 2008), 120.

45. Ibid., 10.

46. Martin Parker, "Human science as conspiracy theory," 194.

47. Douglas Brinkley, *The Great Deluge* (New York: Harper Perennial, 2006).

48. Reilly Morse posits that "environment racism" prevailed in the settlement pattern of the region; New Orleans's landscape reflects the power relations between and within the communities that settled in the city, dividing it into various quarters according to ethnic and class dynamics. Morse argues that the modern racial geography of New Orleans emerged after the Civil War when "whites selected areas for Blacks to occupy that had various disadvantages, such as flooding, unhealthy air, or inadequate streets, water and sewage. A typical geographic marginalization of Blacks was toward low-value, flood-prone swamplands at the edge of the city, far from basic urban infrastructure, such as the original Tremé." Reilly Morse, "Environmental Justice Through the Eye of Hurricane Katrina" (Wahington DC, Joint Center for Political and Economic Studies, Inc., 2008). The document can be accessed online: <http://www.jointcenter.org/hpi/sites/all/files/EnvironmentalJustice.pdf> (accessed on February 2, 2014).

49. John M. Barry, *Rising Tide, The Great Mississippi Flood of 1927 and How it Changed America*, 285–286, 313–317.

50. Cathy Caruth, *Unclaimed Experience, Trauma, Narrative, and History* (Baltimore, MD: The John Hopkins University Press, 1996), 17.

51. Thomas Doherty, Movie Review, *The Journal of American History*, 93, no. 3, December 2006, 997–999. <http://jah.oxfordjournals.org/content/93/3/997.2.full> (accessed on March 11, 2014).

52. "In history everything begins with the gesture of *setting aside*, of putting together, of transforming certain classified objects into 'documents.' This new cultural distribution is the first task. In reality it consists in producing such documents by dint of copying, transcribing, or photographing these objects simultaneously changing their locus and their status. This gesture consists in 'isolating' a body—as in physics—and 'denaturing' things in order to turn them into parts, which will fill the lacunae inside an a priori totality." Michel de Certeau, *The Writing of History*, translated by Tom Conley (New York: Colombia University Press, 1988), 72–73.

53. Manning Marable, *Living Black History, How Reimagining the African-American Past Can Remake America's Racial Future* (New York: Basic *Civitas* Group, 2006), xx.

54. Ibid.

55. Susan Sontag, *Regarding the Pain of Others* (New York: Picador, 2003), 91.

56. Christine Acham, "We Shall Overcome: Preserving History and Memory in *4 Little Girls*" in ed. Paula Massood, *The Spike Lee Reader*, 165.

57. Dora Apel, *Imagery of Lynching: Black Men, White Women, and the Mob* (New Brunswick, NJ: Rutgers University Press, 2004), 9.

58. See chapter 3 "The 'Crime' of Blackness: Lynching Imagery in *The Crisis*" in Amy Helene Kirschke, *Art in Crisis, W. E. B. Du Bois and the Struggle*

for African American Identity and Memory (Bloomington and Indianapolis, IN: Indiana University Press, 2007), 48–114.

59. Evie Shockley, "The Haunted Houses of New Orleans: Gothic Homelessness and African American Experience" in eds. Keith Wailoo, Kareen M. O' Neil, Jeffrey Dowd and Roland Anglin, *Katrina's Imprint: Race and Vulnerability in New Orleans* (New Brunswick, NJ: Rutgers University Press, 2010), 104.

60. Nicole R. Fleetwood, "Failing Narratives, Initiating Technologies: Hurricane Katrina and the Production of a Weather Media Event," *American Quarterly* 58, no. 3, "Rewiring the 'Nation': The Place of Technology in American Studies" (Sept., 2006), 774.

61. Walter Benjamin, "The Work of Art in the Age of Mechanical Reproduction," 236.

62. Anna Hartnell, "*When the Levees Broke*: Inconvenient Truths and the Limits of National Identity" forthcoming *African American Review* 45.2 (2012).

63. Bill Nichols, *Blurred Boundaries: Questions of Meaning in Contemporary Culture* (Bloomington, IN: Indiana University Press, 1994, 2001), 38.

Chapter 3

1. Mark P. Orbe and A. Elizabeth Lyons, "Spike Lee as Entrepreneur: Leveraging 40 Acres and a Mule" in eds. Janice D. Hamlet, Robin R. Means Coleman, *Fight the Power, The Spike Lee Reader*, 378.

2. Robert Hariman and John Louis Lucaites, *No Caption Needed* (Chicago: The University of Chicago Press, 2007). See the chapters on *Migrant Mother* (49–92) and on *Accidental Napalm* (171–207).

3. Ibid., 36.

4. Bill Nichols, *Introduction to Documentary*, 187.

5. Richard Dyer, "White" in *Screen*, 29, no. 4 (1988), 47.

6. Cornel West, *Race Matters* (Boston: Beacon Press, 1993), 124–125.

7. Brian A. Monahan, *The Shock of the News, Media Coverage and the Making of 9/11* (New York and London: New York University Press, 2010), 3. See my review of the book: Delphine Letort, "Brian A. Monahan, *The Shock of the News: Media Coverage and the Making of 9/11*," *InMedia* 2, 2012. <http://inmedia.revues.org/479> (accessed on February 1, 2014).

8. Monahan, *The Shock of the News, Media Coverage and the Making of 9/1*, xii–xiii.

9. "Simulation is no longer that of a territory, a referential being or a substance. It is the generation by models of a real without origin or reality: a hyperreality." Jean Baudrillard, *Simulacra and Simulation*, translated by Sheila Faria Glaser (Ann Arbor, MI: University of Michigan Press, 1994; French edition: Editions Galilee, 1984), 1.

10. Keith Wailoo, Kareen M. O'Neil, and Jeffrey Dowd, "Introduction: Katrina's Imprint" in eds. Keith Wailoo, Kareen M. O'Neil, Jeffrey Dowd, and Roland Anglin, *Katrina's Imprint: Race and Vulnerability in New Orleans*, 1.

11. Ibid.

12. Nancy Boyd-Franklin, "Racism, Trauma, and Resilience, The Psychological Impact of Katrina" in Ibid., 89.

13. Mia Bay, "Invisible Tethers, Transportation and Discrimination in the Age of Katrina" in Ibid., 24.

14. James Jennings and Louis Jushnick, "Poverty as Race, Power and Wealth" in eds. Louis Jushnick and James Jennings, *A New Introduction to Poverty: The Role of Race, Power, and Politics* (New York: New York University Press, 1999), 6.

15. Mary Pattillo-McCoy, *Black Picket Fences: Privilege and Peril among the Black Middle Class* (Chicago: University of Chicago Press, 1999), 2. The author notes: "Welfare debates, discussions of crime and safety, urban policy initiatives, and even the cultural uproar over things like rap music are focused in the situation of poor African Americans. [. . .] But rarely do we hear the stories of the other three-fourths, of the majority of African Americans, who may be the office secretary, the company's computer technician, a project manager down the hall, or the person who teaches our children." Ibid., 2.

16. Douglas Brinkley, *The Great Deluge*, 366.

17. The footage is online: <http://www.youtube.com/watch?v=6v9ZVD9jjpI> (accessed January 13, 2011).

18. "Whether on radio, television, or in the papers, journalists were suddenly and surprisingly taking adversarial positions with officials, and even informing those officials about the realities of the situation at hand. [. . .] It was a heady moment. Everywhere one tuned, there seemed to be an impassioned journalist expressing public outrage and seeking to hold officials accountable." W. Lance Bennett, Regina G. Lawrence, and Steven Livingston, *When the Press Fails, Political Power and the News Media from Iraq to Katrina* (Chicago: The University Press of Chicago, 2007), 65.

19. Douglas Brinkley writes: "Racism was in play, to some degree. If thousands of storm-ravaged citizens were stranded in Boston's Back Bay, caught on some portion of the Massachusetts Turnpike during a flood and if they were white, you can be sure it wouldn't have taken days for them to be evacuated. Whatever the conditions, it wouldn't have taken officials four days to rescue them." Douglas Brinkley, *The Great Deluge*, 465.

20. "The voice reclaims black space. It demands public spatial arrangements that enhance black American citizenship." Mark Frederick Baker and Houston A. Baker, "Uptown Where We Belong, Space, Captivity, and the Documentary of Black Community" in eds. Phyllis R. Klotman and Janet K. Cutler, *Struggles for Representation*, 219.

21. "In the early days after Katrina struck, media reporting and images of anarchy served to justify the manner in which disaster response operations were carried out. For example, within three days after Katrina made landfall, the governor of Louisiana and the Mayor of New Orleans suspended lifesaving operations in New Orleans and ordered emergency responses to concentrate on arresting looters and deterring crime instead." Russel R Dynes and Havidan Rodriguez,

"Finding and Framing Katrina: the Social Construction of Disaster" in eds. David Brunsma, David Overfelt and Steve Picou, *The Sociology of Katrina: Perspectives on a Modern Catastrophe* (Lanham: MD: Rowman & Littlefield, 2007), 24.

22. Michael Eric Dyson, *Come Hell or High Water, Hurricane Katrina and the Color of Disaster* (New York: Basic Civitas, 2006), x–xi.

23. Richard Mizelle, Jr., contends that displacement contributed to increasing New Orleanians' traumatic loss: "In the aftermath of both the Great Mississippi Flood of 1927 and Katrina, many survivors were displaced from their land and homes and migrated to cities in the urban South and the North. Displacement can have another meaning, though, equally linked to the idea of loss. The loss of neighborhood familiarity, support networks, longtime health-care providers, or something as seemingly banal as the neighborhood market where you bought fresh fish every Friday morning all constitute displacement. [. . .] This emotional and psychological distress, I would argue, can lead to exacerbated physical ailments." Richard Mizelle, Jr., "Second-lining the Jazz City: Jazz Funerals, Katrina, and the Reemergence of New Orleans" in eds. Keith Wailoo, Kareen M. O'Neil, Jeffrey Dowd, and Roland Anglin, *Katrina's Imprint: Race and Vulnerability in New Orleans*, 73.

24. Geoffrey Nunberg, *The Years of Talking Dangerously* (New York: Public Affairs, 2009), 194–195.

25. John Fiske, *Media Matters: Race and Gender in U.S. Politics*, (Minneapolis: University of Minnesota Press, 1996), 2.

26. Mike Wayne, "Documentary as critical and creative research" in eds. Thomas Austin and Wilma de Jong, *Rethinking Documentary, New Perspectives, New Practices*, (New York: Open University Press, 2010), 90. The author also mentions Michael Moore's *Bowling for Columbine* (2004) and *Fahrenheit 9/11* (2004), which "mirror academic criticism of US television news and bring it to the mainstream." Ibid., 90.

27. Thomas W. Benson and Brian J. Snee, "New political documentary" in eds. Thomas W. Benson and Brian J. Snee, *The Rhetoric of the New Political Documentary* (Carbondale, IL: Southern Illinois University, 2008), 14.

28. Nancy Boyd-Franklin, "Racism, Trauma, and Resilience, The Psychological Impact of Katrina" in eds. Keith Wailoo, Kareen M. O'Neil, Jeffrey Dowd, and Roland Anglin, *Katrina's Imprint: Race and Vulnerability in New Orleans*, 81.

29. Michael Eric Dyson, *Between God and Gangsta Rap: Bearing Witness to Black Culture* (Oxford, New York: Oxford University Press, 1997), 199.

30. Myisha Priest, "Langston Hughes Writing the Body of Emmett Till" in eds. Harriet Pollack and Christopher Mettress, *Emmett Till in Literary Memory and Imagination* (Baton Rouge, LA: Louisiana State University, 2008), 58.

31. His words echo Frantz Fanon's remarks on the fact of blackness: "I came into the world imbued with the will to find a meaning in things, my spirit filled with the desire to attain to the source of the world, and then I found that I was an object in the mist of other object. Sealed into that crushing objecthood, I turned beseechingly to others. Their attention was a liberation, running over my body

suddenly abraded into nonbeing, endowing me once more with an agility that I had thought lost, and by taking me out of the world, restoring me to it." Frantz Fanon, *Black Skin, White Masks* (New York: Grove Press, 1986), 109.

32. Bernard D. Haley, "'Black on Black' Crime: The Myth and the Reality," *Crime and Social Justice* 20 (1983), 52–53.

33. Pauline Lipman, *High Stakes Education: Inequality, Globalization and Urban School Reform* (London, New York: Routledge, 2004), 169.

34. Gloria Yamato, "Something about the Subject Makes it Hard to Name" in eds. Jo Whitehorse Cochran, Donna Langston, and Caroly Woodward, *Changing Our Power: An Introduction to Women's Studies* (Dubuque, IA: Kendall-Hunt, 1988), 3.

35. Matthew C. Whitaker, ed., *African American Icons of Sport, Triumph, Courage and Excellence* (Westport, CT; London: Greenwood Press, 2008), 50.

36. Jim Brown, with Steve Delsohn, *Out of Bounds* (New York: Kensington Publishing Corp., 1989).

37. The book includes a study of wrestling in the chapter entitled "In the Ring" and of bicycle racing in "The Tour de France." Roland Barthes, *Mythologies* (Paris: Seuil, 1970).

38. Roland Barthes, *What is sport?* translated by Richard Howard (New Haven and London: Yale University Press, 2007), 59–61. Barthes furthers "What is sport? Sport answers this question by another: who is best? But to this question of the ancient duels, sport gives a new meaning: for man's excellence is sought here only in relation to things. Who is the best man to overcome the resistance of things, the immobility of nature?" Ibid., 63.

39. Guy Debord, *Society of the Spectacle* (Detroit: Black and Red, 1967, 1983), 18.

40. Kathryn Jay, *More than Just a Game: Sports in American Life since 1940*, 7.

41. Patrick B. Miller, "The Anatomy of Scientific Racism: Racialist Responses to Black Athletic Achievement" in *Journal of Sport History;* 25 (Spring 1998), 125.

42. Ben Carrington, *Race, Sports and Politics: the Sporting Black Diaspora*, 79.

43. Brown is the topic of another written biography: Mike Freeman, *Jim Brown, The Fierce Life of an American Hero* (New York, London, Toronto, Sydney: Harper Entertainment, 2007).

44. Jim Brown quoted in Roberta J. Newman, "Jim Brown: The Rise and Fall (and Rise) of a Cultural Icon" in eds. David C. Ogden and Joel Nathan Rosen, *From Fame to Infamy, Race, Sport and the Fall from Grace* (Jackson, MS: University Press of Mississippi, 2010), 188.

45. Pero Gaglo Dagbovie and Amaris J. White, "Jim Brown" in ed. Matthew C. Whitaker, *African American Icons of Sport, Triumph, Courage and Excellence*, 50.

46. Kathryn Jay, *More than Just a Game: Sports in American Life since 1940* (New York: Columbia University Press, 2004), 3.

47. Patrick B. Miller and David K. Wiggins, *Sport and the Color Line, Black Athletes and Race Relations in Twentieth-Century America*, x.

48. Kathryn Jay, *More than Just a Game: Sports in American Life since 1940*, 106.

49. Kathryn Jay argues that the NFL (like other sports organizations) was affected by a series of deregulations: "Starting with the move of the Oakland Raiders to Los Angeles in the early 1980s, the NFL embarked on a roller-coaster ride of teams movement. Several developments encouraged owners to consider moving their teams to new locales. First, the coming of free agency dramatically raised player salaries. [. . .] The NFL grew much more aggressive in licensing and marketing its products, and all clubs agreed in 1982 to give NFL Properties exclusive usage of all team logos and league marks. NFL Properties then sold logo rights to companies such as Coca-Cola and Reebok for use in advertisements [. . .]" Ibid., 208. See the chapter "Competing on the open market." Ibid., 180–216.

50. Mike Freeman, *Jim Brown, The Fierce Life of an American Hero*, 124.

51. Michael Messner, "Masculinities and Athletic Careers" in eds. Margaret L. Andersen, Patricia Hill Collins, *Race, Class, and Gender: An Anthology*, fifth edition (New York: Wadsworth, 2004), 199. The author notes that a sports career is no longer deemed attractive to young white men who would rather put for their academic performance as a sign of masculine status: "The white, middle-class institutional context, with its emphases on education and income, makes it clear to them that choices exist and that the pursuit of an athletic career is not a particularly good choice. Where the young male once found sports to be a convenient institution within which to construct masculine status, the postadolescent and young adult man from a higher-status background simply *transfers* these same strivings to other institutional contexts: education and careers." Ibid., 195.

52. Mikel J. Koven, *Blaxploitation Films*, (Herts, England, Kamera Books, 2010), 13.

53. Sam Kelly, "Sidney Poitier: héros intégrationniste" in eds. Mark Reid, Janine Euvrard, Francis Bordat, Raphaël Bassan, *Le Cinéma noir américain* (Condé sur Noireau: Editions Corlet, Collection *CinémAction*, 1988), 69.

54. Donald Bogle writes: "Black audiences were consciously aware for the first time of the great tomism inherent in the Poitier character, indeed in the Poitier image." Donald Bogle, *Toms, Coons, Mulattoes, Mammies, and Bucks: An Interpretive History of Blacks in American Films*, (New York/London: Continuum, 1973), 182.

55. Jim Brown, with Steve Delsohn, *Out of Bounds*, 27. Brown writes: "When a back circled around the end, go for a little pass over the middle, defensive guys could stick out their forearm, catch you in the neck. That could knock you out, but it was legal. So was hitting a guy in the back of his knees when he wasn't looking, another sweetheart move that could end a career. The headslap couldn't maim you, only knock your brain out of your ear. Now outlawed, all that used to be legal and standard [. . .]." Ibid.

56. Ibid., 11.

170 / Notes to Chapter 3

57. Ed Guerrero, *Framing Blackness, The African American Image in Film* (Philadelphia: Temple University Press, 1993), 78. He adds: "Jim Brown was able to do what Poitier was denied in his career to that point, to act in a violent assertive manner and express his sexuality freely." Ibid., 79.

58. See Delphine Letort, "*Sweet Sweetback's Baadasssss Song* (Melvin Van Peebles, 1971): Exégèse d'un film militant" in ed. Eliane Elmaleh, *Usages et contre-usages du stéréotype chez les Afro-américains*, Revue LISA—Vol. VII—no. 1, 2009, Presses Universitaires de Caen, 74–88. <http://lisa.revues.org/index790.html> (accessed on March 14, 2014).

59. Ed Guerrero, *Framing Blackness, The African American Image in Film*, 79–80.

60. Huey P. Newton, "He won't bleed me, A Revolutionary Analysis of *Sweet Sweetback's Baadasssss Song*, With an Introduction by Bobby Seale, June 19, 1971" in ed. Toni Morrison, *To Die for the People*, (San Francisco, CA: City Light Books, 1995; First edition: New York: Random House, 1972), 112–148.

61. Ben Carrington, *Race, Sports and Politics: The Sporting Black Diaspora*, 79.

62. Charlene Regester, "From the Gridiron and the Boxing Ring to the Cinema Screen: The African-American Athlete in pre-1950 Cinema" in eds. J. A. Mangan and Andrew Ritchie, *Ethnicity, Sport, Identity: Struggle for Status* (London: Routledge, 2004), 278.

63. Mike Freeman, *Jim Brown, The Fierce Life of an American Hero*, 146–147, 165, 204.

64. "Like those daytime melodramas, it was a multiple 'family saga' with villains and victims, glacial pace, meandering twists of plot, pregnant pauses, paucity of action, and abundance of talk, and with cuts to commercials during recess or after dramatic pieces of testimony." Linda Williams, *Playing the Race Card, Melodramas of Black and White From Uncle Tom to O. J. Simpson* (Princeton, NJ: Princeton University Press, 2002), 263.

65. "The famous *Time* mug shot that digitally darkened his skin, froze his movement, and wiped the confident smile off his face represented a radical reversal of the smiling athlete who had so gracefully faked out opponents or leaped with casual ease through airport. The demeanor of this charismatic, and now emphatically "black," celebrity was, finally the most compelling reason the American jury-audience could not stop watching the Simpson trial day after long day." Ibid., 269.

66. Jonathan Mathew Finn, *Capturing the Criminal Image: From Mug Shot to Surveillance Society* (Minneapolis, MN: University of Minnesota Press, 2009), 1.

67. Douglas Kellner, *Media Spectacle*, 93–125. According to Kellner, the media spectacle around O. J. Simpson "intensified racial divisions and conflict, and helped promote a white backlash." Ibid., 116.

68. "No single film in the silent era is more important to the critical history of stereotype than is D. W. Griffith's *The Birth of a Nation* (USA, 1915). Here,

the late-nineteenth image of the African American male as rapist turns to pure spectacle in the ideologically weighted aesthetics of black-and-white film. In Gus, played in blackface by Walter Long, we have the filmic birth of what Donald Bogle (1989) call the 'brutal black buck,' a sexually uncontrollable figure who lusts after white women." Robyn Wiegman, "Race, ethnicity, and film" in eds. John Hill and Pamela Church Gibson, *The Oxford Guide to Film Studies* (Oxford: Oxford University Press, 1998), 162.

69. See Martha Menchaca, *Recovering History, Constructing Race, The Indian, Black and White Roots of Mexican Americans* (Austin, TX: University of Texas Press, 2001, 2003).

70. Ed Guerrero, *Framing Blackness, The African American Image in Film*, 34.

71. Mikel J. Koven, *Blaxploitation Film*, 99.

72. Ibid. The author compares *Slaughter* to *Superfly TNT* (Ron O'Neal, 1973) in order to demonstrate that white Blaxploitation films differ to black Blaxploitation productions: "This [*Superfly TNT*] is one of the most intelligent, perceptive and political of the Blaxploitation films. Not surprising, since the screenplay is by black activist and author Alex Haley (*Roots* and *The Autobiography of Malcolm X*). [. . .] Unlike some of the white-made Blaxploitation films discussed below, particularly *Slaughter*, the torture and degradation that Priest experiences at the hands of his white captors is not exploitative. Instead, these scenes of torture are ideological: what these white soldiers do to Priest is what white colonial governments have long been doing to the black bodies of Africa." Ibid., 61–62.

73. "While imprisoned, Newton became identified with the warrior hero of the famous poster, and many Panther supporters came to believe that Newton's release from prison would make the real beginning of 'the revolution.' Newton, however, felt conscious of the fact that he was not the heroic warrior figure, or even the dynamic public performer, that the role required." Judith Lowder Newton, *From Panthers to Promise Keepers: Rethinking the Men's Movement—New Social Formations* (Lanham, MD: Rowman and Littlefield Publisher, 2005), 67.

74. Rhonda Y. Williams, "Black Women, Urban Politics, and Engendering Black Power" in ed. Peniel E. Joseph, *The Black Power Movement, Rethinking the Civil Rights—Black Power Era*, (New York/London: Routledge, 2006), 90.

75. Judith Lowder Newton, *From Panthers to Promises Keepers, Rethinking the Men's Movement,* 63.

76. Newton explains: "The phrase 'All Power to the People' was meant to turn this around, to convince Black People that their rewards were due in the present, that it was in their power to create a Promised Land *here and now*." Huey P. Newton, *Revolutionary Suicide* (New York: Penguin Books, 2009; first edition: Harcourt Brace Jovanovich, 1973), 179.

77. Newton refers to Mao to advocate self-defense in his writings: "One successful practitioner of the art and science of national liberation and self-defense, Brother Mao Tse-tung, put it this way: 'We are advocates of the abolition of war,

we do not want war; but war can only be abolished through war, and in order to get rid of the gun it is necessary to take up the gun.'" Huey P. Newton, "In Defense of Self-Defense" June 20, 1967, in ed. Toni Morrison, *To Die for the People, The Writings of Huey P. Newton*, 84.

78. Malcolm X used the phrase in a speech delivered at Audubon ballroom on June 28, 1964. Malcolm X, "The Second Rally of the OAAU" in *By Any Means Necessary: Malcolm X* (New York: Pathfinder Press, 1992), 102. Newton presents himself as heir to Malcolm X: "But they [the black masses] learned from Malcolm that with the gun they can recapture their dreams and make them a reality. The heirs of Malcolm now stand millions strong on their corner of the triangle, facing the racist dog oppressor and the soulless endorsed spokesmen." Huey P. Newton, "In Defense of Self-Defense" July 3, 1967, in ed. Toni Morrison, *To Die for the People, The Writings of Huey P. Newton*, 88.

79. Jama Lazerow and Yohuru R. Williams, *In Search of the Black Panther Party: New Perspective on a Revolutionary Movement* (Durham, NC: Duke University Press, 2006), 256.

80. Jane Rhodes, *Framing the Black Panthers, The Spectacular Rise of a Black Power Icon,* (New York/London: The New Press, 2007).

81. *Martin A. Berger, Seeing Through Race: A Reinterpretation of Civil Rights Photography (Berkeley and Los Angeles. CA: University of Berkeley Press, 2011),* 7.

82. Gladys L. Knight, *Icons of the African American Protest: Trailblazing Activists of the Civil Rights Movement, Vol. 1* (Westport, CT: Greenwood Press, 2009), 71.

83. Sam Durant, *Black Panther, The Revolutionary Art of Emory Douglas* (New York: Rizzoli, 2007), 28. The book includes artworks by Emory Douglas and published in *Black Panthers*, illustrating the mottos and ideas of the Party.

84. Toni Morrison, *To Die for the People, The Writings of Huey P. Newton*.

85. Christopher P. Lehman, *The Colored Cartoon, Black Representation in American Animated Short Films 1907–1954* (Amherst, MA: University of Massachusetts Press, 2007), 10.

86. Martin A. Berger, *Seeing Through Race: A Reinterpretation of Civil Rights Photography*, 68.

87. Dennis Carlson, "Troubling Heroes: Of Rosa Parks, Multicultural Education, and Critical Pedagogy" in Greg Dimitriadis and Dennis Carlson, *Promises to Keep: Cultural Studies, Democratic Education, and Public Life* (New York: Routledge, 2003), 197.

88. "Of course, King was a genuine leader with an unequalled following. Still, his adoption by whites gave him an ambiguous status—one reason why many white Americans wanted to have his birthday made a holiday was to ensure that this honor would go to someone with whom they could feel comfortable. Blacks could not object, nor was that their wish. At the same time, they sensed that he was essentially a white choice." Andrew Hacker, *Two Nations, Black and White, Separate, Hostile, Unequal* (New York: Charles Scribner's Sons, 1992), 63.

Chapter 4

1. Andrew Dewaard, "Joints and Jams: Spike Lee as Sellebrity Auteur," in eds. Janice D. Hamlet, Robin R. Means Coleman, *Fight the Power, The Spike Lee Reader*, 359.

2. General William T. Sherman issued Special Field Order No. 15 on January 16, 1865, which granted forty acres of tilled land and a mule to freed black families. By June 1965, some forty thousand freed people had settled on four hundred thousand acres of "Sherman land" along coastal South Carolina and Georgia. However, President Andrew Johnson revoked the order after his election and returned the land to its white dispossessed owners. Jeffrey R. Kerr-Ritchie, "Forty Acres, or, An Act of Bad Faith" in eds. Michael T. Martin and Marilyn Yaquinto, *Redress for Historical Injustices in the United States. On Reparations for Slavery, Jim Crow and Their Legacies* (Durham, NC & London: Duke University Press, 2007), 222–237.

3. Manning Marable, *The Great Wells of Democracy: the Meaning of Race in American Life* (New York: Basic Civitas Group, 2006), 230.

4. Ibid., 252.

5. Manning Marable, *Living Black History: How reimagining the African-American Past Can Remake America's Racial Future* (New York: Basic Civitas Group, 2006), 33.

6. The full speech can be accessed online <http://www.blackpast.org/?q=1964-malcolm-x-ballot-or-bullet> (accessed on January 26, 2014).

7. "Let us endeavour to invent a man in full, something which Europe has been incapable of achieving." Frantz Fanon, *The Wretched of the Earth*, translated by Richard Philcox (New York: Grove Press, 2004; first edition: 1961), 55.

8. The full speech can be accessed online <http://www.blackpast.org/?q=1964-malcolm-x-s-speech-founding-rally-organization-afro-american-unity> (accessed on January 26, 2014).

9. Charles T. Banner-Haley, *The Fruits of Integration: Black Middle-Class Ideology and Culture 1960–1990* (Jackson, MS: University Press of Mississippi, 1994), 165.

10. Less than 10 percent of whites live in poverty compared with more 27 percent of African American and 25 percent of Hispanics (Source: U.S. Department of Health and Human Services).

11. Brian Ward, *Just My Soul Reponding: Rhythm and Blues, Black Consciousness and Race Relations* (London: UCL Press, 1998).

12. Although Michel Chion comments on the use of music in fiction films, I argue that Lee uses music to achieve the same effects in the documentary: "Music can directly express its participation in the feeling of the scene, by taking on the scene's rhythm, tone, and phrasing; obviously such music participates in cultural codes for things like sadness, happiness, and movement. In this case we can speak of *empathetic music*, from the word empathy, the ability to feel the

feelings of others." Michel Chion, *Audio-Vision: Sound and Screen*, translated by Claudia Gorsman, (New York: Columbia University Press, 1994), 8.

13. "It was in New Orleans, by contrast, where black people not only found themselves able to retain a number of African cultural practices, such as drumming, that were illegal elsewhere but also chose to stay, generation upon generation, in favor of going too climates that were colder (in both senses of the word). [. . .] Insofar as French and Spanish attitudes that helped to shape New Orleans culture were less invested in suppressing and erasing African influences, those influences became integral to the way of life in that city. [. . .] African American could look to New Orleans for speech patterns, cuisine, rituals, philosophies, and, significantly, music that were as close as we might get to the unknowable African past." Evie Shockley, "The Haunted Houses of New Orleans: Gothic Homelessness and African American Experience" in eds. Keith Wailoo, Kareen M. O'Neil, Jeffrey Dowd, and Roland Anglin, *Katrina's Imprint: Race and Vulnerability in New Orleans* (New Brunswick, NJ: Rutgers, 2010), 102.

14. Michael E. Crutcher, *Tremé, Race and Place in a New Orleans Neighborhood* (Athens, GA: The University of Georgia Press, 2010), 28.

15. Richard Mizelle, Jr., "Second-lining the Jazz City: Jazz Funerals, Katrina, and the Reemergence of New Orleans" in eds. Keith Wailoo, Kareen M. O' Neil, Jeffrey Dowd and Roland Anglin, *Katrina's Imprint: Race and Vulnerability in New Orleans*, 69. The author depicts the jazz funeral as follows: "During a jazz funeral, a brass band traditionally awaits outside of the church or funeral home for the services to be completed, then begins to play processional or mournful music like 'Nearer My God to Thee.' Before older cemetery in the city became full, the entire procession, including the band, would proceed to the gravesite. . . . The dancers and marchers who follow the band as the entire scene moves through the streets of NO are called the second line. These individuals as a unique component of this cultural performance, having at times various connections to the deceased and to a particular community. . . . Some second-liners bring their own brass instruments or drums and join in the band, while others elaborately decorate umbrellas that can be seen from blocks away." Ibid., 70.

16. Janet Walker, "Rights and return: perils and fantasies of situated testimony after Katrina," in eds. Bhaskar Sarkar and Janet Walker, *Documentary Testimonies, Global Archives of Suffering*, 110.

17. Douglas Brinkley, *The Great Deluge*, 33–34. The author further writes: "New Orleans poverty figures had to be juxtaposed against its proportion of elderly, which was above average, and its noticeably large percentage of African Americans. Many social historians have traced the lively cultural personality of New Orleans and its jazz music to that disproportionately large percentage of the city's population, but in the face of a natural disaster, the world of the poor in New Orleans, particularly that of the poor black, and the poor elderly, couldn't be romanticized in a Harry Connick Jr. croon or a Kermit Ruffins horn riff. [. . .] Selling the world on the historic stage set that was so much of picturesque New Orleans, the city seemed not to care about its other decaying side." Ibid., 33.

18. Ellen C. Scott, "Sounding Black, Cultural Identification, Sound, and the Films of Spike Lee" in eds. Janice D. Hamlet, Robin R. Means Coleman, *Fight the Power, The Spike Lee Reader*, 232.

19. Matthew D. Lassiter and Joseph Crespino, *The Myth of Southern Exceptionalism* (Oxford: Oxford University Press, 2009), 159.

20. <http://www.youtube.com/watch?v=3QX7apebWaE> (accessed on January 28, 2014).

21. The full program: 1. We want freedom. We want power to determine the destiny of our Black Community; 2. We want full employment for our people; 3. We want an end to the robbery by the CAPITALIST of our Black Community; 4. We want decent housing, fit for the shelter of human beings; 5. We want education for our people that exposes the true nature of this decadent American society. We want education that teaches us our true history and our role in the present-day society; 6. We want all black men to be exempt from military service; 7. We want an immediate end to POLICE BRUTALITY and MURDER of black people; 8. We want freedom for all black men held in federal, state, county and city prisons and jails; 9. We want all black people when brought to trial to be tried in court by a jury of their peer group or people from their black communities, as defined by the Constitution of the United States; 10. We want land, bread, housing, education, clothing, justice and peace. And as our major political objective, a United Nations supervised plebiscite to be held throughout the black colony in which only black colonial subjects will be allowed to participate, for the purpose of determining the will of black people as to their national destiny.

22. "We want an end to the robbery by the CAPITALIST of the black community."

23. "The economic relationship of America's black communities to the larger society also reflects their colonial status. The political power exercised over those communities goes hand in glove with the economic deprivation experienced by the black citizens." Kwame Ture (formerly known as Stokely Carmichael) and Charles V. Hamilton, *Black Power, The Politics of Liberation in America* (New York: Vintage Books, 1992; First edition: 1967), 16.

24. Newton recounts that he went to the penitentiary in search of "justice," but all he found was "just us."

25. Newton's puns in the play illustrate Saussure's explanation that "meaning exists only within a system." Through puns and anecdotes, the actor interpreting Newton tries to subvert the system to which words as "signifiers" refer. See the chapter "Semiotics" in eds. Robert Lapsley and Michael Westlake, *Film Theory: an Introduction* (Manchester: Manchester University Press, 1988), 33–34.

26. Mikhail Bakhtin, translated by Caryl Emerson, *Problems of Dostoevsky's Poetics* (Minneapolis: University of Minnesota Press, 1984), 127. Bakhtin adds: "Laughter embraces both poles of change, it deals with the very process of change, with crisis itself." Ibid.

27. Averintsev writes "Laughter is not freedom but the process of becoming free" and is quoted by Gergana Vitanova, "Authoring the Self in a NonNative

Language" in eds. Joan Kelly Hall, Gergana Vitanova, Ludmila Marchenkova, *Dialogue with Bakhtin on Second and Foreign Language Learning: New Perspectives* (Hillsdale, NJ: Lawrence Erlbaum Associates, Inc., 2005), 154.

28. J. Edgar Hoover, "Memorandum to Special Agent in Charge," Albany, New York, August 25. 1967, in ed. William L. Van Deburg, *Modern Black Nationalism: From Marcus Garvey to Louis Farrakhan* (New York: New York University Press, 1997), 134.

29. Stokely Carmichael settled in Guinea whereas Eldridge Cleaver and his wife eventually fled to Algeria; Angela Davis followed Huey P. Newton and Bobby Seale in prison. Ward Churchill looks back to Cointelpro's secret war strategies and analyses their disruptive effects within the Black Panther Party. Ward Churchill, "'To Disrupt, Discredit, and Destroy': the FBI's Secret War against the Black Panther Party" in eds. Kathleen Cleaver and Georges Katsiaficas, *Liberation, Imagination, and the Black Panther Party: a New Look at the Panthers and their Legacy* (New York: Routledge, 2001), 78–117.

30. Newton wrote: "Black people must move, from the grassroots up through the perfumed circles of the Black bourgeoisie, to seize by any means necessary a proportionate share of the power vested and collected in the structure of America. We must organize and unite to combat by long resistance the brutal force used against us daily." Huey P. Newton, "In Defense of Self-Defense" June 20, 1967, in ed. Toni Morrison, *To Die for the People, The Writings of Huey P. Newton*, 84.

31. Maulana Karenga developed another nationalist group (US Organization) in Los Angeles at the same time as the Panthers. Karenga put the emphasis on the African cultural heritage to achieve cultural liberation. Scot Brown, *Figthing for US: Maulana Karenga, The US Organization, and Black Cultural Nationalism* (New York: New York University Press, 2005).

32. Huey P. Newton, "To the Black Movement" May 15, 1968, in ed. Toni Morrison, *To Die for the People, The Writings of Huey P. Newton*, 90.

33. "The cultural nationalists are concerned with returning to the old African culture and thereby regaining their identity and freedom. In other words, they feel that the African culture will automatically bring political freedom. Many times cultural nationalists fall into line as reactionary nationalists." Ibid., 90.

34. Ronald D Smith, *Strategic Planning for Public Relations*, fourth edition (New York: Routledge, 2013), 294.

35. Melissa T. Brown, *Enlisting Masculinity. The Construction of Gender in US Military Recruiting* (New York: Oxford University Press, 2012), 94.

36. <http://www.spikeddb.com/work/mlk/> (accessed on January 26, 2014).

37. Clayborne Carson, "Martin Luther King, Jr: Charismatic Leadership in a Mass Struggle," *Journal of American History* 74, September 1987, 448–454.

38. <http://www.spikeddb.com/work/jaguar-2/> (accessed on January 27, 2014).

39. Paul Gilroy, *Against Race: Imagining Political Culture beyond the Color Line* (Cambridge, MA: Harvard University Press, 2000), 203.

40. "Beauty and strength are, after all, understood by Riefensthal as exclusively natural attributes rather than cultural achievement." Ibid., 174.

41. Spike Lee quoted by Yvette Caslin. <http://rollingout.com/business/executive-suite/spike-lee-joins-chevrolets-table-of-brotherhood-tour-challenges-blacks-to-get-education/> (accessed on January 26, 2014).

42. He explains: "I refer to charter schools as freedom schools—the freedom to have a longer year, a longer day; the freedom to make hiring decisions based on qualification; the freedom of parents to pick their school. All of our schools are open-enrolment schools. If you have superior curriculum and instructional models, if you are able to recruit the best and the brightest and half the teachers in this district—charter and noncharter combined—are in their 20s, they're from many of the elite universities, they bring great content mastery, energy; they thing a 180-day school year is a part-time job [. . .]. That's the reason you've been able to lengthen our school year to eleven months and our school day to 8.5 hours. I've always been a strong advocate of a longer school year and a longer school day." Paul Vallas [*IGIW*, Part 2, 10:42]

43. There was an unprecedented explosive growth of charter schools in New Orleans (70 percent are now chartered), which makes it a unique experiment all over the country. Charter schools were devised as an alternative to the public school system which was dogged by financial mismanagement, corruption, high drop-out numbers, and poor student results. Although the state retains the power to renew or not the charters of the schools, depending on whether they success or fail to achieve the expected results, privately operated charters eliminate public participation in the governance of the schools. While they are still financed by tax money, they are also entitled to raise funds and to resort to private investments. See Adrienne Dixson, "Whose Choice? A Critical Perspective on Charter Schools" in Cedric Johnson, *The Neoliberal Deluge: Hurricane Katrina, Late Capitalism and the Remaking of New Orleans*, (Minneapolis: University of Minnesota Press, 2011), 130.

44. She contends that the teachers' ideological dispositions: "(a) influence how they defined and label students and (b) affect their pedagogical choices." Pauline Lipman, *Race, Class, and Power in School Restructuring* (Albany: State University of New York Press, 1998), 26. She furthers explains: "The values, behaviors, language, and knowledge of white, middle-class students is often the standards in schools, and those whose identities do not reflect this standard are marginalized and/or pressured to change and conform. [. . .] Student resistance to the marginalization of their identity may lead to affirmation and strength, but it may also result in denial of educational opportunities, for example, when schooling is constructed in such a way that African American students define academic success as "acting white." McDermott (1974) argues that school failure for some students of color becomes something to be "achieved," a way to protect their personal integrity and dignity in the face of degrading policies, practices, and beliefs of educators." Ibid., 28.

178 / Notes to Chapter 4

45. Not only did Spike Lee endorse the Jordan Spiz'ikes, but he also designed the G-Shock watches for Casio. <http://www.javys.com/casio/series.php?series_id=GT0013> (accessed on January 26, 2014).

46. Charles Banner-Haley, *The Fruits of Integration: Black Middle-Class Ideology and Culture 1960–1990*, 170.

47. Note the company's website address: <http://www.spikeddb.com>. Spike Lee states his goals as following: "Our mission is to create positive, thought-provoking work that entertains and helps boost our client's bottom line. But we've also made it our business to help marketers stay on top of the cultural shifts in America that other guys ignore until it's too late. For over 15 years, we've done so for clients like Pepsi, Jaguar, State Farm, HBO, TNT, Mountain Dew, Johnson & Johnson and Chevrolet." See <http://www.spikeddb.com/about-us/> (accessed on March 22, 2014).

48. Brian Wilson and Robert Sparks, "Michael Jordan, Sneaker Commercials and Canadian Youth Culture" in ed. David L. Andrews, *Michael Jordan Inc., Corporate Sport, Media Culture, and Late Modern America* (Albany: State University of New York Press, 2001), 218.

49. Todd Boyd, "The Day the Niggaz Took Over: Basketball, Commodity Culture and Black Masculinity" in eds. Aaron Baker and Todd Boyd, *Out of Bounds: Sports, Media, and the Politics of Identity* (Bloomington, IN: Indiana University Press, 1997), 138.

50. Ben Carrington, *Race, Sports and Politics: the Sporting Black Diaspora*, 105.

51. Ed., Matthew C. Whitaker, *African American Icons of Sport, Triumph, Courage and Excellence* (Westport, CT; London: Greenwood Press, 2008).

52. Matthew C. Whitaker mentions the "furor that greeted Ali's decision [. . .]. Ali received constant death threats and was menaced by cruel phone calls at home. [. . .] When Ali refused to serve, he was stripped of his title, sentenced to prison, and fined $10,000." Matthew C. Whitaker, "Muhammad Ali," Ibid., 5.

53. Megan Falater, "Tommie Smith and John Carlos," Ibid., 251.

54. Shaun Powell, *Souled Out?: How Blacks are Winning and Losing in Sports* (Champaign IL: Human Kinetics, 2008), 28–30. The author explains: "The possibility of backlash is what frightens those black athletes who do have a social pulse. [. . .] Although it's true that the activist pioneers who risked their public image did pay a price for doing so, history ultimately pardoned them and repaid them handsomely." Ibid., 30.

55. Douglas Kellner, "The Sports Spectacle, Michael Jordan, and Nike," 313. The author draws on Michael Jordan to hammer home his point: "As a polysemic signifier, Jordan thus presents a figure that mobilizes many fantasies (i.e., athletic greatness, wealth, success, and upward mobility) for the national and global imaginary, providing a spectacle that embodies many desirable national and global features and aspirations. Yet Jordan is extremely black and his race is a definite signifier of his spectacle, though his blackness too has conflicting connotations. [. . .] Jordan's blackness is overdetermined and has also served to

signify black transgressions, as when his gambling behavior became a subject of negative media presentation and his father's murder led to speculation on connections with organized crime. In these images, Jordan is presented as the threatening black figure, as the negative fantasy figure of black deviance from white norms." Ibid., 311.

56. The story appears both in the film and in his autobiography. Jim Brown, with Steve Delsohn, *Out of Bounds*, 53–54.

57. Brown explains: "St. Simons is a very unique place because even though we talk about slavery and we talk about racism, I've never really felt racism. [. . .] Segregation gave us an ability to deal with ourselves. So I was always very secure in the community and family and belonging. [. . .] As I learned about my spirit and my attitude, I think a lot of it comes from being here, from being black, being with a black family, a black community, and understanding that the Ebos came here and refused to become slaves" [06:52 to 08:32].

58. "Sadly, a lot of the history and culture is getting bulldozed, literally. White developers and land prospectors now outnumber black natives. Many of the blacks are selling their lands to the whites. My mom still lives on St. Simons and we're holding onto our land. I'm afraid we're in the minority." Jim Brown, with Steve Delsohn, *Out of Bounds*, 53.

59. Kathryn Jay, *More than Just a Game: Sports in American Life since 1940*, 114–115.

60. Mike Freeman, *Jim Brown, The Fierce Life of an American Hero*, 170.

61. Eds., Margaret L. Andersen and Patricia Hill Collins, *Race, Class, and Gender: An Anthology*, 77.

62. Kathryn Jay, *More than Just a Game: Sports in American Life since 1940*, 23.

63. Thomas McLaughlin, *Give and Go, Basketball as a Cultural Practice* (Albany: State University of New York Press, 2008), 209. The author comments on the opening sequence of Lee's film to hammer home his point: "It moves from the rural to the urban, from the all-American players bathed in sunlight to the ghetto courts of the city, from white to black. Lee wants simultaneously to claim basketball as the *American* game and to claim it as the *black* game, played by men and women in desperate racist circumstances, in a corrupt and dangerous world. The sequence expresses a utopian desire and a harsh realism—in fact, it ends with a black man shooting a ball in a maximum-security prison." Ibid., 198.

64. Margaret L. Andersen and Patricia Hill Collins, eds., *Race, Class, and Gender: An Anthology*, 77.

65. Spike Lee notes: "Nowadays guys make a lot of money and there's very few players out there whose fans really believe they want to win anymore. Michael Jordan wants to, whether it's Ping-Pong, bid whist, pitching pennies or whatever. But I bring up the question to a lot of athletes today, black and white, whether they have the will to win. Everybody wants to win on Saturday afternoon or Sunday afternoon when the game begins and the cheerleaders are out there and everybody tunes in. But the games are won in the preparation—are they willing

180 / Notes to Chapter 4

to do what it takes to win before the game ever starts? Seems like some of them just are making so much money that they don't care." Spike Lee and Ralph Wiley, *The Best Seat in the House: A Basketball Memoir*, 273.

66. Ibid., 246. He writes: "Division One college basketball players should be paid. Stipend. Trust fund. Work-study. Whatever you want to call it. No doubt in my mind they should be salaried. They are not stupIbid. They are not blind to the big picture. They see everybody is salaried, from the coach to the school to the conference and its employees, to the concierge and the desk help in the hotels, to the airline pilot, to the commentators in network blazers, to TV producers and technicians, to sneaker manufacturers, to the sneaker reps—everybody under the sun making a good living off the annual contesting of these college games." Ibid., 245.

67. Jeffrey Lane, "Mortgaging Michael Jordan's Reputation" in eds. David C. Ogden and Joel Nathan Rosen, *From Fame to Infamy, Race, Sport and the Fall from Grace,* 128.

68. Mary G. McDonald, "Michael Jordan" in ed. Matthew C. Whitaker, *African American Icons of Sport, Triumph, Courage and Excellence,* 150.

69. Kamal Dean Parhizgar and Robert Parhizgar, *Multiculturall Business Ethics and Global Managerial Moral Reasoning* (Lanham, MD: University Press of America, 2006), 462.

70. <http://watch.nba.com/nba/video/channels/tnt_overtime/2012/11/26/20121126-knicks-nets-spike-tease-tnt.nba> (accessed on January 24, 2014).

71. http://www.highsnobiety.com/2012/12/24/video-royalty-is-big-nba-commercial-directed-by-and-featuring-spike-lee/> (accessed on January 24, 2014).

72. <http://www.highsnobiety.com/2012/03/21/video-the-chance-nike-sportswear-share-your-story-featuring-spike-lee/> (accessed on January 24, 2014).

73. Kathryn Jay, *More than Just a Game: Sports in American Life since 1940,* 4.

74. He declared: "*Hoop Dreams* is the best basketball film I've seen. Even though it was a documentary, it had a great dramatic arc, a fine narrative twist, and was so real. Just goes to show, you can make it up, but you can't make it up as well as life." <http://espn.go.com/page2/s/questions/spikelee.html> (accessed on January 24, 2014).

75. Andrew Dewaard states: "The check from Nike CEO Phil Knight that bailed Lee out when *Jim Brown: All American* went over budget is certainly less publicized." Andrew Dewaard, "Joints and Jams: Spike Lee as Sellebrity Auteur," in eds. Janice D. Hamlet, Robin R. Means Coleman, *Fight the Power, The Spike Lee Reader,* 351.

76. Evie Shockley, "The Haunted Houses of New Orleans: Gothic Homelessness and African American Experience" in eds. Keith Wailoo, Kareen M. O'Neil, Jeffrey Dowd, and Roland Anglin, *Katrina's Imprint: Race and Vulnerability in New Orleans,* 95.

77. Shawn Escoffery explains from a studio that New Orleans will never be the same, especially the Lower Ninth Ward: "There is not a lot of means to rebuild in parts of the Ninth Ward considering the majority of the population

there was extremely poor. Some people sold their home to the Road Home, got a fraction of what it would cost to actually build a new home and they can't come back. Then you have new houses being built up all the time. You have the Make It Right Brad Pitt houses, the Lower Nine Nena and other groups that are working to rebuild the Ninth Ward but the task at hand is daunting" [*IGIW*, Part 1, 47:00].

78. Quoted in Adelaide H. Villemoare and Peter G. Stillman, "Civic Culture and the Politics of Planning for Neighborhoods and Housing in Post-Katrina," in ed. M. B. Hacker, *Culture after Hurricanes, Rhetoric and Reinvention on the Gulf Coast* (Jackson, MS: University Press of Mississsippi, 2010), 28. The authors interpret the mayor's declaration: "In effect, the mayor as authority figure was saying both that people could come back (and even had a right to do so) and that it would be better if they did not (and that the city would not be investing in them, providing services for them, or reintegrating their neighborhoods into the city as a whole." Ibid.

79. Ibid., 20. Joseph Canizaro made a public statement to define the commission's goals: "New Orleans will be a sustainable, environmentally safe, socially equitable community with a vibrant economy. Its neighborhoods will be planned with its citizens, and connected to jobs and the region. Each will preserve and celebrate its heritage of culture, landscape and architecture." Urban Planning Committee: Action Plan for New Orleans Executive Summary, January 30, 2006. <http://www.nolaplans.com/plans/BNOB/Land%20Use%20Committee%20Attachment%20A.pdf> (accessed on January 26, 2014).

80. Peirce F. Lewis notes that the Superdome has been a bone of contention from the moment it was conceived: "Never mind if skeptics sneered that the Superdome would be filled only half a dozen times a year, and then its departing crows would create Texas-sized traffic jams. Never mind that its legislative foundation was slippery, and the cost of retiring bonds might hang like an incubus on New Orleans' financial back for generations to come. [. . .] If Houston had its Astrodome, New Orleans would have its Superdome, bigger and perhaps better." Peirce F. Lewis, *New Orleans: The Making of an Urban Landscape*, (Santa Fe, NM, and Staunutn, VA: The Center for American Places, 2003), 94.

81. Robert Baade and Victor Matheson, "NFL Governance and the Fate of the New Orleans Saints: Some Observations" in eds. Plácido Rodríguez, Stefan Késenne, Jaume García, *Governance and Competition in Professional Sports Leagues* (Oviedo: Ediciones de la Universidad de Oviedo, 2007), 142. The authors explain that the NFL confronted the Saints' owner Tom Benson on the issue, but managed to garner positive publicity by making him stay while he was interested in a better deal than New Orleans could offer.

82. Kathryn Jay, *More than Just a Game: Sports in American Life since 1940*, 208–210. The author gives several examples of relocations that devastated the residents of the cities the football teams originated from. She mentions the Cleveland Browns, who were moved to Baltimore in 1996 and were renamed the Ravens after the team owner Art Modell agreed to provide Baltimore fans with an NFL team, receiving in return all the publicly financed stadium's revenues. Ibid., 212.

83. Jeff Duncan quoted in Robert Baade and Victor Matheson, "NFL Governance and the Fate of the New Orleans Saints: Some Observations," 162.

84. Brad R. Humphreys, Dennis Ramsay Howard, *The Business of Sports: Perspectives on the Sports Industry* (Westport, CT: Greenwood Publishing Group, 2008), 85.

85. Peirce F. Lewis, *New Orleans: The Making of an Urban Landscape*, 36. Professor Peirce F. Lewis considered the construction of the superdome epitomized a mentality change: "It [the Superdome] is a symbol of fundamental change in New Orleans psychology from the old days when the city was run by a handful of old-timers [. . .]. The old, closed, conservative city was open fir business, and open with a vengeance, all with a very strong flavor of Texas and Hollywood. Blue bloods watched in horror, as a new Mardi Gras krewe called "Bacchus" was organized—its membership publicly bourgeois. Bacchus' fourth king, for example, was not an old-time Bourbon, but comedian Bob Hope, specially imported from Hollywood to play the role. In olden days, Hope might have been challenged to a duel under the oaks at dawn. In the early 1970s, a millions Orleanians and tourists cheered him down Canal Street [. . .]." Ibid., 94–95.

86. Mary Lou Widmer explains that New Orleans changed in the 1960s: "With the movement of the population into the suburb, city officials began to think of reconstructing the Central Business District in order to draw big business back to the heart of the city. Poydras Street, with its many small businesses and deteriorating buildings, seemed the ideal place to make this transformation." The International Trade Mart (1965), the Convention Center (1968) and the Superdome (1975) are located at the end of Poydras Street. Mary Lou Widmer, *New Orleans in the Sixties* (Gretna, LA: Pelican Publishing Company, Inc., 2000), 57.

87. "It was the new breed of businessmen—Lester Kabacoff, David Dixon, Joseph Canizaro, Pip Brennan, Clancy Dupee, Blaine Kern, and others, who eclipsed the old elite and, in concert with city hall, charted a tourism-dominated course in the city." Jonathan Mark Souther, *New Orleans on Parade: Tourism and the Transformation of the Crescent City*, (Baton Rouge: Louisiana State University Press, 2006), 164.

88. Bill Nichols states: "Recording instruments (cameras and sound recorders) register the imprints of things (sights and sounds) with great fidelity. It gives these imprints value as documents in the same way as fingerprints have value as documents. This uncanny sense of a document, or image that bears a strict correspondence to what it refers to, is called its indexical quality. The indexical quality of an image refers to the way in wich its appearance is shaped or determined by what it records." Bill Nichols, *Introduction to Documentary*, 34.

89. Adam Jaworski and Crispin Thurlow, "Introduction" in eds. Adam Jaworski and Crispin Thurlow, *Semiotic Landscape, Language, Image, Space* (London & New York: Continuum International Publishing Group, 2010), 31.

90. Julia Hell and Andreas Schönle, "Introduction" in eds. Julia Hell and Andreas Schönle, *Ruins of Modernity* (Durham, NC: Duke University Press, 2010), 7.

91. Laurence J. Vale, "Restoring Urban Viability" in eds. Eugenie Ladner Birch, Susan M. Wachter, *Rebuilding Urban Places after Disaster: Lessons from Hurricane Katrina* (Philadelphia: University of Pennsylvania Press, 2006), 156.

92. The author writes: "The broken levees act as physical evidence of this tragedy while the Lower Ninth Ward itself is framed as 'the place to see' in terms of disaster, destruction and also, now, reconstruction. In addition, these sights/sites undergo a process of sacralization through the repetitive play of images and stories in the mass media and internet." Kevin Dowler, "X Marks the Spot: New Orleans under Erasure" in ed. Tristanne Connolly, *Spectacular Death: Interdisciplinary Perspectives on Mortality and (Un)representability* (Chicago: The University of Chicago Press, 2011), 184.

93. Evie Shockley, "The Haunted Houses of New Orleans: Gothic Homelessness and African American Experience" in eds. Keith Wailoo, Kareen M. O'Neil, Jeffrey Dowd, and Roland Anglin, *Katrina's Imprint: Race and Vulnerability in New Orleans*, 106.

94. Anna Hartnell, "*When the Levees Broke*: Inconvenient Truths and the Limits of National Identity," *African American Review*, 45.2 (2012).

95. Evie Shockley, "The Haunted Houses of New Orleans: Gothic Homelessness and African American Experience" in eds. Keith Wailoo, Kareen M. O'Neil, Jeffrey Dowd, and Roland Anglin, *Katrina's Imprint: Race and Vulnerability in New Orleans*, 108.

96. Hazel Denhart, "Deconstructing Disaster: Psycho-social Impact of Deconstruction in Post-Katrina New Orleans," *Cities* 26, issue 4, August 2009, 196.

97. "Rents increased in the city due to the limited supply of undamaged rental housing, which was made worse by the fact that owners of rental property benefitted from a very small percentage of the recovery grants allocated by HUD's Community Development Block Grant (CDBG)." Matthew J. Scire, *Disaster Housing: FEMA Needs More Detailed Guidance and Performance Measures*, Report to Congressional Requesters, United States Government Accountability Office, August 28, 2009, 11–14. (The full report can be accessed on Google Books.)

98. "The city initially deemed homeowners to have been put on notice of the demolition by the red stickers it placed on the doomed houses, *despite* the fact that large numbers of the residents remained in postevacuation exile all over the country. Further, as residents began to challenge the plan, they discovered that houses that had not suffered structural damage—completely recoverable buildings—were among those that had been selected for bulldozing." Evie Shockley, "The Haunted Houses of New Orleans: Gothic Homelessness and African American Experience" in eds. Keith Wailoo, Kareen M. O'Neil, Jeffrey Dowd, and Roland Anglin, *Katrina's Imprint: Race and Vulnerability in New Orleans*, 109.

99. "New Orleans was among the first American cities to build large-scale public housing for low-income people. The first major "project" was the Iberville complex, completed in 1941, just lakeside of the French Quarter [. . .]. It was classic New Deal "slum clearance" where undesirable neighborhoods were demolished and replaced by building where people in need could find orderly,

sanitary, and agreeable places to live. In many instance it was assumed that public housing would serve an urgent but temporary need [. . .]. Meantime, there was Iberville: about 850 units, in well-built brick units, three stories high, with spacious, grassy courtyards shaded by spreading oaks. It was an uncrowded, highly domestic atmosphere, and a very pleasant one." Peirce F. Lewis, *New Orleans—The Making of an Urban Landscape*, 113.

100. Peirce F. Lewis explains that New Orleans' suburban population exploded "into the swamps" in the late 1950s. "Jefferson officials, who suddenly found taxes deliciously rising, promptly dubbed the parish "Progressive Jefferson" and began to build new levees and streets as revenues accumulated. [. . .] The area's high average income did not result from any large influx of the very rich. Rather it was a combination of middle and upper middle income migration of whites, together with the fact that poor people and black people were discouraged from moving to Jefferson by economic and other constraints." Ibid., 76.

101. Ibid., 77.

102. "These demolitions happened without prior notice to the building owner (Nossiter, 2006) and even inadvertently included the demolition of houses undergoing renovation (Denhart, 2006). This left many homeowners, especially impoverished ones whose sum wealth resided in the broken structure, living in a state of anxiety wondering if their home might be next." Ibid., 195.

103. In January 2014, 100 houses were about to be finished. The progress made can be checked on: <http://www.makeitrightnola.org> (accessed on January 28, 2014).

104. Quoted in Adelaide H. Villemoare and Peter G. Stillman, "Civic Culture and the Politics of Planning for Neighborhoods and Housing in Post-Katrina," in ed. M. B. Hackler, *Culture after Hurricanes, Rhetoric and Reinvention on the Gulf Coast*, 26.

105. Hazel Denhart evokes another program which promotes "deconstruction" as an alternative to demolition. He presents Mercy Corps as a nonprofit, humanitarian relief and development agency that has allowed low-income owners to retake control of their property. His study attempts to demonstrate that the deconstruction process has a positive psychological impact insofar as it empowers the owners who discover the value out of the ruin, for example materials that can be reused, and are encouraged to move toward green practices. Hazel Denhart, "Deconstructing Disaster: Psycho-social Impact of Deconstruction in Post-Katrina New Orleans," *Cities* 26, issue 4, August 2009, 195–201.

106. See chapter 2 "Why Are Ethical Issues Central to Documentary Filmmaking?" in Bill Nichols, *Introduction to Documentary*, 42–66.

107. <http://www.documentary.org/content/what-do-about-documentary-distortion-toward-code-ethics-0> (accessed on January 20, 2014).

108. Eric Barsam, *Non-Fiction Film, A Critical History* (Bloomington, IN: Indiana University Press, 1973, 1992), 305.

109. "To me, it's to find out some important aspect of our society by watching our society, by watching how things really happen as opposed to the social

image that people hold about the way things are supposed to happen." Richard Leacock quoted in Calvin Pryluck, "Ultimately We Are All Outsiders: the Ethics of Documentary Filmmaking" in eds. Alan Rosenthal and John Corner, *New Challenges for Documentary, Second Edition* (Manchester: Manchester University Press, 2005; first edition: 1988), 194.

110. Michael Renov "New Subjectivities: Documentary and Self-Representation in the Post-Vérité Age" in eds. Diane Waldman and Janet Walker, *Feminism and Documentary*, (Minneapolis, MN: University of Minnesota Press, 1999), 88.

111. Documentary theorist Garnet C. Butchart argues that the notion of documentary ethics revolves around three issues: "From the point of view of these three central and related problems—participant consent, the right to know, and the claims of objectivity—debates about ethics in documentary may be understood to have taken shape around a point of incommensurability vis-a-vis the question of individual rights." Garnet C. Butchart, "On Ethics and Documentary: A Real and Actual Truth" in *Communication Theory* 16 (2006), 428.

112. <http://articles.latimes.com/2010/aug/23/entertainment/la-et-spike-20100823> (accessed on April 21, 2014).

113. "Robert Greenwald and Brave New Films are at the forefront of the fight to create a just America, and we want you to join us. Using new media and internet video campaigns, Brave New Films has created a quick-strike capability that informs the public, challenges corporate media with the truth, and motivates people to take action on social issues nationwide. We are an organization that can produce a hard-hitting three-minute video in less than 24 hours that exposes John McCain's double talk, for instance, and receive 9 million views around the world." <http://bravenewfilms.org/> (accessed on March 16, 2011).

114. Edward S. Herman and Noam Chomsky, *Manufacturing Consent* (New York: Pantheon Books, 1988), 307.

115. Cedric Johnson, "Introduction: The Neoliberal Deluge," *The Neoliberal Deluge: Hurricane Katrina, Late Capitalism and the Remaking of New Orleans*, xviii.

116. Ibid., viii.

117. "Although the president's early public statements gave the impression that he would hold BP accountable for the clean-up by working within the established letter of the 1990 Oil Pollution Act, which was passed in the wake of the Exxon Waldez spill, such reassurances rang hollow with many Americans who could not comprehend why neither the White House not BP executives seemed capable of resolving this summer-long crisis. To make matters worse, reports from Obama's own national commission charged that during the critical early weeks, his administration mislead the public about the full scale of the spill. Moreover, Obama's commitment to the 1990 act was itself deeply problematic because the law afforded considerable autonomy to BP and reflected the spirit of individual self-regulation central to neoliberal model." Cedric Johnson, "Preface," *The Neoliberal Deluge: Hurricane Katrina, Late Capitalism and the Remaking of New Orleans*, viii. The author further argues that the media distorted the situation

by highlighting the chaotic chain of events instead of pointing the governance responsibilities: "Disaster planning and evacuation failure at the local, state and national levels reflected a consensus around neoliberal governance. This political reality was lost amid corporate news coverage that portrayed these events as either a string of chaotic, unfortunate missteps, the outcome of partisan gridlock, or simply the result of bureaucratic ineptitude." Ibid., xix.

118. "A state-funded and state-managed public works project along the lines of the Depression era Works Progress Administration might have temporarily provided thousands of jobs to displaced residents and helped the city to retain its population and recover at a much faster rate. Instead of the mass public sector layoffs enacted by Mayor C. Ray Nagin, teachers and employees might have been trained and deployed alongside day laborers and dockworkers in debris removal and clean-up." Ibid., xi.

119. Lisa Margonelli, *Oil on the Brain, Adventures from the Pump to the Pipeline* (New York: Nan A. Talese/Doubleday, 2007).

120. Michael B. McElroy argues that the oil shocks of the 1970s produced a decrease in demand. However, "the mood of the American consumer changed in the 1990s as quickly as it did in the 1980s. The oil crisis was over. The price of gasoline declined and Americans resumed their love affair with large cars. To an increasing extent, light trucks and SUVs emerged as the motor vehicles of choice for American consumers and, as indicated at the outset, fleet average fuel economies dropped accordingly." Michael B. McElroy, *Energy, Perspectives, Problems, and Prospects* (Oxford, New York: Oxford University Press, 2010), 289.

121. Robert A. G. Monks and Nell Minow, *Corporate Governance* (Chichester, UK: John Wiley & Sons, 2011), 354.

122. Stanley Reed & Alison Fitzgerald, *In Too Deep, BP and the Drilling Race that Took it Down* (New Jersey: John Wiley and Sons, Inc., 2011), xii.

123. "Maintaining high-quality, well-run, and safe industrial operations is as much a matter of corporate culture and incentives as it is about money. BP's culture encouraged individuals to take responsibility for their own operations rather than dictating behaviors from the top. It also incentivized things that could be measured. Worker productivity was measured in terms of financial return and safety in terms of incidents. That led them to push people to do more with less, while believing they were safe because they had few-on-the job injuries [. . .]." Ibid., 124.

124. Ibid., xxi.

125. Serge Halimi, "Des patriotes américains contre Wal-Mart," *Le Monde diplomatique* (février 2006). See: <http://www.monde-diplomatique.fr/2006/02/HALIMI/13182> (accessed on March 18, 2014).

126. The film's themes are also developed through an internet multiplatform project: <http://www.landofopportunitymovie.com/> (accessed on February 9, 2014).

127. URL: <http://www.landofopportunitymovie.com/>. A new interactive website was launched after this essay was written, further testifying to the

innovative tools developed to further the viewing of film. It includes three videos that evoke the landscape of the new New Orleans through the portrayals of three residents. <http://landofopportunityinteractive.com>, (accessed on January 12, 2014).

128. <http://nymag.com/daily/intelligencer/2014/02/spike-lee-amazing-rant-against-gentrification.html> (accessed on August 25, 2014)

Conclusion

1. Audrey Thomas McCluskey, "Preface" in eds. Janice D. Hamlet and Robin R. Means Coleman, *Fight the Power, The Spike Lee Reader*, xi.

2. Dewaard explains that artists use their celebrity as a brand to promote their works and dubs them "sellebrities." Andrew Dewaard, "Joints and Jams: Spike Lee as Sellebrity Auteur" in Ibid., 347. See also Yannick Rice Lamb, "Spike Lee as entrepreneur: Leveraging 40 Acres and a Mule" in Ibid., 384.

3. See the whole dossier dedicated to this issue in *Transatlantica* and its introduction by John Dean, "The Businessman as Artist: The Subject Itself," *Transatlantica* 2, 2010. <http://transatlantica.revues.org/5174> (accessed on February 22, 2014).

4. Andrew Dewaard, "Joints and Jams: Spike Lee as Sellebrity Auteur," in eds. Janice D. Hamlet, Robin R. Means Coleman, *Fight the Power, The Spike Lee Reader*, 351.

5. "Lee's own increased economic power has been due in large part to his skill in branding the Spike Lee name, resulting in his transformation into a valuable commodity. From his ability to create controversy incessantly to his numerous and various commercial enterprises, Lee has exploited his celebrity in order to continue his prolific cinematic output over the years." Andrew Dewaard, "Joints and Jams: Spike Lee as Sellebrity Auteur," in eds. Janice D. Hamlet and Robin R. Means Coleman, *Fight the Power, The Spike Lee Reader*, 346.

6. Violaine Roussel, *Voicing Dissent and the War on Iraq* (New York/London: Routledge, 2010), 22.

7. Ibid.

8. Krin Gabbard, *Jamming at the Margins* (Chicago/London: University of Chicago Press, 1996), 155.

9. "What defines his activism is a strong dedication to discursive condemnations of what he sees as malpractices in American foreign and domestic policy, which he combines with practical action in places like New Orleans, Haiti and elsewhere. More recently, [. . .] he has become involved in the build-up of the Haitian nation through financial donations as well as voluntary aid work, including digging trenches, delivering food and medicine to the needy, and going on fundraising trips to Washington and the United Nations." Lisa Tsaliki, Christos A. Frangonikolopoulos, and Asteris Huliaras, *Transnational Celebrity Activism in Global Politics Changing the World?* (Chicago, Bristol: Intellect Ltd., 2011), 75.

10. *Variety* labelled Michael Moore an "agent provocateur" and his films "polemics as performance art." Kendall R. Phillips, *Controversial Cinema: the Films that Outraged America* (Westport, CT: Greenwood Publishing Group, 2008), 153.

11. Wahneema Lubiano, "But Compared to What? Reading, Realism, Representation, and Essentialism in *School Daze, Do the Right Thing*, and the Spike Lee Discourse" in ed. Valerie Smith, *Representing Blackness: Issues in Film and Video* (New Brunswick, NJ: Rutgers Depth of Field, 1997, 2003), 103.

12. George Nelson, *Buppies, B-Boys, Baps and Bohos: Notes on Post-Soul Black Culture* (New York: Harper Perennial, 1992, 1994), 111. The author refers to *She's Gotta Have it* (1986) which was distributed by Island Pictures.

13. Jack Rothman, *Hollywood in Wide Angle: How Directors View Filmmaking* (Lanham, MD: Scarecrow Press, 2004), 99.

14. Julie Dash testifies to the pressures she ran up against as network executives demanded she rearrange the story of Rosa Parks in her television-made film *The Rosa Parks Story* (2001). See Delphine Letort, "The Rosa Parks Story: The Making of a Civil Rights Icon." *Black Camera* 3, no. 2 (2012): 31–50. <http://muse.jhu.edu/> (accessed on May 7, 2012).

15. "In his continuing shift from 'guerrilla' to studio financing, bigger production revenues, and broader-based consumer markets, Lee must confront his most elusive and dangerous demon. Put simply, the real adversary of Lee's creativity and eroding guerrilla stance arises out of the subtle, co-opting currents and crossover pressures of the studio system." Ed Guerrero, *Framing Blackness, The African American Image in Film*, 147.

Bibliography

Alexander, Leslie M. and Walter C. Rucker (eds.). 2010. *Encyclopedia of African American History, Volume 1*. Santa Barbara, California: ABC-CLIO, LLC.

    Article cited: Baggett James L., "Sixteenth Street Baptist Church," 1027–1029.

Andersen, Margaret L., and Patricia Hill Collins (eds.). 2004. *Race, Class, and Gender: An Anthology*, 5th ed. New York: Wadsworth.

    Articles cited: Mantsios, Gregory. "Media Magic, Making Class Invisible," 329–336.

    Messner, Michael. "Masculinities and Athletic Careers," 190–202.

Andrews, David L. (ed.). 2001. *Michael Jordan Inc., Corporate Sport, Media Culture, and Late Modern America*. Albany: State University of New York Press.

    Article cited: Brian, Wilson, and Robert Sparks. "Michael Jordan, Sneaker Commercials and Canadian Youth Culture," 217–258.

Apel, Dora. 2004. *Imagery of Lynching: Black Men, White Women, and the Mob*. New Brunswick, NJ: Rutgers University Press.

Austin, Thomas and Wilma de Jong (eds.). 2008, 2010. *Rethinking Documentary, New Perspectives, New Practices*. New York: Open University Press.

    Articles cited: Nichols, Bill. "Evidence, Rhetoric and Documentary Films," 29–38.

    Mike, Wayne. "Documentary as Critical and Creative Research," 82–94.

Baker, Aaron, and Todd Boyd (eds.). 1997. *Out of Bounds: Sports, Media, and the Politics of Identity*. Bloomington, IN: Indiana University Press.

    Article cited: Todd, Boyd. "The Day the Niggaz Took Over: Basketball, Commodity Culture and Black Masculinity," 123–142.

Bakhtin, Mikhail. 1984. *Problems of Dostoevsky's Poetics*. Translated by Caryl Emerson. Minneapolis: University of Minnesota Press.

Banner-Haley, Charles T. 1994. *The Fruits of Integration: Black Middle-Class Ideology and Culture 1960–1990*. Mississippi: University Press of Mississippi.

Barker, Deborah E. and Kathryn McKee (eds.). 2011. *American Cinema and the Southern Imaginary*. Athens, GA: University of Georgia Press.

> Article cited: Smith, Valerie. "Remembering Birmingham Sunday, Spike Lee's *4 Little Girls*," 179–193.

Barry, John M. 1998. *Rising Tide, The Great Mississippi Flood of 1927 and How it Changed America*. New York: Simon and Schuster Paperback.

Barthes, Roland. 1981. *Camera Lucida*. Translated by Richard Howard. New York: Hill and Wang.

———. 1973. *Mythologies*. Translated by Annette Lavers. London: Paladin.

———. 2007. *What is sport?* Translated by Richard Howard. New Haven, CT, and London: Yale University Press.

Baudrillard, Jean. 1994. *Simulacra and Simulation*. Translated by Sheila Faria Glaser. Ann Arbor: MI: University of Michigan Press.

Benjamin, Walter. 1955. 1968. *Illuminations*. Translated by Harry Zohn. New York: Schocken Books.

Bennett, W. Lance, Regina G. Lawrence, and Steven Livingston. 2007. *When the Press Fails, Political Power and the News Media from Iraq to Katrina*. Chicago: University Press of Chicago.

Benson, Thomas W., and Brian J. Snee (eds.). 2008. *The Rhetoric of the New Political Documentary*. Carbondale, IL: Southern Illinois University.

> Article cited: Benson, Thomas W., and Brian J. Snee, "New political documentary," 1–23.

Berger, Martin A. 2011. *Seeing Through Race: A Reinterpretation of Civil Rights Photography*. Berkeley and Los Angeles: University of Berkeley Press.

Berger, Martin A. "Fixing Images: Civil Rights Photography and the Struggle Over Representation," in Journal of International Association of Research Institutes in the History of Art, October 21, 2010. <http://www.riha-journal.org/Articles/2010/berger-fixing-images> (accessed on February 12, 2014).

Bernard, Sheila Curran. 2007. *Documentary Storytelling, Making Stronger and More Dramatic Nonfiction Films*. Burlington, MA: Elsevier Inc.

Bernstein, Matthew H. (ed.). 2010. *Michael Moore: Filmmaker, Newsmaker, Cultural Icon*. Ann Arbor, MI: University of Michigan Press.

> Article cited: Kellner, Douglas. "Michael Moore and the Aesthetic and Politics of Contemporary Documentary Film," 79–104.

Birch, Eugenie Ladner, and Susan M. Wachter (eds.). 2006. *Rebuilding urban places after disaster: lessons from Hurricane Katrina*. Philadelphia: University of Pennsylvania Press.

    Article cited: Vale, Laurence J., "Restoring Urban Viability," 149–167.

Bloch, Marc. 1992. *The Historian's Craft*. Translated by Peter Putnam. Manchester: Manchester University Press. First edition: Alfred A. Knopf, 1954.

Bogle, Donald. 1973. *Toms, Coons, Mulattoes, Mammies, and Bucks: An Interpretive History of Blacks in American Films*. New York/London: Continuum.

Brinkley, Douglas. 2006. *The Great Deluge*. New York: Harper Perennial.

Brown, Jim, with Steve Delsohn. 1989. *Out of Bounds*. New York: Kensington Publishing Corp.

Brown, Melissa T. 2012. *Enlisting Masculinity. The Construction of Gender in US Military Recruiting*. New York: Oxford University Press.

Brown, Scot. 2005. *Figthing for US: Maulana Karenga, The US Organization, and Black Cultural Nationalism*. New York: New York University Press.

Brunsma, David L., David Overfelt, and J. Steven Picou. 2007. *The Sociology of Katrina: Perspectives on a Modern Catastrophe*. Lanham, MD: Rowman and Littlefield Publishers.

    Articles cited: Dynes, Russel R., and Havidan Rodriguez. "Finding and Framing Katrina: The Social Construction of Disaster," 23–34.

    Picou, J. Steven, and Brent K. Marshall. "Introduction: Katrina as Paradigm Shift: Reflections on Disaster Research in the 21st Century," 1–22.

Carrington, Ben. 2010. *Race, Sports and Politics: The Sporting Black Diaspora*. London: Sage Publications, Inc.

Carson, Clayborne. "Martin Luther King, Jr: Charismatic Leadership in a Mass Struggle." *Journal of American History* 74, September 1987, 448–454.

Caruth, Cathy. 1996. *Unclaimed Experience, Trauma, Narrative, and History*. Baltimore: John Hopkins University Press.

Certeau, Michel de. 1988. *The Writing of History*. Translated by Tom Conley. New York: Colombia University Press.

Chapman, Jane. 2009. *Issues in Contemporary Documentary*. Cambridge UK and Malden USA: Polity Press.

Chion, Michel. 1994. *Audio-Vision: Sound and Screen*. Translated by Claudia Gorsman. New York: Columbia University Press.

Cleaver, Kathleen, and Georges Katsiaficas (eds.). 2001. *Liberation, Imagination, and the Black Panther Party: a New Look at the Panthers and their Legacy.* New York: Routledge.

Cochran, Jo Whitehorse, Donna Langston, and Caroly Woodward (eds.). 1988. *Changing Our Power: An Introduction to Women's Studies.* Dubuque, IA: Kendall-Hunt.

> Article cited: Yamato, Gloria. "Something about the Subject Makes it Hard to Name," 3–6.

Comolli, Jean-Louis. 2004. *Voir et pouvoir, L'innocence perdue: cinéma, télévision, fiction, documentaire.* Paris: Éditions Verdier.

Connolly, Tristanne (ed.). 2011. *Spectacular Death: Interdisciplinary Perspectives on Mortality and (Un)representability.* Chicago: University of Chicago Press.

> Article cited: Dowler Kevin, "X Marks the Spot: New Orleans under Erasure," 169–184.

Crowdus, Gary, and Dan Georgakas. "Thinking about the Power of Images: An Interview with Spike Lee," *Cineaste* 26, no. 2 (2001), 4–9.

Crutcher, Michael E. 2010. *Tremé, Race and Place in a New Orleans Neighborhood.* Athens, GA: University of Georgia Press.

Debord, Guy. 1983. *Society of the Spectacle.* Detroit: Black and Red. First edition: 1967.

Deburg, William L. Van (ed.). 1997. *Modern Black Nationalism: From Marcus Garvey to Louis Farrakhan.* New York: New York University Press.

Denhart, Hazel. "Deconstructing Disaster: Psycho-social Impact of Deconstruction in Post-Katrina New Orleans" in *Cities* 6, issue 4, August 2009, 195–201.

Diawara, Manthia (ed.). 1993. *Black American Cinema.* New York: Routledge.

> Article cited: Baraka, Amiri. "Spike Lee at the Movies," 145–153.

Doherty, Thomas. Movie Review. *The Journal of American History* 93, no. 3, December 2006, 997–999. <http://www.historycooperative.org/cgibin/justtop.cgi?act=justtopandurl=http://www.historycooperative.org/journals/jah/93.3/mr_29.html> (accessed on January 31, 2014).

Durant, Sam. 2007. *Black Panther, The Revolutionary Art of Emory Douglas.* New York: Rizzoli.

Dyson, Michael Eric. 1997. *Between God and Gangsta Rap: Bearing Witness to Black Culture.* Oxford, New York: Oxford University Press.

———. 2006. *Come Hell or High Water, Hurricane Katrina and the Color of Disaster.* New York: Basic Civitas.

Du Bois, W. E. B. 1903. *The Souls of Black Folk.* New York: New American Library, Inc.

Estes, Steve. 2005. *I am a Man! Race, Manhood, and the Civil Rights Movement.* Chapel Hill and London: University of North Carolina Press.

Fabre, Geneviève, and Robert O' Meally (eds.). 1994. *History and Memory in African-American Culture.* New York: Oxford University Press.

> Article cited: Nora, Pierre. "Between Memory and History: Les Lieux de Mémoire," 284–300.

Fanon, Frantz. 1986. *Black Skin, White Masks.* New York: Grove Press. First edition: 1952.

———. 2004. *The Wretched of the Earth*, translated by Richard Philcox. New York: Grove Press. First edition: 1961.

Fenster, Mark. 2008. *Conspiracy Theories, Secrecy and Power in American Culture.* Minneapolis, University of Minnesota Press. First edition: 1999.

Ferrel, Jeff. 1993. *Crimes of Style: Urban Graffiti and the Politics of Criminality.* New York: Garland Publishing.

Finn, Jonathan Mathew. 2009. *Capturing the Criminal Image: from Mug Shot to Surveillance Society.* Minneapolis: University of Minnesota Press.

Fiske, John. 1996. *Media Matters: Race and Gender in U.S. Politics.* Minneapolis: University of Minnesota Press.

Fleetwood, Nicole R. "Failing Narratives, Initiating Technologies: Hurricane Katrina and the Production of a Weather Media Event." *American Quarterly* 58, no. 3, *Rewiring the "Nation": The Place of Technology in American Studies* (Sept., 2006), 774.

Freeman, Mike. 2007. *Jim Brown, The Fierce Life of an American Hero.* New York, London, Toronto, Sydney: Harper Entertainment.

Frisch, Michael. 1990. *A Shared Authority: Essays on the Craft and Meaning of Oral and Public History.* Albany: State University of New York Press.

Gabbard, Krin. 1996. *Jamming at the Margins.* Chicago/London: University of Chicago Press.

Gilroy, Paul. 2000. *Against Race: Imagining Political Culture beyond the Color Line.* Cambridge, MA: Harvard University Press.

Golden, Thelma (ed.). 1995. *Black Male Representations of Masculinity in Contemporary American Art.* New York: Whitney Museum of American Art.

> Article cited: bell, hooks. "Feminism inside: Toward a Black Body Politic," 127–140.

Guerin, Frances, and Roger Hallas (eds.). 2007. *The Image and the Witness, Trauma, Memory and Visual Culture.* London: Wallflower Press.

> Articles cited: Guerin, Frances, and Roger Hallas. "Introduction," 1–20.

Orgeron, Devin, and Marsha Orgeron. "Megatronic Memories: Errol Morris and the Politics of Witnessing," 238–252.

Guerrero, Ed. 1993. *Framing Blackness, The African American Image in Film.* Philadelphia: Temple University Press.

Hacker, Andrew. 1992. *Two Nations, Black and White, Separate, Hostile, Unequal.* New York: Charles Scribner's Sons.

Hackler, M. B. (ed.). 2010. *Culture after Hurricanes, Rhetoric and Reinvention on the Gulf Coast.* Jackson, MI: University Press of Mississsippi.

    Article cited: Villemoare, Adelaide H., and Peter G. Stillman. "Civic Culture and the Politics of Planning for Neighborhoods and Housing in Post-Katrina," 17–43.

Halbwachs, Maurice. 1992. *On Collective Memory* (1941). Edited, translated by Lewis A. Coser. Chicago: University of Chicago.

Haley, Bernard D. "'Black on Black' Crime: The Myth and the Reality." *Crime and Social Justice* 20 (1983), 52–53.

Halimi, Serge. "Des patriotes américains contre Wal-Mart." *Le Monde diplomatique* (février 2006). <http://www.monde-diplomatique.fr/2006/02/HALIMI/13182> (accessed on March 18, 2014).

Hall, Joan Kelly, Gergana Vitanova, Ludmila Marchenkova. 2005. *Dialogue with Bakhtin on Second and Foreign Language Learning: New Perspectives.* Hillsdale, NJ: Lawrence Erlbaum Associates Inc.

    Article cited: Vitanova, Gergana. "Authoring the Self in a NonNative Language," 138–158.

Hamlet, Janice D., Robin R. Means Coleman (eds.). 2009. *Fight the Power, The Spike Lee Reader.* New York: Peter Lang.

    Articles cited: Cobb, Jasmine Nichole, and John L. Jackson. "They Hate Me, Spike Lee, Documentary Filmmaking and Hollywood's 'Savage Slot,'" 251–269.

    Dewaard, Andrew. "Joints and Jams: Spike Lee as Sellebrity Auteur," 345–361.

    Houston, Kerr. "Athletic Iconography in Spike Lee's Early Feature Films," 129–145.

    Lamb, Yannick Rice. "Spike Lee as Entrepreneur: Leveraging 40 Acres and a Mule," 383–398.

    Scott, Ellen C. "Sounding Black, Cultural Identification, Sound, and the Films of Spike Lee," 223–249.

Hariman, Robert, and John Louis Lucaites. 2007. *No Caption Needed.* Chicago: University of Chicago Press.

Hartnell, Anna. "*When the Levees Broke*: Inconvenient Truths and the Limits of National Identity," forthcoming, *African American Review*, 45.2 (2012).

Hell, Julia, and Andreas Schönle (eds.). 2010. *Ruins of Modernity*. Durham, NC: Duke University Press.

> Article cited: Hell, Julia, and Andreas Schönle. "Introduction," 1–16.

Herman, Edward S., and Noam Chomsky. 1988. *Manufacturing Consent*. New York: Pantheon Books, 1988.

Hill, John, and Pamela Church Gibson (eds.). 1998. *The Oxford Guide to Film Studies*. Oxford: Oxford University Press.

> Article cited: Wiegman, Robyn. "Race, ethnicity, and film," 158.

Humphreys, Brad R., Dennis Ramsay Howard. 2008. *The Business of Sports: Perspectives on the Sports Industry*. Westport, CT: Greenwood Publishing Group.

> Article cited: Matheson, Victor A. "Mega-Events: The Effects of the World's Biggest Sporting Events on Local, Regional, and National Economies," 81–100.

Jay, Kathryn. 2004. *More than Just a Game: Sports in American Life since 1940*. New York: Columbia University Press.

Jayamanne, Laleen. 2001. *Toward Cinema and its Double: Cross-Cultural Mimesis*. Bloomington, IN: Indiana University Press.

Jaworski, Adam, and Crispin Thurlow (eds.). 2010. *Semiotic Landscape, Language, Image, Space*. London and New York: Continuum International Publishing Group.

> Article cited: Jaworski, Adam, and Crispin Thurlow. "Introduction," 1–40.

Johnson, Cedric. 2011. *The Neoliberal Deluge: Hurricane Katrina, Late Capitalism and the Remaking of New Orleans*. Minneapolis: University of Minnesota Press.

> Articles cited: Dixson, Adrienne. "Whose Choice? A Critical Perspective on Charter Schools," 130–151.
>
> Johnson, Cedric. "Introduction: The Neoliberal Deluge," xviii–l.

Jushnick, Louis, and James Jennings (eds.). 1999. *A New Introduction to Poverty: The Role of Race, Power, and Politics*. New York: New York University Press.

> Article cited: Jennings, James, and Louis Jushnick. "Introduction: Poverty as Race, Power and Wealth," 1–12.

Kates, R. W., C. E. Colten, S. Laska, and S. P. Leatherman. "Reconstruction of New Orleans after Hurricane Katrina: A Research Perspective" in PNAS

October 3, 2006, 103 no. 40, 14653-14654. <http://www.pnas.org/content/103/40/14653.full.pdf+html> (accessed on January 31, 2014).

Kellner Douglas. 2003. *Media Spectacle*. London and New York: Routledge.

———. 2010. *Cinema Wars: Hollywood Film and Politics in the Bush-Cheney Era*. Chichester, UK: Blackwell Publishing.

Kendall, Diane. 2011. *Framing Class: Media Representations of Wealth and Poverty in America*. Lanham, MD: Rowman and Littlefield Publishers, Inc.

Kirschke, Amy Helene. 2007. *Art in Crisis, W. E. B. Du Bois and the Struggle for African American Identity and Memory*. Bloomington and Indianapolis, IN: Indiana University Press.

Klotman, Phyllis R., and Janet K. Cutler (eds.). 1999. *Struggles for Representation*. Bloomington, IN: Indiana University Press.

> Articles cited: Baker, Mark Frederick, and Houston A. Baker. "Uptown Where We Belong, Space, Captivity, and the Documentary of Black Community," 211-249.
>
> Taylor, Clyde, "Paths of Enlightenment: Heroes, Rebels and Thinkers," 122-150.

Knight, Gladys L. 2009. *Icons of the African American Protest: Trailblazing Activists of the Civil Rights Movement, Vol. 1*. Westport, CT: Greenwood Press.

Koven, Mikel J. 2010. *Blaxploitation Films*. Herts, England: Kamera Books.

Lapsley, Robert, and Michael Westlake (eds.). 1998. *Film Theory: an Introduction*. Manchester: Manchester University Press.

Landsberg, Alison. 2004. *Prosthetic Memory, The Transformation of American Remembrance in the Age of Mass Culture*. New York: Columbia University Press.

Lassiter, Matthew D., and Joseph Crespino. 2009. *The Myth of Southern Exceptionalism*. Oxford: Oxford University Press.

Lazerow, Jama, and Yohuru R. Williams. 2006. *In Search of the Black Panther Party: New Perspective on a Revolutionary Movement*. Durham, NC: Duke University Press.

Leblanc, Phyllis Montana, and Spike Lee. 2009. *Not Just the Levees Broke: My Story During and After Hurricane Katrina*. New York: Atria Books.

Lee, Spike, and Ralph Wiley. 1998. *The Best Seat in the House: A Basketball Memoir*. New York: Random House Inc.

Lehman, Christopher P. 2007. *The Colored Cartoon, Black Representation in American Animated Short Films 1907-1954*. Amherst, MA: University of Massachusetts Press.

Letort, Delphine. "*Sweet Sweetback's Baadasssss Song* (Melvin Van Peebles, 1971): Exégèse d'un film militant" in Eliane Elmaleh (ed.). 2009. *Usages et contre-*

usages du stéréotype chez les Afro-américains. Revue LISA—Vol. VII—no. 1, Presses Universitaires de Caen, 74–88. <http://lisa.revues.org/index790.html> (accessed March 15, 2014).

———. "The Rosa Parks Story: The Making of a Civil Rights Icon." *Black Camera* 3, no. 2 (2012): 31. <50. http://muse.jhu.edu/> (accessed May 7, 2014).

———. "Brian A. Monahan, *The Shock of the News: Media Coverage and the Making of 9/11*." *InMedia* [Online], 2 | 2012, Online since December 19, 2012, connection on January18, 2013. <http://inmedia.revues.org/479>.

Lewis, Peirce F. 2003. *New Orleans: The Making of an Urban Landscape.* Santa Fe, NM and Staunton, VA: The Center for American Places.

Lipman, Pauline. 1998. *Race, Class, and Power in School Restructuring.* New York: State University of New York Press.

Lipsitz, George. 1990. *Time Passages: Collective Memory and American Popular Culture.* Minneapolis: University of Minnesota Press.

Malcolm X. 1992. *By Any Means Necessary: Malcolm X.* New York: Pathfinder Press, 1992.

Mangan J. A., and Andrew Ritchie (eds.). 2004. *Ethnicity, Sport, Identity: Struggle for Status.* London: Routledge.

> Article cited: Regester, Charlene. "From the Gridiron and the Boxing Ring to the Cinema Screen: The African-American Athlete in pre-1950 Cinema," 269–292.

Marable, Manning. 2006. *The Great Wells of Democracy: The Meaning of Race in American Life.* New York: Basic Civitas Group.

———. 2006. *Living Black History: How reimagining the African-American Past Can Remake America's Racial Future.* New York: Basic Civitas Group.

Margonelli, Lisa. 2007. *Oil on the Brain, Adventures from the Pump to the Pipeline.* New York: Nan A. Talese/Doubleday.

Marks, Peter. "A Huey P. Newton Story." *New York Times.* Theater Reviews, February 13, 1997.

Martin, Michael T., and Marilyn Yaquinto (eds). 2007. *Redress for Historical Injustices in the United States. On Reparations for Slavery, Jim Crow and Their Legacies.* Durham, NC and London: Duke University Press.

> Article cited: Kerr-Ritchie, Jeffrey R. "Forty Acres, or, An Act of Bas Faith," 222–237.

Massood Paula J. (ed.). 2007. *The Spike Lee Reader.* Philadelphia: Temple University Press.

> Article cited: Acham, Christine. "We Shall Overcome: Preserving History and Memory in 4 Little Girls," 159–174.

McElroy, Michael B. 2010. *Energy, Perspectives, Problems, and Prospects.* Oxford, New York: Oxford University Press.

McLaughlin, Thomas. 2008. *Give and Go, Basketball as a Cultural Practice.* New York, Albany: State University of New York Press.

Menand, Louis. "Nanook and Me: Fahrenheit 9/11 and the Documentary Tradition," *The New Yorker*, August 9 and 16, 2004, 90–96.

Menchaca, Martha. 2001, 2003. *Recovering History, Constructing Race, The Indian, Black and White Roots of Mexican Americans.* Austin: University of Texas Press.

Miller, Patrick B. 2002. *The Sporting World of the Modern South.* Urbana-Champaign: University of Illinois.

Miller, Patrick B., and David K. Wiggins. 2004. *Sport and the Color Line, Black Athletes and Race Relations in Twentieth-Century America.* New York and London: Routledge.

    Articles cited: Kellner, Douglas. "The Sports Spectacle, Michael Jordan, and Nike," 305–325.

        Miller, Patrick B., "The Anatomy of Scientific Racism: Racialist Responses to Black Athletic Achievement" in *Journal of Sport History* 25 (Spring 2008).

Monahan, Brian A. 2010. *The Shock of the News, Media Coverage and the Making of 9/11.* New York and London: New York University Press.

Monks, Robert A. G., and Nell Minow. 2011. *Corporate Governance.* Chichester, UK: John Wiley and Sons.

Morris Errol. Interview with *The Believer*. April 2004. <http://www.errormorris.com/content/interview/believer0404.html> (accessed on March 10, 2014).

Morrison, Toni (ed.). 1972, 1995. *To Die for the People, The Writings of Huey P. Newton* San Francisco, CA: City Lights Books.

    Articles cited: Newton, Huey P. "To the Black Movement," May 15, 1968, 90–93.

    ———. "In Defense of Self-Defense," June 20, 1967, 80–84.

    ———. "HE WON'T BLEED ME: A Revolutionary Analysis of Sweetback's Baadasssss Song With an Introduction by Bobby Seale," June 19, 1971, 112–148.

Morse, Reilly. "Environmental Justice Through the Eye of Hurricane Katrina." Wahington, DC, Joint Center for Political and Economic Studies, Inc., 2008. <http://www.jointcenter.org/hpi/sites/all/files/EnvironmentalJustice.pdf> (accessed on February 2, 2014).

Nelson, George. 1992, 1994. *Buppies, B-Boys, Baps and Bohos: Notes on Post-Soul Black Culture*. New York: Harper Perennial.

Newton, Judith Lowder. 2005. *From Panthers to Promise Keepers: Rethinking the Men's Movement—New Social Formations*. Lanham, MD: Rowman and Littlefield Publisher.

Newton, Huey P. 1973, 2009. *Revolutionary Suicide*. New York: Penguin Books.

Nichols, Bill. 1994, 2001. *Blurred Boundaries: Questions of Meaning in Contemporary Culture*. Bloomington, IN: Indiana University Press.

———. 2010. *Introduction to Documentary*. Second edition. Bloomington, IN: Indiana University Press.

———. 1994. *Representing Reality: Issues and Concepts in Documentary*. Bloomington, IN: Indiana University Press.

Nunberg, Geoffrey. 2009. *The Years of Talking Dangerously*. New York: PublicAffairs.

Ogden, David C., and Joel Nathan Rosen (eds.). 2010. *From Fame to Infamy, Race, Sport and the Fall from Grace*. Jackson, MS: University Press of Mississippi.

    Articles cited: Lane, Jeffrey. "Mortgaging Michael Jordan's Reputation," 122–144.

    Newman, Roberta J. "Jim Brown: The Rise and Fall (and Rise) of a Cultural Icon," 170–190.

Paris, Jane, and Martin Parker (eds.). 2001. *The Age of Anxiety: Conspiracy Theory and the Human Sciences*. Oxford: Blackwell Publishers.

    Articles cited: Featherstone, Mark. "The obscure politics of conspiracy theory," 31–45.

    Paris, Jane. "The Age of anxiety," 1–16.

    Spark, Alasdair. "Conjuring Order: The New World Order and Conspiracy Theories Of Globalization," 46–62.

    Skinner, Jonathan. "Taking conspiracy seriously: fantastic narratives and Mr Grey the Pan-Afrikanist on Montserrat," 93–111.

Parhizgar, Kamal Dean, and Robert Parhizgar. 2006. *Multiculturall Business Ethics and Global Managerial Moral Reasoning*. Lanham, MD: University Press of America.

Pattillo-McCoy, Mary. 1999. *Black Picket Fences: Privilege and Peril among the Black Middle Class*. Chicago: University of Chicago Press.

Pearson, Hugh. 1994. *The Shadow of the Panther: Huey Newton and the Price of Black Power in America*. Reading, MA: Addison-Wesley Publishing Company.

Peniel, Joseph E. (ed.). 2006. *The Black Power Movement, Rethinking the Civil Rights—Black Power Era*. New York/London: Routledge.

    Articles cited: Williams, Rhonda Y. "Black Women, Urban Politics, and Engendering Black Power," 79–104.

    Williams, Yohuru. "A Red, Black and Green Liberation Jumpsuit," 167–192

Perry, Garry. "New Orleans Survivors: a People Without a Home" in *Freedom Socialist*, August 2007. <http://www.socialism.com/drupal-6.8/?q=node/513> (accessed on February 3, 2014)

Phillips, Kendall R. 2008. *Controversial Cinema: The Films that Outraged America*. Westport, CT: Greenwood Publishing Group.

Pollack, Harriet, and Christopher Mettress (eds.). 2008. *Emmett Till in Literary Memory and Imagination*. Baton Rouge: Louisiana State University.

    Article cited: Priest, Myisha. "Langston Hughes Writing the Body of Emmett Till," 53–74.

Powell, Shaun. 2008. *Souled Out?: How Blacks are Winning and Losing in Sports*. Champaign IL: Human Kinetics.

Radstone, Susannah. 2010. *Memory: Histories, Theories, Debates*. New York: Fordham University Press.

Reed, Stanley, and Alison Fitzgerald. 2011. *In Too Deep, BP and the Drilling Race that Took it Down*. New Jersey: John Wiley and Sons, Inc.

Reid, Mark, Janine Euvrard, Francis Bordat, and Raphaël Bassan (eds.). 1988. *Le Cinéma noir américain*. Paris: Cerf, CinémAction.

    Article cited: Sam Kelly. "Sidney Poitier: héros intégrationniste," 68–73.

Reid Mark A. (ed.). 1997. *Spike Lee's Do the Right Thing*. New York: Cambridge University Press.

    Articles cited: Pouzoulet, Catherine. "The Cinema of Spike Lee: Images of a Mosaic City," 31–49.

Renov, Michael (ed.). 1993. *Theorizing Documentary*. New York and London: Routledge.

Rhodes, Jane. 2007. *Framing the Black Panthers, The Spectacular Rise of a Black Power Icon*. New York/London: The New Press.

Ricœur, Paul. 1983. *Temps et récit, Tome 1: L'Intrigue et le récit historique*. Paris: Seuil.

———. 2000. *La Mémoire, l'histoire, l'oubli*. Paris: Seuil.

———. 2004, 2006. *Memory, History, Forgetting*. Translated by Kathleen Blamey and David Pellauer. Chicago: University of Chicago Press.

Rothman, Jack. 2004. *Hollywood in Wide Angle: How Directors View Filmmaking*. Lanham, MD: Scarecrow Press.

Rodríguez, Plácido, Stefan Késenne, and Jaume García (eds.). 2007. *Governance and Competition in Professional Sports Leagues*. Oviedo: Ediciones de la Universidad de Oviedo.

>Article cited: Baade, Robert, and Victor Matheson. "NFL Governance and the Fate of the New Orleans Saints: Some Observations," 141–170.

Romano, Renee C., and Leigh Raiford (eds.). 2006. *The Civil Rights Movement in American Memory*. Athens, GA: University of Georgia Press.

>Articles cited: Dwyer, Owen J. "Interpreting the Civil Rights Movement: Contradiction, confirmation, and the Cultural Landscape," 5–27.
>
>Romano, Renee C. "Narratives of Redemption, The Birmingham Church Bombing Trials and the Construction of Civil Rights Memory," 96–133.

Roscoe, Jane, and Craig Hight. 2011. *Faking it, Mock Documentary and the Subversion of Factuality*. Manchester: Manchester University Press.

Rothman, Jack. 2004. *Hollywood in Wide Angle: How Directors View Filmmaking*. Lanham, MD: Scarecrow Press.

Roussel, Violaine. 2010. *Voicing Dissent and the War on Iraq*. New York/London: Routledge.

Rubie, Peter. *The Elements of Narrative Nonfiction, How to Write and Sell the Novel of True Events*. 2009. Fresno, CA: Quill Driver Books.

Sarkar, Bhaskar, and Janet Walker (eds.). 2010. *Documentary Testimonies, Global Archives of Suffering*. New York/Oxon: Routledge.

>Articles cited: Sarkar, Bhaskar, and Janet Walker. "Introduction: Moving Testimonies," 1–34.
>
>Walker Janet. "Rights and return: perils and fantasies of situated testimony after Katrina," 83–114.

Saussure, Ferdinand de. 1949. *Cours de linguistique générale*. Paris: Payot

———. 1974. *Course in General Linguistics*. Translated by Wade Baskin. Glasgow: Fontana/Collins.

Scire, Matthew J. *Disaster Housing: FEMA Needs More Detailed Guidance and Performance Measures*. Report to Congressional Requesters, United States Government Accountability Office, August 28, 2009, 11–14. (The full report can be accessed on Google Books.)

Seale, Bobby. 1970, 1991. *Seize the Time, The Story of the Black Panther Party and Huey P. Newton*. Baltimore, MD: Black Classic Press.

Smith, Ronald D. 2013. *Strategic Planning for Public Relations*. Fourth edition. New York: Routledge.

Smith, Valerie (ed.). 1997, 2003. *Representing Blackness: Issues in Film and Video*. New Brunswick, NJ: Rutgers Depth of Field.

> Article cited: Lubiano, Wahneema. "But Compared to What? Reading, Realism, Representation, and Essentialism in School Daze, Do the Right Thing, and the Spike Lee Discourse," 97–122.

Sontag, Susan. 1979. *On Photography*. London: Penguin Books.

———. "Photography," *New York Review of Books* (October 18, 1973). Reprinted in *Anthology: Selected Essays from Thirty Years of the New York Review of Books*. 1993. New York: New York Review of Books.

———. 2003. *Regarding the Pain of Others*. New York: Picador.

Souther, Jonathan Mark. 2006. *New Orleans on Parade: Tourism and the Transformation of the Crescent City*. Baton Rouge: Louisiana State University Press.

Sterritt, David. *Spike Lee's America*. 2013. Cambridge, UK/Malden USA: Polity Press.

Tierney, Kathleen, Christine Bevc, and Erica Kuligowski. "Metaphors Matter: Disaster Myths, Media Frames, and Their Consequences in Hurricane Katrina." *The Annals of the American Academy of Political and Social Science* 604, March 2006, 57–81.

Tsaliki Lisa, Christos A. Frangonikolopoulos and Asteris Huliaras. 2011. *Transnational Celebrity Activism in Global Politics Changing the World?* Chicago/Bristol: Intellect Ltd.

Ture, Kwame (formerly known as Stokely Carmichael) and Charles V. Hamilton. 1967, 1992. *Black Power, The Politics of Liberation in America*. New York: Vintage Books.

Van Peebles, Melvin. 1995. *Panther*. New York: Thunder's Mouth Press.

Wailoo, Keith, Kareen M. O'Neil, Jeffrey Dowd, and Roland Anglin (eds.). 2010. *Katrina's Imprint: Race and Vulnerability in New Orleans*. New Brunswick, NJ: Rutgers University Press.

> Articles cited: Bay, Mia. "Invisible Tethers, Transportation and Discrimination in the Age of Katrina," 21–33.
>
> Boyd-Franklin, Nancy. "Racism, Trauma, and Resilience, The Psychological Impact of Katrina," 78–94.
>
> Mizelle, Richard, Jr. "Second-lining the Jazz City: Jazz Funerals, Katrina, and the Reemergence of New Orleans," 69–77.

Shockley, Evie. "The Haunted Houses of New Orleans: Gothic Homelessness and African American Experience," 95–114.

Wailoo, Keith, Kareen M. O'Neil, and Jeffrey Dowd. "Introduction: Katrina's Imprint," 1–6.

Waldman, Diane, and Janet Walker. 1999. *Feminism and Documentary*. Minneapolis, MN: University of Minnesota Press.

Ward, Brian. 1998. *Just My Soul Reponding: Rhythm and Blues, Black Consciousness and Race Relations*. London: UCL Press.

West, Cornel. 1993. *Race Matters*. Boston: Beacon Press.

Whitaker, Matthew C. (ed.). 2008. *African American Icons of Sport, Triumph, Courage and Excellence*. Westport, CT/London: Greenwood Press.

    Articles cited: Dagbovie, Pero Gaglo, and Amaris J. White. "Jim Brown," 49–60.

        Falater, Megan. "Tommie Smith and John Carlos," 243–253.

        McDonald, Mary G. "Michael Jordan," 145–155.

        Whitaker, Matthew C. "Muhammad Ali," 1–12.

Widmer, Mary Lou. 2000. *New Orleans in the Sixties*. Gretna, LA: Pelican Publishing Company, Inc.

Williams, Linda. 2002. *Playing the Race Card, Melodramas of Black and White from Uncle Tom to O. J. Simpson*. Princeton, NJ: Princeton University Press.

Williams, Linda. "Mirrors without memories: truth, history and the new documentary," *Film Quarterly*, 46 (3; Spring), 1993, 9–21.

Wood, Joe (ed.). 1992. *Malcolm X: In Our Own Image*. New York: St. Martin's Press.

Young, James Edwards. 1988. *Writing and Rewriting the Holocaust: Narrative and the Consequences of Interpretation*. Bloomington, IN: Indiana University Press.

Online Interactive Sites

PBS website on *A Huey P. Newton Story:* <http://www.pbs.org/hueypnewton/>

Spike DDB: <http://www.spikeddb.com/about-us/>

The Make It Right Foundation: <http://www.makeitrightnola.org>

Brave New Films: <http://bravenewfilms.org/>

Land of Opportunity: <http://www.landofopportunitymovie.com/>

Index

40 Acres and a Mule, 115, 103, 104 149, 154

A Huey P. Newton Story, xiii, 3, 12–15, 28, 65, 96, 98, 102, 111–116
A Hundred Rifles, 94
Acham, Christine, 59
advertising, 8, 89, 103, 115, 116, 118, 119, 124, 126, 149, 150, 151, 152, 169n49
aesthetic strategies in Lee's documentaries: 4, 30, 31, 103, 128, 141, 149, 159n40, 170n68
African American athletes, 3, 11, 30, 31, 64, 82, 83, 84, 86, 87, 88, 89, 90, 92, 96, 116, 119–126, 152, 170n62, 170n65, 178n54
Aldrich, Robert, 90
Ali Baba Goes to Town, 92
Ali, Muhammad, 120, 122, 124
American flag, 11, 62
Andersen, Margaret L., 123, 124, 169n51
Apel, Dora, 59
Aquin, Hubert, 84
archival footage, 5, 7, 10, 12–15, 21–23, 28–29, 34, 37, 38, 39, 42, 43, 45, 48, 53, 54, 56, 57, 58, 60, 62, 63, 65, 66, 68, 69, 76, 83, 84, 87, 97, 99, 110, 112, 113, 114, 118, 134, 144, 145, 154, 158n25, 159n34, 160n4

Armstrong, Louis, 107
authenticity, 3, 9, 10, 22, 64

Bad 25, 3, 4, 21, 30, 32, 110, 149
Baez, Joan, 12, 13
Bakhtin, Mikhail, 113
Bamboozled, 1
Banner-Haley, Charles T., 105, 119
Barry, John M., 53, 54, 163n38, 163n42
Barthes, Roland, 44, 45, 84, 85
basketball, xi, 1, 2, 27, 30, 31, 32, 87, 88, 119, 123, 124, 150, 152, 159, 179n63, 180n66, 180n74
Baudrillard, Jean, 65n, 165n9
BBC, 71
Benjamin, Walter, 42, 61
Berger, Martin A., 47, 99, 101, 161n44
biographical documentary, 2, 3, 4, 9, 10, 18, 27, 28, 30, 82, 84, 87, 88, 105, 111
Birmingham, 12, 40, 42, 46–50, 58, 60, 161n12, 162n28
black nationalism, 1, 7, 38, 89, 102–106, 110–117, 120, 125
Black Panther Party, 10, 13–15, 29, 62, 64–65, 96–97, 101, 111–114, 150–151, 157n12, 171n73, 175n21, 176n29, 176n31
black power, 29, 89, 99, 104, 105, 110, 112, 120
Black Starz, 3

205

Blanchard, Terence, 25, 35, 36, 108, 132
Blanco, Kathleen Babineaux, 57, 68, 77, 117
Bloch, Marc, 66, 178n30
Bogle, Donald, 91, 93, 169n54, 171n68
Boyd-Franklin, Nancy, 69, 77
Brando, Marlon, 14, 159n34
Brinkley, Douglas, 55, 71, 109, 110, 138, 139, 142, 144, 152, 166n19, 174n17
British Petroleum (BP), 25, 36, 106, 138, 143, 144, 145, 178n30, 185n117, 186n123
Brown, James, 106
Brown, Jim, 2, 8, 26, 27, 64, 82–96, 102, 106, 120–122, 124, 138, 169n55
Brown, Melissa T., 115
Bryant, Kobe, 2, 3, 8, 24, 26, 27, 30–32, 122–123, 138, 150, 152–153
business, 1, 6, 54, 106, 118, 122, 123, 125, 126, 128, 129, 138, 140, 148, 149, 150, 152, 178n47
Bush, George W., 144

Canizaro, Joseph, 127, 129, 181n79
capitalism, 60, 81, 102, 105, 112, 147, 152
Carlos, John, 120, 124
Carmichael, Stokely, 97, 99, 112, 103, 175n23, 176n29, 187n5
Carrington, Ben, 86, 92, 120
Carson, Clayborne, 115
Caruth, Cathy, 56
Certeau, Michel de, 164n52
Chambliss, Robert, 40, 41, 49
Chapman, Jane, 16, 26, 158n17
characterization, 6, 12, 14, 15, 16, 26, 27, 28, 29, 34, 35, 98, 109, 114
charter schools, 81, 117, 118, 147, 177n42, 177n43
Cheney, Dick, 142

Chevrolet, 115, 116, 150, 177n41, 178n48
Chomsky, Noam, 142
Citizen Kane, 30
civil rights movement, xiii, 2, 3, 6, 10, 13, 34, 38, 39, 40, 47, 48, 50, 51, 52, 55, 71, 80, 99, 100, 101, 110, 116, 118, 121, 131, 150, 143, 161n12, 161n24, 162n29
class inequalities 106, 150
Cleaver, Eldridge, 96, 176n29
Clockers, 1, 11
collective memory, 6, 37, 38, 40, 48, 121, 126
Collins, Addie Mae, 12, 40, 45
Collins, Patricia Hill, 123, 124, 169n51
colorblind 59, 64, 101, 116
Comolli, Jean-Louis, 6
conspiracy theory, 32–33, 54–56, 137, 160n41, 163n41, 163n43
Convention Center, 35, 53, 62, 69, 70, 71, 72, 77, 129, 158n25, 182n86
corporate culture, 19, 20, 65, 103, 106, 116, 118, 119, 124, 125, 126, 132, 137, 138, 141, 144, 146, 147, 148, 150, 152
crime, 1, 3, 11, 20, 21, 40, 47, 51, 53, 54, 65, 66, 71, 73, 76–81, 92, 93, 94, 116, 147, 151
Crispin, Thurlow 130
Crutcher, Michael E., 107
Cutler, Janet K. 2, 166n20

Davis, Angela, 14, 176n29
De Antonio, Emile, xii, xiii, 13, 23
De Bois, W. E. B., 59, 69
Debord, Guy, 86
Denhart, Hazel, 133
Desohn, Steven, 84
Dewaard, Andrew, 103, 187n5
discrimination, 12, 39, 50 55, 57, 75, 87, 105, 113, 125, 131, 133, 135, 137, 148, 150

Do the Right Thing, 1, 11, 16, 24, 119, 150
documentary modes: poetic, 9, 13, 20, 22, 28, 43; expository, 9, 10, 13, 28, 54, 163n40; observational, 4, 9, 28; participatory, 5, 6, 9, 16, 28, 64; reflexive, 6, 7, 9, 10, 15, 27, 28–36, 37, 76, 77, 87, 141, 159n40; performative, 5, 9, 16–23, 28, 160n42
Douglas, Emory, 100
Dowd, Maureen, 144
Drew, Robert, 141
Dynes, Russel R., 73, 166n21
Dyson, Michael Eric, 55, 74, 80

economic empowerment, 103, 104, 105, 106, 121, 122, 154
education, 19, 21, 34, 66, 70, 78, 81, 90, 104, 105, 116–118, 142, 151, 168N51, 177n 44
Eisenstein, Sergei, 23
ESPN, 3, 31, 123, 126, 150, 180n74
ethical issues, 27, 126, 140–148
ethnicity, 11, 38, 106, 106, 123, 130, 133, 136, 153, 159n35, 164n48

fact and fiction, 11, 54
family photographs, 42, 43, 45, 46, 47, 57, 58, 62
Fanon, Frantz, 105, 167n31, 173n7
Farrakhan, Louis, 104
Fenster, Mark, 54, 55, 163n41
Ferro, Marc, 6, 37, 39
fiction, 1, 2, 3, 4, 5, 10, 11, 12, 13, 15, 16, 24, 26, 28, 29, 34, 35, 54, 123, 150
fiction and nonfiction, 2, 11, 13, 15, 26, 28, 29, 150
financing, 3, 103, 123, 126, 152, 153, 154, 188n15
Fingers, 94
Fiske, John, 76
Fleetwood, Nicole R., 60

football, 2, 24, 26, 82, 83, 84, 85, 86, 87, 88, 89, 90, 91, 92, 93, 121, 125, 128, 129, 130, 181n82
Four Little Girls, xiii, 3, 6, 7, 12, 13, 21, 26, 28, 38, 40–45, 47–49, 52, 58–60, 116, 150
Francesca, Mike, 95
Freeman, Mike, 89
Frisch, Michael, 48

Gabbard, Krin, 151
Garvey, Marcus, 103
General Motors, 103, 105, 115
gentrification, xi, 121, 137, 148, 187n128
Gilroy, Paul, 116
Greenwald, Robert, 77, 141, 147–148, 185n113
Greenwood, Preston, 116
Grierson, John, 9
Guerrero, Ed, 15, 91, 94, 153, 170n57, 188n15
Guess Who's Coming to Dinner?, 91
Gulf Coast, 20–21, 24, 26, 28, 66, 141, 143, 144, 145, 147, 148

Halbwachs, Maurice, 40, 42
Halimi, Serge, 147
Hamilton, Charles V., 112, 175n23
Hampton, Fred, 14, 113, 157n12
Hanes, Arthur, Jr., 49, 59
Hariman, Robert, 63–64, 101
HBO, 3, 34, 142, 129
He Got Game, 1, 123, 124
Headly, Bernard, 81
Hell, Julia, 130
Herman, Edward, 142
Herrington, Donnell, 79, 80, 81
Hight, Craig, 32, 159n40, 160n42
Hoop Dreams, 123, 126, 180n74
Hoover, J. Egdar, 14, 29, 113, 114
housing projects, 23, 127, 131, 133, 134, 135, 136, 137, 140, 147
Humble, 25, 36, 139

Hurricane Katrina, xiii, 3, 4, 7, 10, 11, 17, 18, 19, 21, 22, 32–39, 52–57, 60, 62, 65–77, 79, 102, 107–109, 117, 127–131, 133, 135–138, 140, 143–144, 147, 148, 150, 152–153, 157, 162n36, 163n38, 164n48, 166n19, 166n21, 167n23
Hutton, Bobby, 14, 113, 159n34

Ice Station Zebra, 90
iconic photographs, 3, 34, 39, 46, 48, 57–62, 63, 64, 99, 100, 114
If God Is Willing and Da Creek Don't Rise, 3, 4, 6, 7, 17, 18, 19, 20, 21, 23, 24, 34, 35, 36, 56, 61, 68, 75, 78, 81, 82, 106, 116, 117, 126–131, 133–134, 137, 138, 142, 144, 150, 152
In the Year of the Pig, 23

Jackson, Alphonso, 136
Jackson, Jesse, 151
Jackson, Michael, 2, 3, 8, 21, 30, 32, 106, 110, 111, 120, 149
Jaworski, Adam, 130
Jay, Kathryn, 88, 89, 121, 123, 126, 128, 181n82
jazz, 1, 31, 60, 61, 107–110, 174n15
Jeanette, Joe, 92
Jennings, James, 70
Jim Brown: All American, 3, 26, 38, 64, 82, 83, 84, 85, 87, 89, 93, 120, 126, 180n75
Johnson, Cedric, 114, 114, 145, 147, 177n43
Johnson, John Lester, 92
Jordan, Michael, 3, 8, 31, 119, 120, 124, 125, 178n55, 179n65
journalism, 71, 72, 77, 93, 166n18
Juakali, Endesha, 24, 131, 137
Jungle Fever, 1
Jushnick, Louis, 70

Karenga, Maulana, 114, 175n31

Kellner, Douglas, 30, 31, 93, 120, 158n21
King, Martin Luther, Jr., 3, 14, 101, 102, 105, 115, 118
Klotman, Phyllis R., 2, 166n20
Kobe Doin' Work, 3, 27, 30–32, 122–123, 150, 152–153
Koven, Mikel J., 94
Kracauer, Siegfried, 43
Ku Klux Klan, 60

Landrieu, Mitch, 24, 35, 138, 143
Landsberg, Alison, 38
Lane, Jeffrey, 124
Leacock, Richard, 141, 185n109
Lewis, Peirce F., 129, 134, 135, 181n80, 182n85, 184n99, 184n100
Lipman, Pauline, 81, 117, 177n44
Lipsitz, George, 52
Lower Ninth Ward, é22, 24? 33, 35, 53, 70, 118, 126, 127, 131, 132, 134, 139, 140, 152, 180n77, 183n97
Lucaites, John Luis, 63–64, 101
lynching, 25, 58, 59, 60, 80

Malcolm X, 1, 11, 38, 62, 141
Malcolm X, 14, 97, 98, 104, 105, 106, 110, 112, 122, 131, 171n72, 172n78
Manhood, 91, 97, 162n29
Marable, Manning, 57, 58, 104
Margonelli, Lisa, 142, 145
McLaughlin, Thomas, 123, 179n63
McNair, Chris, 44, 46, 48, 49, 50
McNair, Denise, 12, 40, 42, 44? 46, 48, 49, 50
McNair, Maxine, 50, 51
Make It Right Foundation, 139, 140, 152, 180n77, 203
Messner, Michael, 90, 169n51
Micheaux, Oscar, 149
middle-class values, 70, 71, 77, 105, 135, 150
Miller, Patrick D., 86, 88

Miracle at St. Anna, 2
Mizelle, Richard, Jr., 168, 167n23
Mo' Better Blues, 1
Modell, Art, 86, 87, 90, 181n82
Mohammed, Elijah, 104
Monahan, Brian A., 65
money, 52, 70, 89, 104, 116, 117, 118, 123, 124, 125, 132, 133, 137, 147, 150, 152, 154
Montana-Leblanc, Phyllis, 17–20, 25, 26, 27
Moore, Michael, 21, 141, 158n21, 188n10
Morial, Marc, 57, 67
Morris, Errol, xiii, 13, 157n10
Morrison, Toni, 100
music, 2, 3, 5, 12, 14, 16, 22, 30, 31, 35, 52, 58, 60, 61, 68, 89, 94, 103, 106–111, 117, 128, 133, 142, 145, 149, 157n15, 173n12, 174n13, 174n15, 174n17
music videos, 110, 117

Naggin, Ray C., 57, 67, 68, 77, 127, 128, 135, 136, 137, 181
NBC, 71, 154
Nelson, George, xi, 152
New Orleans, 2, 3, 4, 10, 18–22, 24–24, 33–39, 52–56, 60–21, 66–79, 81, 107–108, 126–148, 150–153, 174n13, 174n17, 177n43, 180n77, 181n79, 181n80, 181n81, 182n85, 182n86, 183n99, 184n100
Newton, Huey, 10, 13, 14, 15, 29, 64, 91, 97, 98, 99, 100, 101, 102, 105, 111, 112, 113, 114, 115, 116, 150
Newton, Judith, 77
Nichols, Bill, 3, 4, 9, 13, 16, 28, 29, 36, 62, 140, 156n4, 157n11, 163n40, 182n88
Nike, 8, 103, 118, 119, 123, 124, 125, 126, 152, 154
Nora, Pierre, 39
Nunberg, Geoffrey, 75

Obama, Barack, 36, 118, 144, 145, 185n117
oil, 20, 25, 36, 38, 141–147, 151
oral history, 39, 48–52, 56, 58
Outfoxed: Rupert Murdoch's War on Journalism, 77
Owens, Jesse, 116

Parker, Martin, 160n41, 163n43
Parks, Rosa, 100, 101, 110, 188n14
Penn, Sean, 152
Pennebaker, D. A., 141
photography, 13, 16, 28, 31, 36, 37, 42–48, 57–65, 74, 75, 93, 96, 99, 101, 112, 114, 117, 118, 134, 139, 161n24
Pitt, Brad, 21, 35, 139, 152, 181
Poitier, Sidney, 91, 169n54, 170n57
poverty, 19, 20, 54, 66, 69, 70, 77, 81, 106, 110, 135, 136, 137, 174n11
Pouzoulet, Catherine, 11

race and class, 1, 2, 7, 8, 21, 24, 39, 48, 53, 71, 106, 116, 124, 127, 133, 136, 143, 150, 151
racial issues, 10, 19, 70, 88, 120, 154
racism, xi, xiii, 10, 11, 22, 24, 49, 56, 58, 59, 60, 64, 65, 69, 72, 73, 75, 76, 77, 80, 86, 87, 88, 96, 99, 101, 112, 120, 132, 150
rap music, 18, 72, 78, 79, 80, 110
Radstone, Susannah, 51
refugee, 56, 75
reconstruction, 2, 21, 34, 35, 38, 52, 53, 57, 66, 81, 109, 127, 128, 129, 131, 132, 134, 136, 137, 138, 139, 140, 143, 147, 148, 151, 153, 157n15, 163n92
Reid, Mark A., xi–xiii
Renov, Michael, 15, 141
Rhodes, Jane, 99
Ricœur, Paul, 39–40, 160n7
Riefenstahl, Leni, 116, 177n40
Riot, 91

Robertson, Carole, 12, 40, 41, 42
Rodriguez, Havidan, 166
Roosevelt, Franklin Delano, 24, 63, 134, 136, 137, 145
Roscoe, Jane, 32, 159n40, 160n42
Roussel, Violaine, 151
Russel, Honore L., 77

Schöle, Andreas, 130
School Daze, 1, 11
Seale, Bobby, 29, 97, 176n29
segregation, 12, 40, 42, 46, 48, 49, 50, 51, 53, 55, 58, 60, 73, 87, 89, 100, 114, 134, 150, 179n57
She Hate Me, 1
She's Gotta Have it, 1, 103, 119, 154, 188n12
Shockley, Evie, 60, 127, 131, 132, 134, 174n13, 182n98
skin color, 38, 81, 93
Slaughter, 91
slavery, 73, 117, 121, 138, 154, 173n2, 179n57
Smith, Roger Guenveur, 13–15, 29, 96–98, 101, 111, 159n34
Smith, Tommie, 120, 124
Smith, Valerie, 45, 48
Sontag, Susan, 43, 46, 58
soundtrack, 79, 82, 84, 94, 96, 112, 139, 145, 157n15
Sparks, Robert, 119
Spike DDB, 103, 115, 119, 149, 203
sports documentary, 3, 11, 26, 32, 82–95, 106, 113, 119, 129, 138, 150–152
stereotypes, 1, 2, 7, 8, 10, 36, 63, 65, 70, 76, 82, 93, 94, 95, 96, 99, 100, 101, 106, 110, 130
Superdome, 35, 69, 70, 77, 127, 128–131, 137, 158, 181n80, 182n85, 182n86
Sweet Sweetback's Baadasssss Song, 90, 91, 92, 94

Syracuse University, 87, 88, 89, 90

Take a Hard Ride, 91
Tarzan's Revenge, 92
television, 3, 5, 7, 9, 11, 14, 15, 17, 31, 38, 48, 60, 63, 65, 66, 68–74, 76, 77, 84–85, 89, 93, 96, 101, 107, 113, 115, 129, 137, 141, 145, 149, 153, 154
The Dirty Dozen, 90, 91
Till, Emmett, 80
Tse-Tung, Mao, 98, 171n77
trauma, 22, 46, 48, 50, 51, 55, 56, 66, 72–76, 80, 107, 117, 127, 129, 130, 135, 140, 167n23

Vale, Lawrence J., 130
Vallas, Paul, 117
Van Peebles, Melvin, 91
Vietnam, 14, 23, 112, 120
voice-over commentary, 24, 27, 32, 54, 61, 68, 78, 82, 84, 86, 89, 113, 115, 116, 125, 152

Welch, Raquel, 94
Wesley, Cynthia, 12, 40
West, Cornel, 64
When the Levees Broke: A Requiem in Four Acts, 3, 4, 7, 17, 19, 22, 25, 26, 32, 33–36, 39, 52, 55, 57, 60, 61, 65, 66, 70, 76, 78, 107, 108, 109, 116, 131, 137, 141, 142, 146, 150, 157n15, 160n42
Wiggins, David K., 88
Wild Man from Borneo, 92
Wiley, Ralph, 88, 124, 159n35
Williams, Linda, 93, 170n64
Wilson, Brian, 119
Wooten, John, 121

Yamato, Gloria, 81